Thomas Mangel

Inter-Vehicle Communication at Intersections:
An Evaluation of Ad-Hoc and Cellular Communication

Inter-Vehicle Communication at Intersections: An Evaluation of Ad-Hoc and Cellular Communication

by
Thomas Mangel

Dissertation, Karlsruher Institut für Technologie (KIT)
Fakultät für Informatik
Tag der mündlichen Prüfung: 5. Juli 2012

Impressum

Karlsruher Institut für Technologie (KIT)
KIT Scientific Publishing
Straße am Forum 2
D-76131 Karlsruhe
www.ksp.kit.edu

KIT – Universität des Landes Baden-Württemberg und
nationales Forschungszentrum in der Helmholtz-Gemeinschaft

KIT Scientific Publishing 2012
Print on Demand

ISBN 978-3-86644-899-5

Inter-Vehicle Communication at Intersections: An Evaluation of Ad-Hoc and Cellular Communication

zur Erlangung des akademischen Grades eines

Doktors der Ingenieurwissenschaften

von der Fakultät für Informatik
des Karlsruher Instituts für Technologie (KIT)

genehmigte

Dissertation

von

Thomas Mangel

aus Rheda-Wiedenbrück

Tag der mündlichen Prüfung: 5. Juli 2012

Erster Gutachter: Prof. Dr. rer. nat. Hannes Hartenstein
Karlsruher Institut für Technologie (KIT)

Zweiter Gutachter: Prof. Dr. rer. nat. Frank Kargl
Universität Ulm

Acknowledgments

First of all, I would like to express sincere thanks and gratitude to my supervisor Prof. Dr. Hannes Hartenstein for his great support and invaluable feedback. I am especially thankful that I always got all the support I needed despite the geographic distance. I also wish to thank Prof. Dr. Frank Kargl, who was the co-evaluator of this dissertation.

The results presented in this dissertation were obtained during my work at BMW Group Research and Technology in the city of Munich. I want to thank Timo Kosch and Karl-Ernst Steinberg for enabling me to write this thesis at BMW. I especially have to thank Timo for providing me the amount of freedom I needed to execute my research. A special thanks goes to Benjamin Weyl and Markus Strassberger for their mostly hard, but very helpful feedback. I want to thank Oliver Klemp for the enlightening discussions on wireless technology and my work. Thanks go to Matthias Michl for his assistance regarding the reception measurements. Further, I also want to thank all the other colleagues and friends who contributed with feedback and technical discussions to this thesis.

A big thank you goes to Dennis Burgkhardt and Oliver Klemp for proof reading this thesis and providing very valuable feedback in the process.

I want to thank the members of the Decentralized Systems and Network Services Research Group, in particular Jens Mittag, for always welcoming me despite my seldom presence, for the technical discussions, administrative help, as well as bringing the numerous updates of my thesis website online.

To my fellow team members at BMW: Timo, Benjamin, Markus, Marc, Ilse, Benno, Alexandre, Max and Markus again: it has been a great pleasure and a lot of fun working with all of you.

Further, I would like to take this opportunity to thank my friends, as well as the Ph.D. candidates at BMW, who accompanied me in the wonderful last three years.

Last but not least, thanks to my parents: You always supported me and believed in me. I know this is not self-evident. Thank you so much.

Thomas Mangel – Munich, August 2012

Abstract

Inter-vehicle communication promises to increase movement and behavior awareness of vehicles compared to existing technologies like radar. The idea is that every
vehicle regularly transmits information such as position, speed and heading in
Cooperative Awareness Messages (CAMs) to surrounding vehicles. The periodic
CAMs are foreseen to be sent via 5.9 GHz IEEE 802.11p ad-hoc communication.

While the properties of this direct ad-hoc communication have been intensively investigated in recent years, knowledge about radio propagation at inner-city
intersections with potential Line-Of-Sight (LOS) obstruction was scarce at the
start of this thesis, although the suboptimal radio propagation properties due to
the relatively high frequency of 5.9 GHz impact radio-coverage in this scenario.

Furthermore, cellular systems—in principle also able to handle the information exchange—promise a better coverage in the inner-city intersection scenario
due to the high position of base stations and a lower frequency. The potential
limitations of ad-hoc communication on the one hand and possible advantages of
cellular communication on the other hand motivate to compare the suitability of
both communication technologies in a challenging communication environment.

A scenario investigation revealed that cross-traffic assistance at inner-city
intersections represents the desired high demand scenario. It relies on the capacity-
intense regular CAM exchange and needs a high status update rate, raising capacity
concerns especially in cellular networks. Furthermore, a building placement analysis shows that Non-Line-Of-Sight (NLOS) reception is needed in this scenario
in terms of ad-hoc communication.

In order to tackle the lack of knowledge on 5.9 GHz NLOS propagation, an
extensive NLOS measurement campaign was performed at eight intersections in
the city of Munich. A systematic selection of measured intersections enabled the
detailed evaluation of certain influence factors on NLOS reception quality. The
measurements revealed that NLOS reception is well feasible at application critical
distances to intersection center. In a second step, a dedicated 5.9 GHz NLOS path
loss and fading model was deduced. Multi-dimensional fitting enabled a reliable
quantification of the identified influence factors. A comparison to existing models
shows that they mostly differ substantially to reality at 5.9 GHz.

Finally, NLOS reception quality under network competition is being evaluated by performing packet-level network simulations, leveraging the proposed NLOS propagation model. The simulations revealed that high transmission power levels are usable in critical traffic conditions. While reception rates in NLOS are degraded due to network competition, the resulting reception quality seems still tolerable.

In terms of cellular communication, capacity, latency and costs are major concerns. The capacity demand of the investigated application in a cellular system is investigated by an environment analysis. It combines information about base station position, street network, and vehicle flow on streets in order to predict the number of communicating vehicles, and in a second step the inter-vehicle communication driven network load per cell. A high load demand of several thousand CAM/Cell/s is identified.

Available capacity and resource efficient delivery of CAMs are evaluated by a technical analysis of the Universal Mobile Communication System (UMTS) and Long Term Evolution (LTE) cellular standards. Cell broadcasts in the downlink and a random access driven uplink delivery are proposed to prevent duplication overhead in the downlink and potentially under-utilized static connections. While UMTS does not provide sufficient capacity, LTE does due to its higher spectral efficiency and ability to use wider frequency bands. UMTS is characterized by a high latency, while LTE round trip times turn out reasonably low. In conclusion, LTE can enable cross-traffic assistance from a technical perspective.

However, modifications at base stations would be required to support the proposed efficient delivery. Furthermore, a non-negligible amount of bandwidth consumption is found, directly translating into considerable operational costs.

Finally, the ability of ad-hoc and cellular communication to enable cross-traffic assistance at inner-city intersections is compared based on the found results. While both systems can technically enable the application, ad-hoc communication provides a slight advantage regarding latency and reliability. More importantly however, utilizing ad-hoc communication inherits a considerable cost advantage compared to a cellular communication based information delivery.

Zusammenfassung

Vehicle-to-Vehicle (V2V)-Kommunikation bietet die Möglichkeit, die Reichweite des Bewegungswissens über umliegende Verkehrsteilnehmer eines Fahrzeuges gegenüber existierenden Technologien wie zum Beispiel Radar zu erhöhen. Hierdurch können potentiell neue proaktive Sicherheitssysteme realisiert werden. Die Idee ist, dass jedes Fahrzeug Zustandsinformationen wie seine Position, Geschwindigkeit und Fahrtrichtung regelmäßig in Cooperative Awareness Messages (CAMs) an alle umliegenden Fahrzeuge verschickt. Hierdurch kann jedes Fahrzeug ein detailliertes Umgebungsabbild und Bewegungsprognosen erstellen. Für die Kommunikation ist im letzten Jahrzehnt eine spezielle dezentrale Ad-Hoc-Funktechnologie entwickelt worden. Sie arbeitet auf 10 MHz breiten Frequenzbändern bei 5,9 GHz. Die physikalische Schicht und der Medienzugriff sind als IEEE 802.11p standardisiert.

Während die Eigenschaften dieser Ad-Hoc-Funktechnologie intensiv erforscht worden sind, wurde dem Funkverhalten an innerstädtischen Kreuzungen mit potentieller Sichtlinienverdeckung wenig Beachtung geschenkt. Dabei stellen die aufgrund der hohen Frequenz nicht optimalen Funkausbreitungseigenschaften eine große Herausforderung hinsichtlich ausreichender Funkabdeckung dar. In diesem Szenario versprechen darüber hinaus zellulare Kommunikationssysteme, im Prinzip genauso geeignet für den Informationsaustausch, aufgrund der hohen Position der Basisstationen und niedrigeren Frequenzen eine bessere Abdeckung. Die im Fahrzeug nötige zellulare Hardware wird hierbei in Zukunft immer häufiger vorhanden sein, weil die Anbindung von Fahrzeugen an das Internet zunehmend wichtiger wird. Dies motiviert zellulare Kommunikationssysteme als Alternative zum dezentralen Funk zu untersuchen.

Ziel der Arbeit ist es daher, die Leistungsfähigkeit sowohl von Ad-Hoc- als auch zellularer V2V-Kommunikation im Umfeld innerstädtischer Kreuzungen und im Kontext einer V2V-Anwendung zu evaluieren. Die untersuchten Kommunikationstechnologien sind hierbei das dezentrale 5,9 GHz IEEE 802.11p sowie die Mobilfunkstandards UMTS und das zukünftige LTE als momentan am weitesten entwickelte zellulare Systeme. Durch die Fokussierung auf eine Anwendung mit hohen Ansprüchen an Latenz, Übertragungskapazität und räumliche Abdeckung des Funkkanals soll der Frage nachgegangen werden, ob und wo die unterschiedlichen Kommunikationstechnologien als Übertragungsmedium für die V2V-Nachrichten an ihre Grenzen stoßen.

Unter den V2V-Anwendungen haben im Allgemeinen die proaktiven Sicherheitsanwendungen die höchsten Anforderungen. Diese basieren grundsätzlich auf den in CAMs übertragenen Informationen, welche eine höhere Last als ereignisbasierte V2V-Nachrichten erzeugen. Querverkehrsassistenz warnt den Fahrer zum Beispiel, falls sich ein aus einer Querstraße kommendes Fahrzeug auf Kollisionskurs befindet. Dies ist die einzige Applikation, welche einen zweidimensionalen Raum überwachen muss (Straße des Fahrzeugs und die Querstraße). Außerdem ist die Applikation empfindlich gegenüber Fehlern in Bezug auf die Richtungsangaben der Fahrzeuge. In der Folge wird eine hohe Nachrichtenrate von 10 Hz sowie geringe Latenz gefordert. Daher stellt diese Anwendung die für die Untersuchung gewünschten hohen Anforderungen an die Kommunikation.

Im Bereich zellularer V2V-Kommunikation haben sich die wenigen bisherigen Arbeiten auf Applikationen beschränkt, die ausschließlich die wesentlich weniger Last erzeugenden ereignisbasierten Nachrichten benutzen. Die für Querverkehrsassistenz nötigen CAMs werfen allerdings Fragen über die in UMTS und LTE verfügbare Kapazität für ebendiese und die zu erwartende Last durch CAMs in Funkzellen auf. Eine effiziente Nutzung der verfügbaren Kapazität ist hier im Speziellen problematisch, da die Kommunikationscharakteristik von CAMs, kurze aber regelmäßige Pakete, mit der typischen Verbindungsorientierung von zellularen Kommunikationssystemen kollidiert. Dies führt leicht zu einer Verschwendung von zugewiesenen Ressourcen. Des Weiteren müssen alle im Uplink übertragenen CAMs an alle Fahrzeuge verteilt werden. Um Ressourcen zu schonen, ist daher eine Downlink-Übertragung via Broadcast wünschenswert.

Zuerst zeigt die Dissertation anhand einer Umgebungsanalyse am Beispiel der Stadt München die zu erwartende Last pro Funkzelle auf. Die Analyse kombiniert Informationen über die Abdeckung einzelner Zellen, Straßen pro Zelle sowie Verkehrsfrequenzdaten pro Straßenabschnitt, um die Menge der Fahrzeuge pro Funkzelle abzuschätzen. Es zeigt sich, dass über 600 am Verkehr teilnehmende Fahrzeuge in einer Funkzelle existieren können. Auf diesen Zahlen aufbauend wird in der Arbeit dargelegt, dass unter den milderen Annahmen von nur 5 Hz Nachrichtenrate und einer Übertragung ausschließlich im Kreuzungsbereich etwa 1700 CAM/Funkzelle/Sekunde in der Rush-Hour übertragen werden müssten.

Um diese Zahl bewerten zu können, wird die verfügbare Kapazität und ressourceneffiziente Übertragung von CAMs via UMTS und LTE in der Arbeit durch eine technische Analyse der Standards untersucht. Auch die zu erwartende Latenz durch den Umweg über die Infrastruktur wird in diesem Rahmen betrachtet.

Die Analyse zeigt, dass sich die ungünstigen stehenden Verbindungen durch eine Benutzung des Random Access im Uplink und von Broadcast im Downlink umgehen lassen. Allerdings bedingt der Random Access in UMTS eine erhöhte Latenz und eine gewisse Kapazitätslimitierung, wobei aber auch der Downlink bei der erforderlichen robusten Codierung nicht genügend Kapazität für die gefundenen maximalen Mengen an CAMs bietet. LTE wiederum ist mit einer niedrigen Latenz und mehr Kapazität pro Frequenzband technisch durchaus in der Lage, Querverkehrsassistenz zu ermöglichen. Allerdings unterstützt der jetzige Softwarestand in den Basisstationen beider Systeme die theoretisch aufgezeigten Übertragungswege nicht. Des Weiteren hat sich gezeigt, dass für eine ressourcenoptimale Übertragung Standardisierung notwendig wäre.

Die Fähigkeit des dezentralen 5,9 GHz IEEE 802.11p-Standards, Querverkehrsassistenz an innerstädtischen Kreuzungen zu ermöglichen, steht und fällt mit der Frage nach der Notwendigkeit, Informationen unter Non-Line-Of-Sight (NLOS)-Bedingungen zu übertragen, und wie gut dies funktionieren würde. Die Arbeit zeigt durch eine systematische Analyse der Bebauung in München, dass zum Zeitpunkt einer erforderlichen Warnung an den Fahrer, etwa 3 Sekunden vor einem potentiellen Unfall, nur etwa 20 % aller Kreuzungsecken eine Sichtline zwischen zwei sich synchron aus schneidenden Straßen nähernden Fahrzeugen bieten. Unter der Annahme, dass nicht jede Kreuzung mit einem Repeater ausgestattet sein wird, ist es daher angebracht, die Qualität von NLOS-Empfang zu untersuchen. Vor dieser Arbeit existierten nur NLOS-Pfadverlust-Modelle aus dem Mobilfunk für Basisstationen innerhalb einer Häuserschlucht und meist nur für Frequenzen bis 2 GHz. Ein Vergleich der Modelle, wenn rekonfiguriert auf 5,9 GHz, zeigte Unterschiede zwischen den Modellen im prognostizierten NLOS-Pfadverlust von bis zu 20 dB, was deren Verwendbarkeit in Zweifel zieht.

Im Zuge dieser Arbeit ist daher eine umfangreiche Messkampagne an acht Kreuzungen in München durchgeführt worden. Eine systematische Auswahl der getesteten Kreuzungen, basierend auf Clustering-Ergebnissen aus der Bebauungsanalyse, ermöglichte sowohl eine Generalisierung der Ergebnisse als auch die Beurteilung von Einflussfaktoren wie der Weite der Bebauung oder Unterschiede zwischen Stadt- und Vorstadtkreuzungen. Die Messungen haben gezeigt, dass selbst unter Worst-Case-Bedingungen ein guter Empfang in Warndistanz zur Kreuzung existiert. Die Daten der Messungen werden in der Arbeit in einem zweiten Schritt in ein Pfadverlust-und Fading-Modell überführt. Die Ableitung der Pfadverlust-Formel über mehrdimensionales Fitting ermöglichte eine verlässliche Quantifizierung der Einflussfaktoren.

In einem letzten Schritt wird in der Arbeit das Empfangsverhalten im NLOS unter Last untersucht. Hierzu wurden Paket-Level-Simulationen basierend auf dem erstellten Kanal-Modell im ns-2-Netzwerksimulator durchgeführt. Eine Verkehrs-simulation (SUMO) diente der Findung applikationsrelevanter Verkehrsszenarien und damit realistischer Netzwerklast-Level. Es konnte gezeigt werden, dass es in kritischen Situationen möglich ist, mit den gleichen hohen Sendeleistungen wie bei den Messungen zu operieren. Die Empfangsrate im NLOS sinkt zwar durch unter Last entstehende Paket-Kollisionen ab, allerdings ergeben sich immer noch tolerierbare Empfangsraten in der kritischen Phase der Kreuzungsannäherung.

Zusammenfassend wird in der Arbeit am Beispiel einer V2V-Anwendung mit höchsten Anforderungen an die Kommunikation der Grad der Eignung von Ad-Hoc und zellularem Funk für V2V-Kommunikaton verglichen. Die Schwachstelle des dezentralen 5,9 GHz IEEE 802.11p-Systems im Rahmen der Querverkehrsassistenz an innerstädtischen Kreuzungen ist die durch die hohe Frequenz eingeschränkte Fähigkeit zum Empfang im NLOS. Im Zuge der Arbeit wurde umfangreiches Wissen über den NLOS-Empfang aufgebaut und in ein Simulationsmodell überführt. Darauf aufbauend durchgeführte Simulationen erlauben eine Bewertung der in realen Situationen (unter Last) zu erwartenden Empfangseigenschaften. Zwar sind die gefundenen Empfangsraten im NLOS bei 5,9 GHz IEEE 802.11p im Worst-Case relativ gering, dennoch zeigt die Arbeit, dass der nötige NLOS-Empfang im Allgemeinen im Rahmen der Anforderungen gut funktioniert. Zellulare Systeme sind vor allem aus zwei Gründen problematisch: Die Anzahl an Fahrzeugen pro Zelle ist erwartbar hoch und das Übertragungsschema der zu übermittelnden Nachrichten passt nicht zur Auslegung der Systeme auf Punkt-zu-Punkt-Verbindungen. Die Arbeit analysiert die zu erwartende Last und zeigt Wege auf, wie große Mengen CAMs effizient über zellulare Systeme übertragbar sind. Während die Kapazität stark von variablen Parametern abhängt, zeigt die Analyse dennoch, dass sich UMTS schlecht für Querverkehrsassistenz eignet. Ferner wurden Nebenbedingungen gefunden, die eine Umsetzung der Applikation über zellulare Systeme erschweren. Die in zellularen Systemen anfallenden Übertragungskosten sind ein weiteres Hindernis für den Einsatz dieser Technologie.

Im Fazit zeigt der 5,9 GHz IEEE 802.11p Ad-Hoc-Funk trotz der schwierigen Empfangsbedingungen eine annehmbare Leistung. Querverkehrsassistenz über das zellulare LTE-System ist zwar technisch möglich, allerdings lassen Kosten, Leistungs-Einschränkungen und Nebenbedingungen die zellulare Technologie im Nachteil erscheinen.

Contents

1

Introduction

1.1 Motivation

Most automotive safety systems in today's vehicles rely on onboard sensors. Well functioning systems have been realized with this paradigm. Nevertheless, there are clear limitations. Those sensors use visible light or radar to detect objects. In result a line of sight to safety relevant objects is needed. Therefore, these systems are limited in detection range and proximity coverage.

Radio technology based Vehicle-to-Vehicle (V2V) communication systems have the potential to increase range and coverage of location and behavior awareness. As a result, these systems might enable new highly developed pro-active safety systems that warn drivers about dangerous situations before they are even able to see them. Such systems have been investigated in numerous governmental research projects[1] in Europe, the United States (U.S.), and Japan.

The common idea is that each vehicle communicates information like position, speed, and heading periodically to other vehicles in Cooperative Awareness Messages (CAMs). Secondly, vehicles inform others in case of sudden behavior changes such as hard breaking in an event driven fashion. In combination, vehicles are enabled to deduce a highly accurate environment picture, used as basis for movement prediction. Algorithms have been designed that detect different types of dangerous situations based on this knowledge. One simple use case, "extended emergency break light", is presented exemplarily in Figure 1.1.

---

[1]An overview on the V2V communication research project history is given in Section 2.1.1.

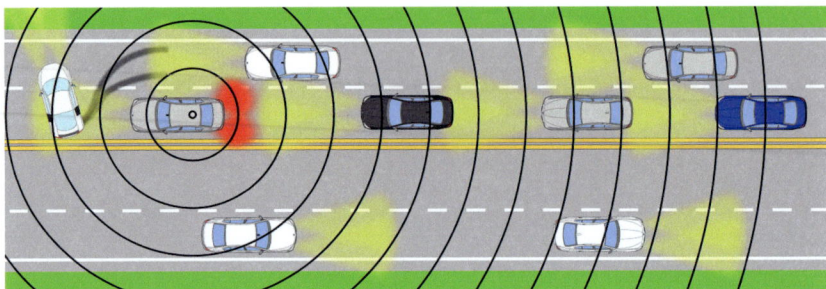

Figure 1.1: Example for a V2V communication application: Extended emergency break light – An event driven message warns surrounding vehicles about an emergency breaking. The blue vehicle on the right can warn its driver way ahead of the danger because it receives a message issued by the breaking vehicle.

For information delivery, a dedicated direct ad-hoc communication technology has been developed in the last decade. The system works on 10 MHz wide frequency bands at 5.9 GHz in the U.S. and Europe. Medium and physical access is standardized as IEEE 802.11p [1]. While many properties of this ad-hoc technology have been intensively investigated in recent years, the knowledge on radio propagation at inner-city intersections with potential Line-Of-Sight (LOS) obstruction has been pretty limited at the start of this thesis, although the suboptimal radio propagation properties due to the relatively high frequency of 5.9 GHz lead to challenges in terms of radio-coverage in this scenario.

Furthermore, cellular communication systems—in principle also able to handle the information exchange—promise a better coverage in the inner-city intersection scenario due to the high position of base stations and a lower frequency. Since the demand for Internet connectivity is rising, cellular modules become more and more common in vehicles. Due to this fact, there is also a trend in the industry to favor cellular systems to enable first simple—low communication demand[2]—connected vehicle applications like the communication of traffic light timings. However, the question arises, if applications with high communication demand might be feasible with cellular systems too.

The potential limitations of ad-hoc communication on the one hand, and possible advantages of cellular communication on the other hand, motivate to compare the suitability of both communication technologies for inter-vehicle communication in a challenging communication environment. Such an environment manifests itself in the inner-city intersection scenario as investigated in this thesis.

---

[2]"communication demand" is characterized and discussed in detail in Section 2.2.1.

1.2 Problem Description

The suitability of ad-hoc and cellular communication to enable inter-vehicle communication at intersections will become most obvious in eventual limitations to support a high demand application. In general, applications that rely on CAMs that are transmitted several times a second will impose the highest demands.

However, such applications are not only challenging in terms of the induced network load, but also depend on the environment. In terms of inner-city intersections, there exist impact factors like the position of buildings or the amount of intersections in a certain area. Such factors influence the two different communication systems each in its own way.

In terms of ad-hoc communication at intersections, the question arises how often Non-Line-Of-Sight (NLOS) reception is needed. The closer buildings are located to an intersection the less view into a crossing street exists, leading to a higher need for NLOS reception. Cellular communication is influenced by the environment primarily in a different way. Each cell in the system covers a certain area. The density of intersections in a city influences the number of communicating vehicles in a single cell coverage area, determining the capacity to be provided by a cellular technology to support CAM transmissions.

In order to judge the performance of both systems in the intersection scenario, it is needed to evaluate the impact of those environmental factors; a task that had not been done before (despite the factor of vehicle density on linear roads).

The second important problem domain is the evaluation of technical factors that influence the performance of the systems. In terms of the ad-hoc communication, knowledge about the ability of 5.9 GHz IEEE 802.11p to support NLOS reception is needed. If the LOS is blocked, diffraction, reflection, and refraction of radio waves potentially enable NLOS reception. However, the relatively high frequency of 5.9 GHz and a difficult radio fading environment will complicate the NLOS reception of packets. Detailed knowledge about NLOS propagation is especially needed to enable a simulation based evaluation of achievable packet reception rates under network competition.

The existing knowledge about 5.9 GHz inter-vehicle NLOS reception was limited however. There only existed NLOS path loss models for cellular base stations inside of building canyons, for example at traffic lights. Most of those models are only specified for an operation frequency of up to 2 GHz. A comparison showed that the predicted NLOS path loss varies by up to 20 dB between the models when parameterized to 5.9 GHz, questioning their usability. In consequence, a reliable NLOS propagation model for 5.9 GHz IEEE 802.11p communication is an open question.

Regarding cellular systems, the available capacity for CAM transmissions is certainly one of the main open questions. Capacity is in particular problematic, as the communication characteristic of CAMs—a broadcast of regular but short messages—conflicts with the point-to-point connection orientation of cellular networks. This easily leads to a waste of scheduled resources. Therefore, a resource efficient way to transmit CAMs is one of the main challenges.

While there was a first research project on cellular inter-vehicle communication [2], it only demonstrated the feasibility of a safety application with low, purely event-driven, information demand. The efficient transmission of CAMs as well as the available capacity for such applications remained open questions. Latency concerns, due to the infrastructure detour, are another problem that needs to be examined in terms of a high demand application.

1.3 Goals

The goal of this thesis is to provide knowledge about the suitability of ad-hoc as well as cellular communication for inter-vehicle communication at inner-city intersections. In particular, a goal is to investigate whether the different communication technologies are able to support a high demand application. This way, the thesis might identify potential weak points in their general ability to support inter-vehicle communication applications.

In a first step, an application with very high communication demand has to be identified. Demand is assumed to express itself in a need for high network capacity, low latency, and reliable communication in a challenging propagation environment.

The goals in terms of cellular systems are to identify the communication demand and to investigate the ability to handle the found demand efficiently. Furthermore, knowledge about the achievable latency is desired. The identification of potential constraints in adopting as well as costs involved in operating the investigated application via cellular communication are a further goal of this thesis.

Based on the identified challenges in the problem description, a first goal of the ad-hoc communication evaluation is to provide knowledge about the NLOS reception necessity. In case NLOS reception is needed, the thesis needs to provide in-depth knowledge on the NLOS reception properties of 5.9 GHz IEEE 802.11p. A dedicated NLOS propagation model and knowledge on the wireless channel behavior under network competition at an inner-city intersection is desired.

In the end, this thesis is intended to compare both communication technologies regarding their performance and potential limitations in the envisioned demanding scenario.

1.4   Approach

First of all, the selection of the investigated application and scenario is performed via a demand comparison between the often assumed inter-vehicle communication applications. Factors taken into account are requirements on latency, communication range, and area coverage, CAM transmission frequency, as well as propagation environment difficulty. The analysis shows that cross-traffic assistance at inner-city intersection is the potentially most challenging application/scenario combination. The following evaluation of the communication systems takes the demands of this application—like warning the driver three seconds before a potential impact—into account in order to provide application relevant performance assessments.

Before investigating the performance of the different technologies, an environment analysis is performed for each technology to identify its special communication demand. A building positioning analysis for intersections in the city of Munich shows the need for NLOS reception in terms of ad-hoc communication driven cross-traffic assistance and identifies common building placements. Such information is needed to perform meaningful measurements and simulations. Regarding cellular systems, an analysis is performed that prognoses the expected number of vehicles per cell in the city of Munich. Based on this number, the needed capacity per cell for CAM transmissions can be concluded.

The investigated cellular systems are Universal Mobile Communication System (UMTS) and the forthcoming Long Term Evolution (LTE), as they are the highest developed systems at the moment. Unfortunately, the performance of these systems is not well measurable, and it is complicated to simulate them in a representative way[3]. In consequence, a theoretic analysis of the standards is performed to examine available capacity, efficient ways of information delivery, and expected latency. The thesis hereby focuses on answering basic questions and identifying dominant influence factors on performance. Also, constraints are identified and discussed that might complicate the adoption of cellular technology for inter-vehicle communication at intersections. Finally, investments as well as operational costs involved in utilizing a cellular system are examined.

Ad-hoc communication is evaluated based on the common 5.9 GHz IEEE 802.11p standard. The technology evaluation first investigates NLOS reception. Based upon the building placement analysis results, NLOS reception measurements were done in eight representative intersections in the city of Munich. The gathered data is transferred into a path loss and fading model afterwards. A fitting based model generation is used to reliably quantify influence factors. In a last step, reception rates under network competition are investigated via packet-level network simulations based on the developed NLOS model. Application relevant

---

[3]The complications in simulating or measuring cellular systems are discussed in Section 3.2.5.

scenarios were identified via traffic simulations. Hence, the results show performance in situations where the application potentially needs to warn the driver.

Finally, the ability of the technologies in supporting the demanding cross-traffic assistance application is compared based on the analysis results.

1.5 Thesis Structure

This section is dedicated to give a short overview about the structure of this thesis as visualized in Figure 1.2.

The thesis starts with an introduction to V2V communication and the selection of the investigated application and scenario in Chapter 2. The technology introduction in Section 2.1 will first of all explain the vision of such a system and introduce the commonly assumed system design as proposed in numerous research projects. Afterwards, the broadcast nature of the transmissions is discussed before an overview on the envisioned applications is given. Based on this brief introduction, the selection of the investigated scenario and application is described

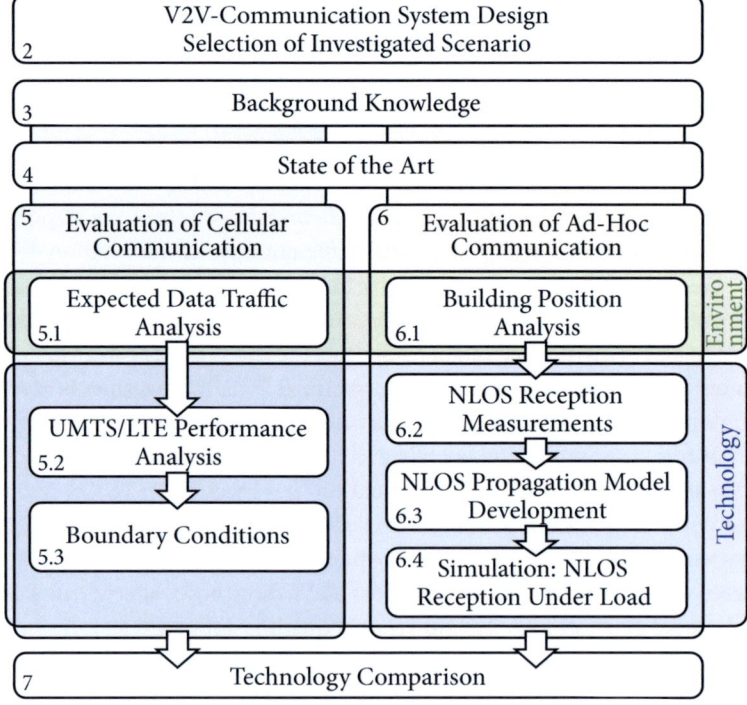

Figure 1.2: Thesis structure.

in Section 2.2. The selection is done via a comparison of the communication demand of the different applications. The selected application and scenario—cross-traffic assistance at inner-city intersections—as well as their implications are described in detail afterwards.

Thesis-specific theoretic background will be discussed in Chapter 3. As visualized in Figure 1.2, the discussion is split by technology. In terms of the 5.9 GHz IEEE 802.11p communication, PHY/MAC, radio channel stress, ad-hoc network simulation, as well as propagation at inner-city intersections are discussed in Section 3.1. The cellular background discussion in Section 3.2 starts with a general system description before discussing implications of inter-vehicle communication in such systems. Afterwards, the basics of UMTS and LTE are explained. Finally, the difficulties to evaluate such systems in the investigated scenario are discussed in order to explain why the performance evaluation of cellular communication in this thesis is done as a theoretic analysis, rather than measurements for example.

The explanation of the theoretic background is followed by a discussion on state of the art research in terms of the thesis topic in Chapter 4. The chapter shows what kind of information is already available and where gaps and weaknesses exist that need to be tackled in the individual parts of the performance analysis in this thesis. It also provides a certain degree of motivation as it discusses some points given in the problem description in Section 1.2 in more detail.

The evaluation of cellular and ad-hoc communication is performed separately in Chapter 5 and 6. As visualized in Figure 1.2, both evaluations first perform an analysis of the environment before evaluating the technical ability of the technologies to handle the application under the identified environment influence factors.

The environment influence investigation in terms of the cellular evaluation in Chapter 5 tries to answer the question how much load is expected due to CAM delivery at inner-city intersections (Section 5.1). The analysis combines data about the size of individual cells, the street network, and vehicle frequency per street segment data in the city of Munich for deriving the expectable number of vehicles per cell. Combining this information with the CAM transmission frequency allows to conclude the number of CAMs that need to be delivered by a cellular system per time. The following performance analysis in Section 5.2 investigates if, and how the determined number of CAMs is transmittable by UMTS and LTE. The analysis examines the transmission options and parameters of the systems to make performance predictions on a theoretic basis. In course of this analysis, some boundary conditions are revealed that are discussed afterwards in Section 5.3, comprising potential rollout constraints, reliability concerns, and a cost analysis.

The evaluation of 5.9 GHz IEEE 802.11p ad-hoc communication in Chapter 6 starts with an analysis of building positions at intersections in Section 6.1. The analysis shows how often NLOS reception is needed in case of cross-traffic assistance information demand and provides information about typical building positions, therefore reference scenarios. Such data is used in the following NLOS measurement campaign in Section 6.2 for selecting representative test intersections. A systematic setup and test environment selection is performed in order to enable the gathering of in-depth knowledge on 5.9 GHz IEEE 802.11p NLOS reception quality under varying influence factors and close to production conditions. In the following Section 6.3, a packet-level NLOS path loss equation and fading characterization is derived from the gathered data. Finally, a packet-level simulation of NLOS reception under network competition is performed in Section 6.4 to gain knowledge on NLOS reception in real-world situations with traffic flow. The simulation uses the newly developed NLOS propagation model to accurately predict NLOS reception.

The results from the two technology evaluations, ad-hoc and cellular, will be set into comparison in Chapter 7. Benefits and issues will be discussed in context of both technologies. Finally, a conclusion and an outlook will be given in Chapter 8.

1.6   Already Published Parts of this Thesis

Most of the evaluations presented in this thesis have already been published in scientific publications:

- The cellular data traffic analysis in Section 5.1 has been published in [3].
- The cellular performance analysis in Section 5.2 is based on [4].
- The building positioning analysis in Section 6.1 has been published in [5].
- The 5.9 GHz IEEE 802.11p NLOS measurement campaign presented in Section 6.2 has been published in [6].
- The NLOS propagation model deduction in Section 6.3 has been published in [7] (conference best paper award) and in an extended version in [8].
- The simulation based investigation of NLOS reception under competition in Section 6.4 has been published in [9].
- The introduction, state of the art, and the background chapter of this thesis are based in parts on passages from the aforementioned papers.
- Publications [3; 6; 7; 8; 9] are accompanied by a website each, providing for example measurement and evaluation visualizations or full evaluation plot sets. A thesis website [10] joins those paper websites. A more detailed description is given in Appendix A.1.

In addition to the papers, parts of this thesis, mainly in the background chapter, are based on passages of the author's Master Thesis [11].

List of Published Papers

[3] T. Mangel and H. Hartenstein, "An Analysis of Data Traffic in Cellular Networks Caused by Inter-Vehicle Communication at Intersections," in *2011 IEEE Intelligent Vehicles Symposium (IV'11)*, Baden-Baden, Germany, Jun. 2011, pp. 473–478. [Online]. Available: http://dx.doi.org/10.1109/IVS.2011.5940495

[4] T. Mangel, T. Kosch, and H. Hartenstein, "A Comparison of UMTS and LTE for Vehicular Safety Communication at Intersections," in *2nd IEEE Vehicular Networking Conference (VNC 2010)*, Jersey City, NJ, USA, Dec. 2010, pp. 293–300. [Online]. Available: http://dx.doi.org/10.1109/VNC.2010.5698244

[5] T. Mangel, F. Schweizer, T. Kosch, and H. Hartenstein, "Vehicular Safety Communication at Intersections: Buildings, Non-Line-Of-Sight and Representative Scenarios," in *8th Int. Conference on Wireless On-Demand Network Systems and Services (WONS 2011)*, Bardonecchia, Italy, Jan. 2011, pp. 35–41. [Online]. Available: http://dx.doi.org/10.1109/WONS.2011.5720197

[6] T. Mangel, M. Michl, O. Klemp, and H. Hartenstein, "Real-World Measurements of Non-Line-Of-Sight Reception Quality for 5.9GHz IEEE 802.11p at Intersections," in *Communication Technologies for Vehicles, (from 3rd Int. Workshop on Comm. Technologies for Vehicles (Nets4Cars 2011))*, ser. Lecture Notes in Computer Science, vol. 6596. Springer Berlin / Heidelberg, Mar. 2011, pp. 189–202. [Online]. Available: http://dx.doi.org/10.1007/978-3-642-19786-4_17

[7] T. Mangel, O. Klemp, and H. Hartenstein, "A Validated 5.9 GHz Non-Line-Of-Sight Path-Loss and Fading Model for Inter-Vehicle Communication," in *11th Int. Conference on ITS Telecommunications (ITST 2011)*, Saint-Pertersburg, Russia, Aug. 2011, pp. 75–80. [Online]. Available: http://dx.doi.org/10.1109/ITST.2011.6060156

[8] T. Mangel, O. Klemp, and H. Hartenstein, "5.9 GHz inter-vehicle communication at intersections: a validated non-line-of-sight path-loss and fading model," *EURASIP Journal on Wireless Communications and Networking*, vol. 2011, no. 1, pp. 182–193, Nov. 2011. [Online]. Available: http://dx.doi.org/10.1186/1687-1499-2011-182

[9] T. Mangel and H. Hartenstein, "5.9GHz IEEE 802.11p Inter-Vehicle Communication: Non-Line-Of-Sight Reception Under Competition," in *3rd IEEE Vehicular Networking Conference (VNC 2011)*, Amsterdam, Netherlands, Nov. 2011, pp. 155–162. [Online]. Available: http://dx.doi.org/10.1109/VNC.2011.6117137

2

The Communication System and Selection of Investigated Scenario

This Chapter will first give a short introduction to inter-vehicle communication in Section 2.1 to provide a solid background for the selection of the investigated application and scenario in the following Section 2.2.

2.1 An Inter-Vehicle Communication System

This section provides a short introduction on inter-vehicle communication and the resulting type of Intelligent Transportation System (ITS). Firstly, the history of inter-vehicle communication is presented before the basic vision and resulting system design is described. Next, the ITS architecture that emerged in recent years is presented. Afterwards, the general communication characteristic is discussed. The introduction is concluded by an overview on the envisioned connected ITS applications.

2.1.1 History, Vision, and System Design

History   The first research on two-way communication between vehicles as well as infrastructure was performed in the 1970s. The Comprehensive Automobile Traffic Control System (CACS) project started 1973, funded by the Japanese Ministry of International Trade and Industry (MITI) [12]. The objectives of this project

- reduction of road traffic congestion
- reduction of exhaust fumes caused by traffic congestion
- prevention of accidents
- enhancement of public and social role of automobiles

still remained valid through the long history of connected vehicle research projects. The very first projects in Europe (Prometheus) and the U.S. (Path) started in 1986.

These three pioneering projects were followed by a huge number of research projects[1] in the last decade. The starting point to those efforts was marked by the availability of low-cost Wireless Local Area Network (WLAN) radio hardware and the availability of the Global Positioning System (GPS) for civilian use. Furthermore, in 1999, the U.S. Federal Communications Commission (FCC) allocated 75 MHz of bandwidth in the 5.9 GHz band for Dedicated Short Range Communication (DSRC) between vehicles and infrastructure [13]. This dedicated bandwidth allocation, close to the 5.2–5.8 GHz band used by IEEE 802.11a, ultimately revived the research interest.

In the U.S., the U.S. Department of Transportation (USDOT) started with VSC a research program in 2002 mainly targeted at vehicle safety that was followed up by VSC-A. The connection between vehicles and infrastructure was investigated in the Vehicle Infrastructure Integration (VII) initiative and CICAS-V project.

In Europe, several Framework 6 and 7 Programs of the European Commission were initiated. The eSafety initiative was started in 2001. In the following, SAFESPOT, COOPERS, CVIS, iTETRIS, and SEVECOM were targeted at special topics of connected ITS. The 2010 finished PRE-DRIVE C2X project and its DRIVE follow-up are intended to prepare European field tests and develop a unified architecture.

Inter-vehicle communication was investigated in several national research projects, too. In terms of Germany, the FleetNet, NoW, Aktiv, and sim^{TD} projects should be mentioned. In particular provides the currently running sim^{TD} project a comprehensively specified architecture and deploys a huge field test.

Harmonization of research activities is performed on a European level in the COMeSafety and COMeSafety 2 projects. Most recent, a U.S.-EU task force was initiated. Another organization coordinating interests is the Car-to-Car Communication Consortium (C2C-CC) consisting of many vehicle manufacturers (OEMs) and industry suppliers. A more in depth history on inter-vehicle communication in Japan, Europe and the U.S. can be found in [14].

---

[1]Note that no references to the websites of the research projects mentioned in this section are given as the page contents and their addresses change frequently. Furthermore, the corresponding websites should be easily discoverable by the given project names.

The work on a dedicated radio interface for vehicular communication started in 2004. The Institute of Electrical and Electronics Engineers (IEEE) created a task group to develop an amendment to the IEEE 802.11 standard, called 802.11p. In addition, a working group was formed to develop specifications on the higher layers of a vehicular protocol stack (IEEE 1609). IEEE 1609 for example handles multi-channel coordination.

Further standardization on Intelligent Transportation Systems has been performed by ETSI, SAE, ISO and others in recent years. Subjects currently in standardization are e.g. the message format or load control on the wireless channel.

While the possibility to use cellular communication was specified and briefly investigated in many of the mentioned projects, dedicated projects that solely investigate the usability of cellular technology for vehicular communication only emerged a few years ago. The CoCar project started in 2006 in context of the German "Aktiv" project and was followed up by the CoCarX project. An analysis on the topics and results of those two projects is given in Section 4.1.3 later on.

Vision The envisioned potential benefits of connected vehicles and infrastructure are basically twofold: Firstly, radio connectivity can improve the awareness of the vehicle and the driver about other road traffic participants. Range and coverage of location awareness can be increased to improve traffic safety. Secondly, an envisioned comprehensive knowledge of traffic conditions can enable improvements in traffic efficiency. On the one hand, the information exchange with infrastructure further increases the environment knowledge of vehicles. On the other hand, it should allow an optimized traffic flow control.

Sensors monitoring the environment in current vehicles rely on ultrasonic sound, radar or recently also lidar (e.g. [15]). These technologies evaluate reflections of their own transmission to detect objects and need an unobstructed line of sight to do so. If a vehicle transmits its position to another vehicle via radio signals, this limitation is relaxed. Radio signals bend around objects up to a certain degree, are reflected or diffracted and will in consequence allow reception in near LOS or even NLOS conditions. The range of radio transmissions is much higher as well, reaching 1–2 km in terms of the envisioned 5.9 GHz communication on highways, while the detection ranges of current commercial long range radar sensors are limited to $\approx$250 m. Radio technology potentially allows to achieve awareness of all road participant in a radius of at least several hundreds of meters around a vehicle. Such data can be used to create a long range environment map, enabling to warn a driver early about dangerous situations ahead or adapt the vehicle systems for energy efficient operation.

Another benefit over traditional sensors is the ability to achieve an information awareness far exceeding simple object localization. For example, a vehicle might distribute rain sensor data to warn others, inform a traffic light about its turn wish to influence its timing, or communicate its envisioned route to central authorities to enable global traffic optimizations. Also, multi-hop communication can in principle extend the range of information delivery beyond the direct radio communication range.

System Design   In order to enable such a vision of connected vehicles, common system design principles emerged throughout the many research projects in the last decade.

Awareness about surrounding vehicles will be achieved by a regular broadcast of CAMs via the 5.9 GHz IEEE 802.11p ad-hoc communication technology. Such messages are transmitted by broadcast several times a second (10 Hz are often assumed) and contain a basic information set containing position, heading, curvature, speed and acceleration. Every vehicle monitors the CAM broadcasts from all other surrounding vehicles, enabling the deduction of a detailed environment picture. Based on this picture, pro-active safety applications can perform movement predictions of other vehicles to detect potentially dangerous situations.

In case of unforeseen behavior changes or dangerous situations, like hard breaking, additional CAMs are transmitted with increased power. Those event-driven CAMs are intended to increase awareness beyond the regular CAM information exchange. Furthermore, detected events such as a traffic-jam-end are geocasted by Decentralized Environmental Messages (DENMs). The event-driven messages in particular support hazard warning applications.

Regular CAMs and event-driven DENMs are envisioned to be transmitted on a dedicated control channel reserved to those safety critical messages. In general, the systems are able to communicate on multiple channels. Most current projects (such as sim^{TD}) proclaim a two transceiver design to support a parallel communication with infrastructure or enable commercial services like billing. Service announcements will be made on the always monitored control channel.

Infrastructure connectivity is enabled via road side stations, containing the same 5.9 GHz IEEE 802.11p hardware as vehicles. However, most inter-vehicle communication systems also envision cellular links to propagate information relevant to vehicles in huge areas or to access for example traffic information along a route.

2.1.2   System Architecture

The numerous research projects came up with a complete communication architecture to support the envisioned system design. Most of those architectures are in principle very similar. The European COMeSafety harmonization project describes a unified architecture view in its "European ITS Communication Architecture" deliverable [16]. The architecture comprises four main ITS communication components, ITS Vehicle Station, ITS Roadside Station, ITS Central Station and ITS Personal Station. An ITS station consists of an Application Unit (AU) and a Communication and Control Unit (CCU). From a network stack perspective, an AU contains the communication protocol layers while a CCU covers the lower layers up to the transport layer.

The envisioned network and protocol stack is visualized in Figure 2.1. The stack basically consists of six components: The four stacked layers "Access Technology", "Network and Transport", "Facility" and "Applications", plus the two cross-layer components "Management" and "Security".

The "Access Technology" layer comprises the physical and data link layer of various communication technologies as shown in Figure 2.1. The communication

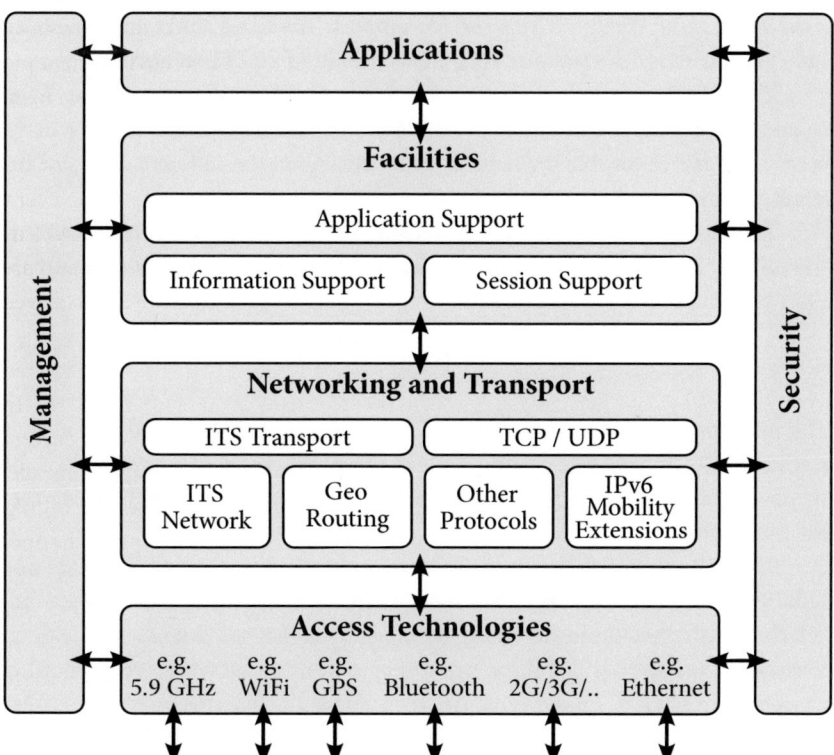

Figure 2.1: The Reference Protocol Stack from the COMeSafety Project ITS Station Reference Architecture – Reproduced with slight simplifications from COMeSafety Deliverable D31 v2.0 [17] and v3.0 [16].

technologies are used for external as well as internal communication and are not necessarily wireless. The complete communication stack is included for some specific non-ITS communication technologies such as cellular 3G/4G or Bluetooth.

The "Network and Transport" layer provides the protocols for data delivery between ITS stations and ITS external stations such as the Internet. It covers ITS specific transport mechanisms like CAM delivery or geo-routing of data to other ITS participants. In this domain, it also handles functions such as congestion control and reliable end-to-end delivery if requested. Communication to non-ITS domains is for example provided via classical TCP/IP.

The "Facilities" layer contains various functions to support applications and to help managing the system. The layer for example enables to address applications and to discover and use new services in the ITS domain or provides Human Machine Interface (HMI) support. It also checks relevance, aggregates, stores, and maintains information such as sensor data or received CAMs. The latter manifests itself in the Local Dynamic Map (LDM) support. The LDM stores and maintains information about the surrounding environment of an ITS station.

The "Applications" layer covers the different ITS applications. The "Management" cross-layer configures the different stack components. The "Security" cross-layer is responsible for security and privacy on the different layers of the stack and manages for example station identities.

Therefore, from an ITS vehicle stations perspective, the ad-hoc as well as the cellular links that are intended to be investigated in this thesis already do exist in today's ITS architecture.

2.1.3 A Pervasive Broadcast System

The main purpose of such an inter-vehicle communication based ITS is environment knowledge, manifesting itself in the LDM. Whatever applications, be it pro-active safety or prospective adjustments of vehicle systems to safe fuel, are built upon it.

The LDM is mainly built upon the information transmitted in CAMs and DENMs. Both message types are transmitted as broadcasts. Therefore, every vehicle within communication range is implicitly addressed as a receiver of those messages. Considering that those messages are transmitted with communication ranges up to 1–2 km, lots of potential receivers exist. Furthermore, the CAMs are transmitted multiple times a second by every vehicle. In combination, each vehicle might receive a high number of CAMs per second from vehicles in its surrounding. Therefore, from a general communication demand perspective, inter-vehicle communication manifests itself as an unbounded pervasive uncoordinated broadcast system [18] with non-negligible network capacity demand.

2.1.4   Applications

In order to conclude this introduction to inter-vehicle communication systems, a short overview on envisioned applications that might be realized with such a system is given in the following. Applications can be classified in three different groups: Safety and Efficiency Applications as well as Value Added Services.

Traffic Safety Applications   represent the first group. They can be subdivided with regard to their information demand in two subgroups. First of all, applications that rely on a complete environment picture; hence rely on the regularly transmitted CAMs:

- *Forward Collision Warning* – A vehicle monitors the movement of vehicles in the same lane ahead and warns if a forward collision becomes likely.
- *Cross Traffic Assistance* – A vehicle approaching an intersection monitors the collision probability to vehicles approaching from the intersecting road based on movement prediction.
- *Overtaking Vehicle* – A vehicle signals its presence in case it overtakes. Other vehicles use this information and their environment knowledge to ensure a secure overtaking process.
- *Lane Change Assistant* – The movement of vehicles on neighboring lanes on a highway is monitored in case a driver wants to change lanes.
- *Merging Assistance* – The driver is assisted in finding a gap while merging onto a highway. The merging region can be taken into account from map data.

Secondly, there are applications that can potentially be realized with event driven notifications only:

- *Approaching Emergency Vehicle* – Emergency vehicles inform others about their presence to speed up their passage.
- *Post Crash Warning, Car Breakdown Warning, Slow Vehicle Warning* – Crashed or immobilized vehicles—representing a hazard—alert approaching vehicles.
- *Emergency Electronic Break Lights* – A vehicle communicates a hard breaking. This way, following vehicles can be warned even if there are vehicles in between obstructing the sight of the driver.
- *Wrong Driving Direction Warning* – A vehicle detects that it is driving in the wrong direction and issues a warning.
- *Decentralized Floating Car Data* – Detected events such as a traffic jam, road works, slippery road, fog, rain or wind are propagated to the surrounding. Geo-cast allows keeping those warnings active in a certain region.

Traffic Efficiency Applications use the environment map or event data to increase traffic efficiency in terms or travel times or fuel consumption:

- *Green Light Optimized Speed Advisory (GLOSA)* – A traffic light propagates its timing to approaching vehicles, enabling them to give a speed advice to the driver for optimizing the time of arrival.
- *Green Wave Assistant* – A variant of GLOSA, trying to optimize green waves.
- *Traffic Information and Recommended Itinerary* – Information is delivered to vehicles to enhance their route decisions.
- *Electronic Traffic Sign* – Signs communicate presence or information to vehicles.
- *Future Speed Profile* – Vehicles predict future speed by monitoring motion on street ahead for saving fuel by optimizing drive train or guiding driver to do so.

Value Added Services are for example a "Point of Interest Notification", "Local Electronic Commerce", "Electronic Toll Collect", "Stolen Vehicle Alert", "Map Download", "Instant Messaging" or "Media Downloading", to name a few. Those services would be operated on one of the service channels.

This section presents the most important applications. A complete list of applications can be found for example in [17].

2.2 Application and Scenario Selection

The goal of this thesis—as discussed in Section 1.3—is to evaluate the suitability of ad-hoc and cellular communication to support a high demand application in a challenging scenario; hence asking the question if they are able to support all of the envisioned applications, or only a subset thereof. Such focusing on a particular application is also intended to limit the scope of the investigation and provide results that take application demands into account.

This section will firstly discuss the reasons to investigate the cross-traffic assistance application in the inner-city intersection scenario. Afterwards, it describes the properties of the selected application and scenario and their implications on communication demand.

2.2.1 Application Communication Demand

The communication paradigms in the ITS reference architecture as presented in Section 2.1.2 are twofold. On the one hand, the system contains the ITS specific communication exchange, and on the other hand the more traditional connection driven mechanisms that are mainly provided to enable management and value added services.

This thesis will concentrate on the ITS specific communication that enables the safety and efficiency applications. Its pervasive broadcast character as described in Section 2.1.3, together with the demands of the envisioned safety applications, leads to a high communication demand and puts challenge on both communication technologies. As the "pervasiveness" of the system, and therefore communication challenge, is strongly bound to the delivery of the regular CAM transmissions, applications that are purely based on event-driven messages with their limited communication demand are not taken into consideration here.

The demand of different safety applications that rely on CAM transmissions is compared in the following. The goal is to find an application with high demand on capacity, latency and spatial coverage of the radio signal. Four different types of application classes are compared in Table 2.1. The comparison is based on three different requirement types: time and range of interest, requirement on information quality and spatial monitoring of the environment.

	Cross Traffic Assistance	Longitude Assistance (e.g. Forward Collision Warning)	Future Speed Profile	Traffic Information (collecting RSU)
Time period being of interest	Past / Now / Future [ms–5s]	Past / Now / Future [ms–min]	Future [s–min]	Past / Now / Future [min–h]
Distance range of interest (movement prediction quality requirement at that range)	Near (very high) to Medium (high)	Near (very high) to Medium (medium)	Near (medium) to Far (low)	Near/ Medium/ Far (low)
Influence factors on movement prediction quality (information quality requirement)	Position (high [m]) + Speed (high) + Heading (very high)	Position (high [m]) + Speed (high)	Position (high [m]) + Speed (middle)	Position (low [m...10m]) + Speed (low) + Destination (low)
Monitored corridor	2D	1D	1D	2 * 1D

Table 2.1: Communication demand comparison of different application classes that rely on CAMs. Quality requirements are judged based on application requirements, but are subjective as studies discussing requirements of applications in the required detail are non-existent to the best of the author's knowledge. For example, range of interest and movement prediction quality requirement were not analyzed in [19].

The "Traffic Information" class comprises use cases that use Road Side Units (RSUs) to monitor traffic based on CAMs. RSUs, for example located at traffic lights, might be used to collect an environment picture and report past, present or prognoses of future traffic information to a central authority or use such data for behavioral adaptation (e.g. adaptive traffic light timing). The general accuracy of such information does not need to be high; an update every second might be sufficient. In general, a line of sight from an RSU to monitored vehicles can be assumed. In terms of spatial coverage, a traffic light RSU at an intersection will monitor two dimensions, but with a one dimensional character from a signal propagation perspective.

The "Longitude Assistance" and "Feature Speed Profile" classes are similar in terms of the monitored area. "Longitude Assistance" comprises applications that monitor the behavior of vehicles ahead to warn the driver or adapt the vehicle speed (cruise control). "Feature Speed Profile" will monitor the upcoming street corridor to predict future speeds and adapt the vehicle drive train for saving fuel or guide the driver to do so. The safety applications from the first class will have higher demands on the accuracy and time resolution of information, whereas the speed profile needs a longer information horizon and therefore a higher communication range. In terms of spatial coverage, both classes only need to monitor a one dimensional corridor in driving direction.

Finally, the "Cross Traffic Assistance" safety application in particular needs a high accuracy of heading and placement information, as small differences will have strong influence on the prognosis about time and place when/where a vehicle will cross an intersection and in consequence collision probability [20; 21]. Probably even more importantly, the application needs information from two dimensions, as it has to "look" into a crossing street. The view is here potentially obstructed by buildings or trees, impacting reception quality.

Traffic information gathering obviously has the lowest requirements. Longitude assistance applications come in second, having high requirements on time resolution leading to a higher capacity demand. Furthermore, reception rates need to be higher as these applications are safety relevant. Cross traffic assistance has the highest demands. It constantly needs to monitor two dimensions with high accuracy to be able to predict potential collisions. Objects might obstruct the line of sight between vehicles approaching an intersection. This challenges the communication link reliability, especially in terms of the ad-hoc communication.

Of course, longitude assistance on multi-lane highways might also impose a high load demand, especially challenging a cellular system. However, the more complicated propagation conditions at an inner city intersection motivate to rather investigate cross-traffic assistance.

In consequence, this thesis evaluates the communication technologies with respect to CAM delivery for cross-traffic assistance. The properties of the application are described in the following section.

2.2.2   Cross Traffic Assistance

Cross traffic assistance constantly monitors vehicles on the crossing street while a vehicle is approaching an intersection. The application prognoses the future trajectory for the vehicle and all close-by vehicles approaching the intersection from the crossing street. In pseudo-code, the prognosis can be expressed simplified as:

$$\text{Position}_{\text{Future}} = \text{Position}_{\text{Last}} + f(\text{Speed}_{\text{Last}}, \text{Heading}_{\text{Last}}, \text{Curvature}_{\text{Last}}, \text{Time}_{\text{ToFuture}})$$

The last known position, speed, heading, and curvature for surrounding vehicles will be taken from the last received CAM transmission from those vehicles. Therefore, not only the quality of received information, but also their age influences the projection quality.

The application will monitor if the own and a crossing vehicles trajectory will intersect in future points in time and classify such event as a potential collision. For a detailed description of a proposed detection algorithm see [20]. The classification accuracy depends especially on the self-positioning as well as heading estimation accuracy of the received information [20]. The latter, as small deviations in heading will considerably change the point of trajectory crossing. As heading might change with time, the age of the last received information becomes even more important.

The application will warn a driver acoustically or visually 3 s before a potential collision. The point of last intervention is roughly 1 s before the potential impact. Both numbers derive from the simple breaking-distance formula:

$$d_{\text{stop}} = v_0 * t_{\text{reac}} + \frac{v_0{}^2}{2a}$$

where v_0 is the initial speed in m/s, t_{reac} the reaction time in seconds, and a the deceleration in m/s^2. Given a typical driver reaction time of 1 s and the maximum user initiated deceleration in normal intersection approaching of $\approx 3.1\,m/s^2$ [20], this leads to roughly 3 s at v_0 speeds of 30–50 km/h. The last intervention point of 1 s before a potential impact roughly corresponds to 0.1 s system reaction time and a maximum vehicle deceleration of $a = 8\,m/s^2$. In terms of the envisioned real algorithm design, the computation is more complicated as guard spaces need to be considered [20]. Also, potential points of collisions in the intersection are dependent on the inflow lanes of both vehicles. This is simplified in this thesis by assuming the intersection center as potential point of collision.

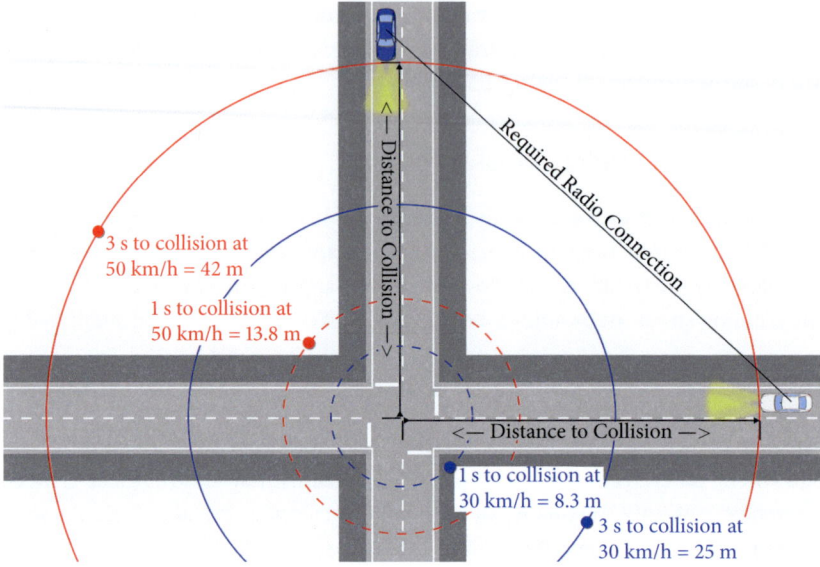

Figure 2.2: Cross-traffic assistance application demands. Warning and last intervention distances at different speeds, determining the required radio connection under simultaneous approaching.

The distance implications of the application are visualized in realistic scaling in Figure 2.2. It shows the warning and intervention distances under simultaneous approaching of crossing vehicles at approaching speeds of 30 and 50 km/h—typical inner-city speed limits in Europe. An ad-hoc communication system has to cover at least the distance between vehicles at those distances to intersection center in a reliable fashion. A cellular system needs to ensure that all vehicles in such circles receive the information propagated by an approaching vehicle. In case cell borders are crossing an intersection, a cellular communication based solution must ensure that information is delivered to all relevant cells.

2.2.3   Inner-City Intersections

Not only the cross-traffic application itself, but also the environment at intersections has implications on the communication.

Inner-city intersections considerably complicate the communication in the cross-traffic assistance use-case compared against rural intersections. Especially the ad-hoc communication suffers from buildings at corners. They can lead to an obstruction of LOS between vehicles in the critical moments of intersection

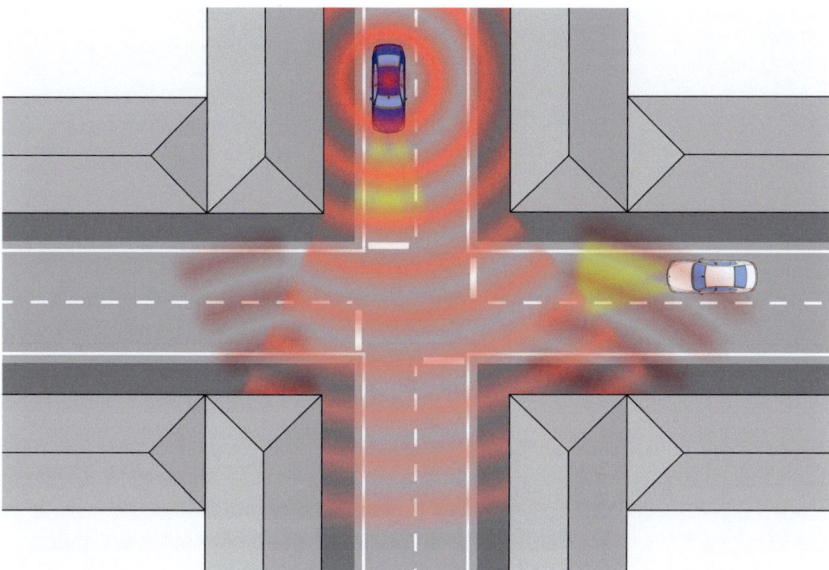

Figure 2.3: Direct ad-hoc communication at inner-city intersection with line-of-sight obstruction by buildings in cross-traffic assistance critical situation: NLOS reception is required and might be enabled by a reflected radio signal component.

approaching, complicating reception. If the LOS is blocked, diffraction, reflection and refraction of radio waves can enable NLOS reception. But, the relatively high frequency of 5.9 GHz and a difficult radio fading environment will complicate the NLOS reception of packets.[2] Figure 2.3 visualizes an inner-city intersection with obstructed LOS. Here, exemplarily a reflection of the transmitted signal reaches the vehicle in the crossing street.

The analysis on building positions in the City of Munich in Section 6.1 shows that NLOS reception is needed. If two vehicles are approaching synchronously at 50 km/h, only 22 % of all intersection corners provide a LOS between the vehicles at the desired warning point of 3 s to a potential impact. While RSUs might re-broadcast messages and reduce the need for NLOS reception, it is unlikely that the majority of crossings will be equipped with a dedicated RSU in the future. Non-equipped intersections will predominantly exhibit NLOS radio link conditions between vehicles, motivating to investigate inner-city intersection and the complicated NLOS reception in this thesis. Also, the existing knowledge about NLOS reception quality of 5.9 GHz IEEE 802.11p was rather limited before this thesis as discussed in Chapter 4.

---

[2]Background Section 3.1.4 provides a more detailed discussion on propagation at intersections.

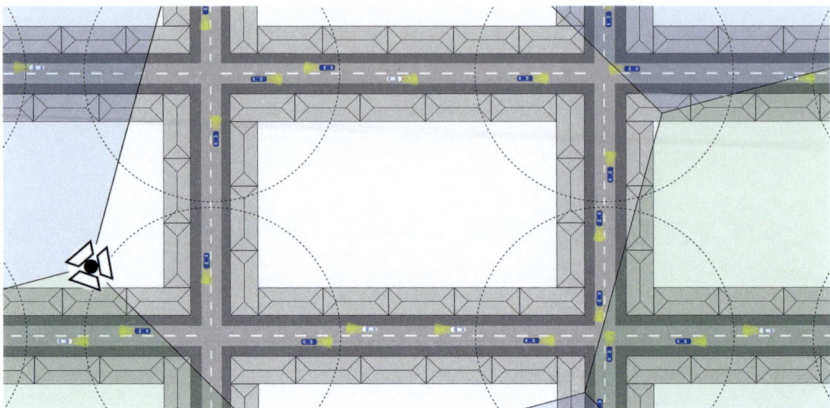

Figure 2.4: Cellular coverage of city – A cell covers multiple intersections and most stretches of streets are close to intersection center (circles show 42 m distance): Even if it is assumed that only vehicles at intersections communicate (blue), most vehicles in a cell would communicate CAMs to enable cross-traffic assistance.

A high density of intersections per area implicates that vehicles often will be located close to intersections and therefore required to communicate CAMs to enable cross-traffic assistance. The analysis on cell sizes and street network in the city of Munich in Section 5.1 reveals for example that 50 % of all street km in the city of Munich are within 42 m (the warning distance at 50 km/h) to an intersection. Furthermore, given the fact that likely high transmission powers are required to enable NLOS reception in intersection vicinity, this implicates high load levels for ad-hoc communication in cities due to increased signal propagation lengths in LOS.[3]

In terms of cellular communication, the high intersection and vehicle densities in cities lead to high numbers of needed CAM transmissions per area. An example on how intersection density, cell size, and application communication demand might lead to many communicating vehicles per cell is visualized in Figure 2.4. The scenario is demanding in terms of capacity, as each cell only provides a certain capacity that must be shared by all nodes in the area it covers. While the cell coverage area (cell size) is certainly smaller in cities as compared to rural areas, the high density of intersections in cities will nevertheless lead to a high communication demand per cell.

In combination, with NLOS reception requirements in terms of the ad-hoc system and capacity per area demands in terms of the cellular system, inner-city intersections lead to the desired difficult environment conditions in terms of both communication technologies.

---

[3] A more detailed explanation on this problem is given in technical background Section 3.1.4.

3

Background Knowledge

This chapter will provide the technical background to the performance evaluations in this thesis. The chapter first discusses the characteristics of the ad-hoc technology and its implications on CAM transmissions at inner-city intersections and their evaluation, before providing the same for cellular communication.

The background discussion in this chapter is certainly not describing the technologies and methods in every detail. Instead, it focuses on aspects that are relevant to the performance evaluations in Chapter 5 and 6 of this thesis.

3.1   Ad-Hoc Communication via 5.9 GHz IEEE 802.11p

Direct ad-hoc communication works without a central coordination entity: the nodes need to coordinate the access to the channel in a cooperative fashion. In consequence, the Physical Layer (PHY) and Medium Access Control (MAC) of the 5.9 GHz IEEE 802.11p technology play an important role in terms of performance. PHY characteristics are further defining reception in different propagation environments. Hence, this section starts with a description of IEEE 802.11p PHY/MAC in Section 3.1.1. Afterwards, the impact of channel load on reception rate is discussed in Section 3.1.2. MAC imperfections are one of the main problems here. The evaluation in Section 6.4 is based on network simulation. The background on such simulations is described in Section 3.1.3. It comprises PHY/MAC simulation as well as propagation modeling. The propagation modeling description also serves as background to the propagation model deduction in Section 6.3. Finally, the basic properties and implications of the special propagation conditions at intersections with NLOS are discussed in Section 3.1.4. Those general NLOS propagation findings serve as important basis for the whole ad-hoc evaluation in Chapter 6.

3.1.1 IEEE 802.11p PHY/MAC and Channels

The term IEEE 802.11p stands on the one hand for an amendment to the IEEE 802.11 standard, and is on the other hand often used to describe the general lower layers of inter-vehicle communication. This section will first describe the allocated frequencies and intended communication channels, before discussing important aspects of the PHY and MAC in the IEEE 802.11p standard [1].

Frequency Allocation and Channels In Europe and the U.S., dedicated frequency bands at 5.9 GHz were reserved for ITS communications. In the U.S., the FCC allocated 75 MHz of spectrum at 5850–5905 MHz [13]. In Europe, 30 MHz of spectrum at 5875–5905 MHz named G5A were granted to ITS by the European Communications Committee (ECC) in 2008 [22]. A G5B named extension at 5855–5875 MHz is in recommended state.

IEEE 802.11p works on 10 MHz wide frequency bands at 5.9 GHz. Therefore, the allocated frequency spectrum is wide enough to contain multiple channels. The allocated frequencies, regulatory power limits and the intended channel usage situation in the U.S. and Europe is visualized in Figure 3.1. As the figure reveals, a single control channel accompanied by two service channels dedicated to safety is common practice. The control channel is used to deliver CAMs and DENMs as

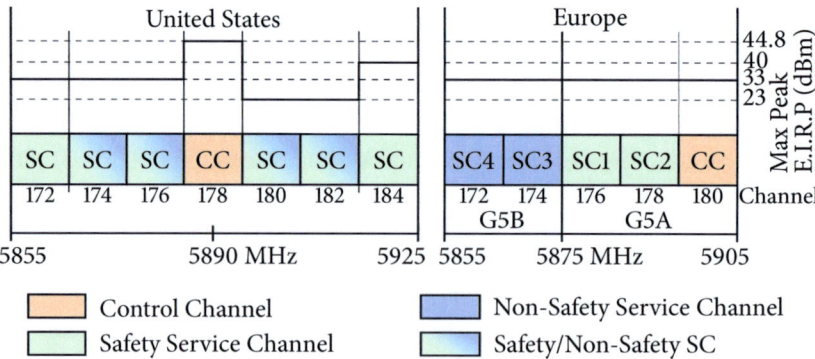

Figure 3.1: Frequency allocation and usage in the U.S. and Europe. Common are one control and two service channels for safety. Power limitations are given as Maximum Peak E.I.R.P.

well as service announcements for services provided on the service channels. The two safety service channels are used for vehicle to roadside and high-availability (U.S.) [23] or geo-routed data (Europe) [16]. Non-safety channels might be used for value added services. As this thesis is intended to investigate CAM delivery, it will focus on the single common control channel in the evaluation.

The allowed radiation power is important, as it effectively limits the communication range. The maximum peak Equivalent Isotropically Radiated Power (E.I.R.P.) is limited in Europe to 33 dBm [22; 24], corresponding to an allowed power density of 23 dBm/MHz. In the US, it is allowed to operate the common control and one safety channel at even higher peak powers of up to 44.8 and 40 dBm [13]. However, currently available IEEE 802.11p hardware (e.g. based on IEEE 802.11p chipsets from Atheros) is limited to a maximal output power of 21–23 dBm. Therefore, an antenna gain of ≈10 dB is allowed in case of no cable loss. More interestingly, the maximal allowed values will likely not be used in any case: it has been proposed to reduce the maximum power on the European SC2, SC3 and SC4 channels to reduce negative inter-channel interference onto the critical CC and SC1 channels [25].

PHY   Physically, packets are modulated onto the 10 MHz wide carrier with Orthogonal Frequency Division Multiplexing (OFDM). OFDM splits the available frequency into a certain number of sub-carriers, where neighboring ones are orthogonal to each other. Due to the orthogonality, no frequency guard spacing is needed between sub-carriers as in normal frequency multiplexing. This way, the frequency spectrum is used efficiently while maintaining the robustness advantages of frequency multiplexing: Small sub-carriers lead to a long symbol duration, having the advantage that a guard interval—covering the time until signal reflections arrive—can be added at little overhead. The guard interval reduces problems with inter-symbol interference, as reflections of one symbol likely arrive within the interval and are therefore not overlaying the next transmitted symbol.

IEEE 802.11p uses 64 sub-carriers with a width of 0.15625 MHz each, where 48 are used for data, 4 for phase reference and 12 as unused spacing distance to the neighboring channels (visualized in Figure 3.2). The Fast Fourier Transformation (FFT) symbol duration is 6.4 μs and the additional guard interval 1.6 μs, leading to a total symbol duration of 8 μs. As the signal propagates at speed of light (roughly $3 * 10^8$ m/s), a reflection detour of up to 480 m is covered.

The PHY layer of IEEE 802.11p is a modification of IEEE 802.11a. IEEE 802.11a uses a 20 MHz channel instead of 10 MHz, but the same number of carriers. In consequence, the data rates in IEEE 802.11p are half of the IEEE 802.11a ones, but the symbol duration and symbol guard period double. Therefore, the robustness against inter-symbol interference has been increased in IEEE 802.11p.

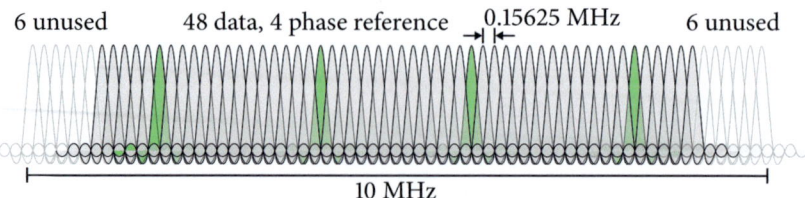

Figure 3.2: Signal modulation on one 10 MHz IEEE 802.11p channel – OFDM modulation with 64 sub-carriers.

IEEE 802.11p provides data rates from 3 to 27 Mbps. Those data rates are generated by four different modulations and three different coding rates. Modulation defines the number of encoded bits per single sub-carrier wave. More bits per waveform translate into less robustness to signal distortions in the decoder. Coding rate defines the forward error control in the signal. Only a certain portion of all bits is used for data, the rest is used for error detection and correction. The available data rates together with their construction are shown in Table 3.1. Simulation studies showed that it is most likely needed to limit the modulation to QPSK to achieve robust CAM transmissions [26]. The study showed that 6 Mbps seems optimal under CAM induced network competition.

The data of a single packet is distributed over all OFDM sub-carriers in IEEE 802.11p. In consequence, a packet is transmitted with the full channel data rate and occupies the full channel frequency bandwidth. Therefore, the MAC

Data Rate (Mbps)	Modulation	Coding Rate	Coded Bits per Subcarrier	Coded Bits per OFDM Symbol	Data Bits per OFDM Symbol
3	BPSK	1/2	1	48	24
4.5	BPSK	3/4	1	48	36
6	QPSK	1/2	2	96	48
9	QPSK	3/4	2	96	72
12	16-QAM	1/2	4	192	96
18	16-QAM	3/4	4	192	144
24	64-QAM	2/3	6	288	192
27	64-QAM	3/4	6	288	216

Table 3.1: IEEE 802.11p data rates and their specification (reproduced from [23]). Modulation leads to "coded bits" while coding rate specifies the final amount of pure data bits per OFDM symbol. In general: the less data bits per symbol, the more robust the transmission.

has to ensure that only one transmission is present on the channel to prevent negative effects of multiple parallel signal components (multi-user interference, discussed in Section 3.1.2).

MAC The MAC serves the purpose of managing the access to the system and wireless medium between multiple users.

The IEEE 802.11 standard defines users in a network as participants of a service set. It is named Basic Service Set (BSS) in the classic infrastructure mode, while an Independent Basic Service Set (IBSS) defines an ad-hoc network between stations. A handshake procedure is performed with the access point or another station when a station wants to join a service set. One of the important amendments in the IEEE 802.11p standard is the ability of stations to operate without joining a service set. This is needed on the control channel, as no central control entity exists and the dynamic forming of service sets in a highly mobile environment would lead to a high coordination overhead. The pure ad-hoc communication in IEEE 802.11p enables the transmission of CAMs and DENMs without management delays.

The multi-user channel access coordination is basically handled by two different coordination functions in IEEE 802.11. The Distributed Coordination Function (DCF) is available in both, ad-hoc (such as in IEEE 802.11p) and infrastructure mode, while the Point Coordination Function (PCF) is an alternative method in infrastructure mode. The DCF is the default method and uses the principle of Carrier Sense Multiple Access with Collision Avoidance (CSMA/CA) to coordinate the access to the wireless medium. CSMA/CA only allows a station to transmit if the channel is not used and provides mechanisms to avoid collisions by parallel access.

The DCF in IEEE 802.11 works as follows: A clear channel assessment information from the PHY layer defines the idle status of the channel. The medium is indicated as busy if the received signal energy level is above a certain threshold. Waiting for a clear channel assessment alone is not sufficient though. Multiple stations wishing to transmit would identify idle state in the same moment, producing parallel transmissions without a countermeasure (collision avoidance). Furthermore, in unicast mode, an acknowledgment needs to be transmitted timely after transmission and has to be protected. An Inter-Frame Space (IFS) mechanism is used to guard acknowledgments and avoid parallel accesses. The mechanism is visualized in Figure 3.3. An acknowledgment might be transmitted if the channel is idle during a Small IFS (SIFS) guard space to the initial packet. The next packet frame transmission might start after the Distributed IFS (DIFS) duration. The DIFS is longer as the SIFS and guards the acknowledgment delivery. The likelihood of parallel transmission of multiple stations is reduced by each station selecting a random backoff slot from a contention window. In case the channel is sensed idle

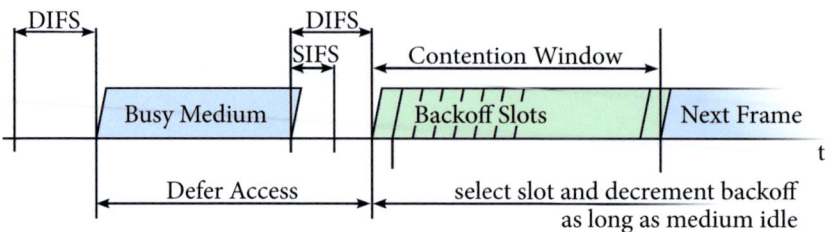

Figure 3.3: The 802.11 Distributed Coordination Function (reproduced from [27], without QoS enhancement).

until the picked slot arrives, a station is allowed to transmit. If it becomes busy in the meantime, the station halts the backoff counter decrement until the channel becomes idle again. When the countdown reaches zero and the channel is idle, the frame is transmitted. This backoff slot mechanism reduces the probability of parallel transmission start on the cost of a small delay.

The IEEE 802.11 standard further describes a Point IFS (PIFS), an exponential backoff mechanism for retransmissions and Quality of Service (QoS) via Enhanced Distributed Channel Access (EDCA). EDCA provides different access classes, which have their own frame queue. Prioritization works via a differing backoff slot amount and contention window minimum/maximum length. IEEE 802.11p defines QoS with four of those access classes. These methods (PIFS, Retransmissions and QoS) are not further discussed here as they are not relevant to the investigated CAM delivery at intersections: CAMs are for example transmitted with a single priority.

The IEEE 802.11p MAC further provides methods for multi-channel advertisements. For example, it provides timing advertisements on the control channel for services that are operated on a service channel. Most research projects (such as the German sim^{TD} [28]) propose to equip vehicles with at least two radios. This way, one radio can always monitor the safety relevant control channel. In consequence, channel switching is also irrelevant for the CAM delivery investigations in this thesis and will not be discussed here further. Information on the not discussed parts of the IEEE 802.11p MAC is available in the standards [27; 1] or for example in [14].

3.1.2 Reception under Radio Channel Stress

Inter-vehicle communication manifests itself as pervasive broadcast system as described in Section 2.1.3. Every time a vehicle wants to transmit a CAM, the radio has to gain access to the medium by performing the DCF procedure as described in Section 3.1.1. The CSMA/CA process suffers under pervasive broadcast conditions from two problems: Firstly, there might be close to or more nodes wanting to transmit as there are available slots in the backoff window, increasing the probability of nodes picking the same slot. Secondly, CAM transmissions are prone to the "hidden terminal problem" [29] of CSMA/CA that inevitably leads to a certain degree of multi-user interference.

The hidden terminal problem is visualized in Figure 3.4. A circle around a node (given as black dot) describes the radio wave of a transmission and its coverage (idealized). The figure visualizes the hidden terminal problem with help of three nodes and two transmissions. The current time is given in a timeline. The left node starts to transmit first. Reception of the message is ongoing at the middle node. In box 2, the right node started its transmission after detecting no ongoing transmission, thus assuming the channel is free. It is not aware of the ongoing reception at the middle node. At this "hidden terminal", the radio wave of the second message interferes with the ongoing transmission: multi-user interference occurs. In consequence, the middle node is eventually not able to receive even one of both messages: one or two packet losses occur.

Packet loss of unicast transmissions can be either prevented by Ready-To-Sent/Clear-To-Sent (RTS/CTS) status exchanges or corrected by a targeted retransmission following a missing Acknowledgement (ACK). However, both methods are not well suitable for broadcast transmissions due to a need for feedback coordination (to prevent interference), an additional channel occupation, and further drawbacks [11]. Due to such problems, IEEE 802.11 does not provide those techniques for broadcasts in ad-hoc mode and they are not used in IEEE 802.11p. In consequence, hidden terminal collisions must be expected and a certain degree of packet loss under communication stress is inevitable.

Also, medium access imperfections such as the hidden terminal problem have direct consequences in terms of network load. A single CAM transmission is much more costly than its pure blocking of the medium during the transmission: each new CAM transmission might introduce new hidden terminal problems on nodes

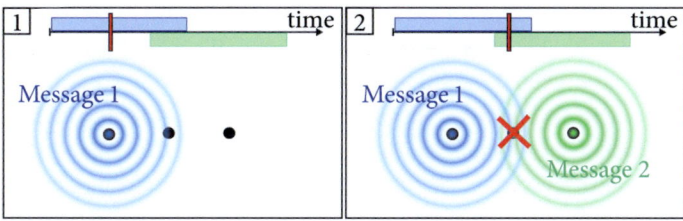

Figure 3.4: The hidden terminal problem: CSMA/CA cannot prevent the radio wave interference at the middle node.

receiving a message. In consequence, reception rates will suffer most in scenarios with many CAM transmissions per area and time. Real-world measurements of reception under such high radio channel stress to assess the impact of multi-user interference on reception rates are unfortunately difficult. Testing with several hundred nodes in real life would be expensive, difficult to coordinate and results would be hard to compare. However, with network simulation, there exists a method to evaluate network behavior at high channel competition levels.

3.1.3   Ad-Hoc Network Simulation / Propagation Modeling

Simulation enables cheap and fast testing of reception under network load as long as it is possible to accurately model the system and its environment. Modeling the communication components of the IEEE 802.11p ad-hoc communication is fortunately relatively easy as they are well defined and of limited complexity compared to cellular standards. Therefore, simulation will be used in Section 6.4 to evaluate the reception behavior under network load in real traffic conditions.

Network simulation is done in a special simulator program. The simulator is configured to reflect a real system. The position of nodes, their network stacks and a virtual program running on every node are modeled. Different propagation conditions can be specified. Each simulation run produces a log file that stores aspects of communication from interest. These can be statistically evaluated afterwards.

This section describes the used tools and theories to achieve meaningful results with regard to a real life IEEE 802.11p system. Furthermore, this section is intended to explain properties of wireless communications like propagation.

The next subsection will explain the simulation of IEEE 802.11p driven inter-vehicle communication. Afterwards, wireless propagation and the used models to simulate it will be discussed. Communication range related considerations follow afterwards in Subsection 3.1.3.3.

3.1.3.1   IEEE 802.11p Simulation with Network Simulator 2 (ns-2)

The simulations in Section 6.4 are based on the widely used packet-level network simulator 2 (ns-2) [30] in the latest[1] 2.34 version. This release includes the IEEE 802.11 MAC simulation overhaul as proposed in [31], making it a good choice for MAC dependent simulations. Proper MAC modeling is needed, as MAC level effects like hidden terminal collisions are a strong impact factor on reception under competition as discussed in Section 3.1.2. IEEE 802.11p modeling can be enabled by a certain parameter configuration of the 802.11 simulation modules.

---

[1]In the writing phase of this thesis, ns-2.35 was released. However, according to the release notes, it does not contain any fixes or improvements regarding the modeling of IEEE 802.11p.

ns-2 simulates networks in a discrete event based manner. It simulates the complete network stack of communication nodes as well as the underlying physical connection between the nodes. The simulation is done in a completely chronological order. In case of any change in the system, the conditions of the change and the implications on all other ongoing events are computed. A system change is for example a scheduled execution of code, the start or end of a transmission or MAC timeouts.

The simulation of transmission success follows this scheme. Every time a physical packet transmission is started, its reception signal strength at all other nodes is determined via signal propagation modeling (see Section 3.1.3.2). The received signal power is determined as the sum of transmission power and antenna gain minus cable loss and power loss due to propagation of the signal. Based on the reception power of a signal, it is newly decided if ongoing transmissions at other nodes are still successful, or interrupted by the new signal. A reception of a transmission is hereby possible if the Signal to Interference-plus-Noise Ratio (SINR) is higher than a threshold. The SINR is computed by

$$SINR = \frac{P_{strongest}}{P_1 + P_2 + ... + P_x + P_{noise\_floor}}$$

where P_1 to P_x are the powers of simultaneously existing signals that are weaker than $P_{strongest}$. The threshold required to be able to decode a signal is dependent on modulation and coding scheme. For example, the required SINR for a successful decoding of a 6 Mbps IEEE 802.11p transmission (QPSK modulation and 1/2 coding) is 8 dB by ns-2.34 default. In order to classify a packet as received, the SINR of a signal has to be higher than the threshold during the whole time of reception.

The IEEE 802.11 MAC simulation module in ns-2.34 models the complete CSMA/CA access control as discussed in Section 3.1.1. The DCF with its inter-frame spacing coordination via SIFS, DIFS and contention window is modeled as a state machine. Each timeout is put into the event chain of the simulator. This way, ns-2 is able to accurately model the medium access and its effect on packet reception.

The PHY/MAC layer simulation also models the "capture effect"[32] supported by modern IEEE 802.11 radios: if a considerably stronger signal as the one being currently received arrives, the radio is able to interrupt the current (destroyed) reception and capture the newly arriving stronger packet.

While ns-2 simplifies certain aspects of the communication to reduce complexity, such as assuming constant reception signal strength over the complete packet duration, especially the MAC is modeled very accurately. As discussed in Section 3.1.2, a proper MAC simulation is needed to allow for a meaningful evaluation of NLOS reception rates under network load in later Section 6.4.

3.1.3.2 Propagation Modeling

This section describes radio signal propagation and how propagation effects are modeled. Also, the internals of propagation modeling reveal information about the sensitivity of radio signals to multi-user interference at different distances.

A packet transmission in wireless communication is technically the process of transmission, propagation and reception of a radio signal. An antenna radiates the signal energy into space. Two basic propagation effects determine the signal energy and receive ability at the receiver. Firstly, the signal strength decreases in free space as the signal spreads the further it travels from its source: the emitted energy is distributed over an increasing area and less power remains at a single spot. The amount of energy loss is further determined by the signal frequency as well as the material the signal travels in. Such energy loss in a line-of-sight path is referred to as free-space loss.

Secondly, the signal might be obstructed, refracted, reflected or diffracted. While an obstruction blocks the signal, the last three effects might lead to multi-path signal components arriving at the receiver. Those components are energy degraded and might be distorted in phase and amplitude and have different angles of arrival at the receiver. Such multi-path components are further delayed with respect to the main LOS signal component. Number, quality and strength of such signal components are changing over time due to the movement of objects. The combination of multi-path signal components at the receiver can either result in cancellation or superposition, resulting in declined or—in rare cases—improved reception conditions compared to a single LOS signal component arriving at the receiver. In a dynamic environment with many obstacles, small shifts of transmitter or receiver will lead to strong changes in multi-path components arriving at the receiver. This channel variation at small-scale position changes, typically less than one half of the wavelength, is referred to as small-scale fading. However, multi-path signal components also occur in a static environment. This motivates the typical modeling of propagation in simulators: free-space loss and a long-term aggregation of multi-path effects are modeled as path loss, before applying a characterization of small-scale fading. In packet level simulations, the time-frequency selective cancellation or superposition of multi-path components is hereby modeled as a power gain or loss per packet.

Path Loss Simulating wireless communication starts with path loss simulation. Path loss can be described in this context as the average power level at different distances to transmitter. Therefore, it is modeled deterministically by an equation with *transmitter (tx)↔receiver (rcv)* distance as input. A very basic path loss construct is Free-Space Path Loss (FSPL) [33]. It describes the free-space loss of a signal not influenced by any multi-path components and radiated from an isotropic antenna that has no directivity at all. In such rather hypothetic conditions, the FSPL in dB is given as:

$$P_{Loss}(d) = 10 * \log_{10} \left(\frac{4\pi d}{\lambda} \right)^2$$

where d is the distance from transmitter in meters and λ the signal wavelength in meters. A second, more variable model is the log-distance path loss model [34]:

$$P_{Loss}(d) = P_0 + 10 * E_L \log_{10} \left(\frac{d}{d_0} \right)$$

where E_L is the loss-exponent and P_0 the path loss at reference distance d_0. The path loss at reference distance is usually computed with the FSPL model. Setting $E_L = 2$ leads to the FSPL model. This model is provided by ns-2 with a modification allowing for three different loss exponents in three different distance stretches.

While the omni-directional antennas usually used in IEEE 802.11p inter-vehicle communication are certainly not isotropic and multi-path components exist, real word experiments have shown that path loss in the IEEE 802.11p radio communication environment is well described by the FSPL model. The results of the LOS measurements described in Section 6.2.1 reveal the same result (Section 6.3.1.2).

The resulting path loss for a transmission power setup that results in a 0.75 reception rate at 200 m on a competition-free channel as computed by ns-2 is shown in Figure 3.5. The noise floor is set to the typical -99 dBm value of current Atheros 802.11 chipsets. 8 dB SINR requirement for a 6 Mbps IEEE 802.11p channel

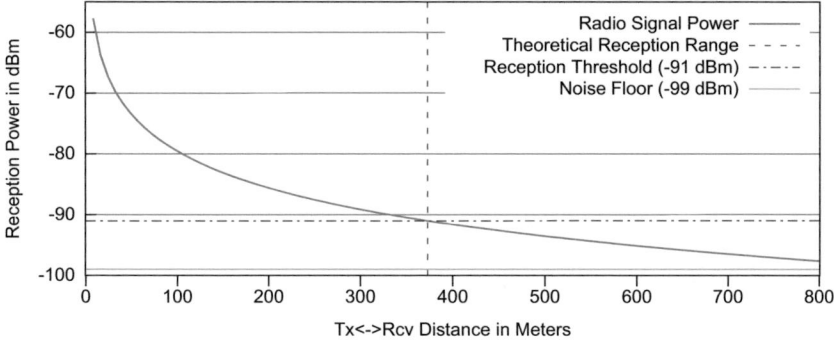

Figure 3.5: Radio wave power loss over distance in simulation. 8.29 dBm transmission power. No antenna gain or cable loss. FSPL path loss model.

result in a reception threshold of -91 dBm on a competition free channel. A node can receive a packet in case of no interference if its signal is stronger than this threshold. The average power drops below the reception threshold at ≈370 m. This range is often referred to as "theoretical reception range". Its distance is almost two times the "intended range"[2] of 200 m the transmission power was calibrated to.

The figure shows that signal power will not drop below the noise floor up to more than 800 m. While the signal is already weak before it reaches this range, it could nevertheless influence ongoing receptions as a noise component. Therefore, the figure illustrates the enormous range where a signal is still able to disturb other ongoing transmissions compared to the intended range of communication.

Small-scale fading Small-scale fading refers to strong fluctuations of the channel at small environmental changes. From a packet level aggregation perspective, it leads to a fluctuating signal power between packets[3]. Small-scale fading is simulated as a stochastic process: The complexity of the number of signal-paths, each signal component strength, delay and phase shift, and the resulting signal power enhancement or loss is abstracted by a stochastic model. It generates the signal gain/loss that every receiver experiences on top of the path loss by picking a random value under a statistical power distribution.

The current state-of-the-art simulation model of small-scale fading for inter-vehicle communication environments is the Nakagami-m [35] distribution as it can be parameterized to different fading characteristics. The Nakagami-m distribution in the signal power domain can be expressed via the gamma distribution. The gamma distribution is given as:

$$g(x; \alpha, \beta) = \frac{\beta^\alpha}{\Gamma(\alpha)} x^{(\alpha-1)} e^{(-\beta x)}$$

where α is the shape parameter and β the inverse scale parameter $\beta = \frac{1}{\theta}$. Given Ω is the expected signal strength, α needs to be set to m and β to $\frac{m}{\Omega}$ to get the Nakagami-m power distribution. The simulator sets $\Omega = P_L$, the power after path loss in mW.

The m-value describes the influence of LOS against reflected signal components. A higher m-value strengthens the influence of the LOS and therefore weakens the influence of multi-path components, resulting in a narrower signal gain/loss distribution. An m-value of 1 reduces the Nakagami-m fading model hereby to the well-known Rayleigh fading model [36]. Rayleigh is a common fading model for urban environments (found via measurements for cellular conditions e.g. in [36],

---

[2]The construct of "intended range" is described in Section 3.1.3.3.

[3]The 5.9 GHz IEEE 802.11p measurements in this thesis reveal the small-scale fading induced power fluctuation between packets, too. For example visualized in Figure 6.17 in Section 6.3.

and inter-vehicle conditions e.g. in [37; 38; 39] and Section 6.3.1.4 of this thesis).

The influence of the m-value parameter on the power distribution (Probability Density Function (PDF)) is given in Figure 3.6. It shows the power distribution for three m-values for a power after path loss value of -60 dBm. The m-value basically defines the amount of signal gain/loss due to fading. The peak of the PDF curve is located at the computed path loss average. As the PDF average is not at the peak, the fading computation influences the average power value at a certain distance in the simulation.

The deterministic computation of path loss would lead to an unrealistic fixed communication range (reception rate 1 or 0) on a competition free channel. The statistical effect of small-scale fading simulation on reception rates is shown in Figure 3.7. It reveals the resulting average reception probability when using the

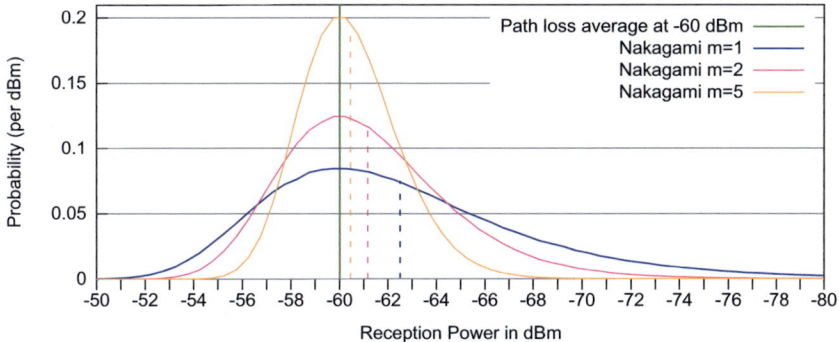

Figure 3.6: The Nakagami-m PDF on top of an exemplary -60 dBm value from path loss. Dashed lines show new average after applying the Nakagami fading.

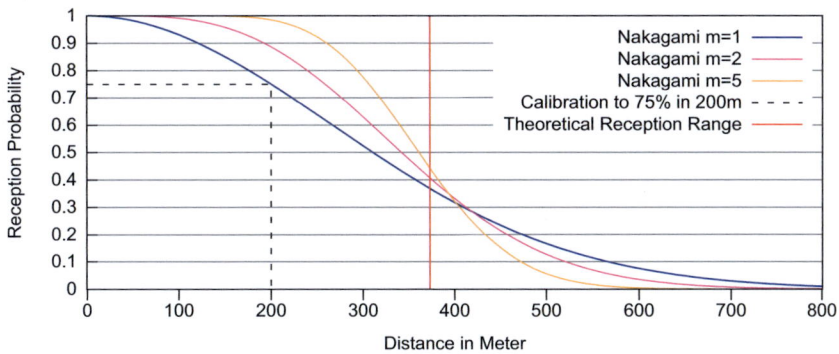

Figure 3.7: Influence of different Nakagami m-values on reception rates in the simulation (on competition free channel). Transmission power calibration.

Nakagami-m distribution with different m-values on a competition free channel (after path loss determination as shown in Figure 3.5). The figure shows how the higher contribution of line of sight in case of higher m-values results in less loss of reception rate (due to more unlikely loss of signal strength) up to the theoretical reception range. On the other hand, it drops more rapidly afterwards. The dashed line points out the power calibration criteria.

3.1.3.3 Transmission Power and Communication Range

Transmissions in simulations are done with a certain power. It determines the communication range. Communication range is a subjective term however: while it might be defined as the theoretic reception range, the application demand plays an important role here too; at theoretic range, reception rates will already be below 0.5 under Nakagami-m fading.

An often-used concept is to select power corresponding to a certain reception quality in a limited area around a node—described by an "intended range" as radius (e.g. in [18; 40]). The quality criteria used in this thesis is an average reception rate of 0.75 exactly at the intended range in case of a competition-free channel and Nakagami-m=1 fading.

The optimal power value for a given intended range value can either be determined by running simulations with different power values and selecting the right one, or by a theoretical examination of the used propagation model. An inverse computation of the used algorithms allows the determination of the exact power value needed to fulfill the reception quality demand.

Section 3.1.3.2 motivates to be very sensitive about intended range and therefore also transmission power selection. The range a message is influencing communication on the channel is much bigger than the intended range of communication. With inverse computation, it is even possible to quantify the difference. The theoretical reception range is 1.86 times the intended range under the simulation assumptions imposed earlier. The range at which the signal is representing a considerable interference component is even higher. This will be especially important in the load simulations in Section 6.4 of this thesis.

3.1.4 Propagation at Inner-City Intersections

This section describes the basic known characteristics of ad-hoc communication propagation in the investigated inner-city intersection scenario. It further discusses predicted influence factors on reception and resulting implications.

The propagation conditions at inner-city intersections differ from the typically simulated linear road communication environment as described in Section 3.1.3.

At inner-city intersection, buildings will be likely located at the corners. They limit the field of view where LOS propagation conditions exist. Buildings obstruct the radio signal from a propagation perspective. Nevertheless, reception behind a building (in NLOS) might be possible via reflected or diffracted signal components. However, radio waves loose energy during each reflection or diffraction. The energy loss depends on the frequency of the signal, the angle of arrival and the material, structure and shape of the surface [41]. A higher frequency in general leads to a higher energy loss.

One of the major factors influencing the radio wave energy distribution in NLOS areas in the investigated inner-city intersection scenario is likely the field of view into the side street. The width of the field of view determines the LOS area and the angle of the first reflection. This first reflection will likely provide the most power in NLOS. This intuitive observation of building positioning influence is visualized Figure 3.8. In the figure it is supposed that the transmitter is still 50 m away from the intersection. In the left intersection, the inter-building distance is only 20 m, in the right a bit wider with 30 m. It becomes obvious that the field of view—corresponding to radio LOS area—is considerably wider in the right intersection. Also, the last point where a first reflection happens is located farther into the side street in the right intersection. Furthermore, the angle of this first reflection is considerably wider. In consequence, the most spreading reflected wave will hit the cross street at a much higher distance to intersection center: in the example at 33 compared to 17.5 m. In consequence, there likely will be a much higher radio wave energy at the same distance to intersection center. In terms of the application, a vehicle coming from the right street leg will have a higher probability of receiving a CAM at the same distance to a potential collision in the intersection center.

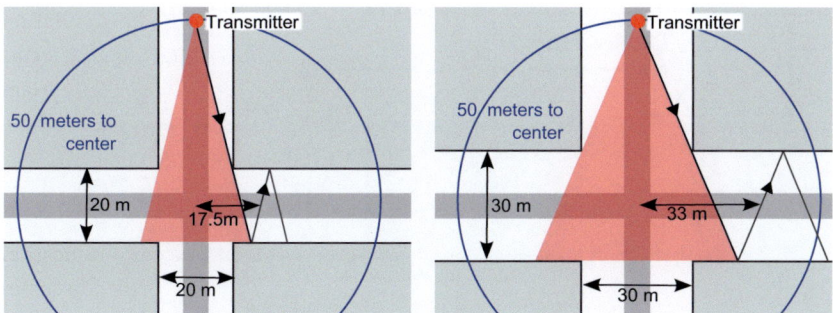

Figure 3.8: Influence of inter-building distance on the size of LOS/NLOS area and propagation due to reflections. Angle of incidence equal to the angle of reflection.

From a modeling perspective, the effects that enable NLOS reception lead to a certain path loss in the NLOS area. In terms of the inner-city intersection scenario, path loss in NLOS can be interpreted as the average power loss over distance in the crossing street when the LOS is obstructed by a building at the corner. Before this thesis, a validated NLOS path loss model for 5.9 GHz inter-vehicle communication did not exist. However, there existed several micro-cellular NLOS path loss models for urban street canyons with below rooftop base stations [42; 43; 44; 45; 46; 47; 48] in the literature. While those models are based on measurements at low frequencies of 0.9–2.1 GHz, without low-profile vehicular antennas and base station heights of about 2–4 m, the environment setup is close to 5.9 GHz IEEE 802.11p conditions at intersections. Therefore, those models have been used parameterized to 5.9 GHz and with vehicle height at receiver and transmitter for inter-vehicle simulations at intersections [49; 50; 51]. While this thesis shows in Section 6.3 that those models are not very accurate with respect to inter-vehicle propagation conditions, they are a good starting point to discuss the influence of different factors on NLOS path loss modeling at intersections.

All of those models split the distance between transmitter and receiver. The dimensions involved in the different equations are visualized in Figure 3.9. The models either use the distances from transmitter and receiver to the corner (d'_t, d'_r) or the center (d_t, d_r) of the intersection and compute the path loss via a virtual source in the intersection. The influence of field of view is expressed by taking the inter-building distance (w_t, w_r) and the distance from transmitter to wall (x_t) into account. All models assume that reflection is the dominant component up to a break-even distance, while diffraction dominates afterwards. The break-even distance depends on transmit and receive antenna mounting height.

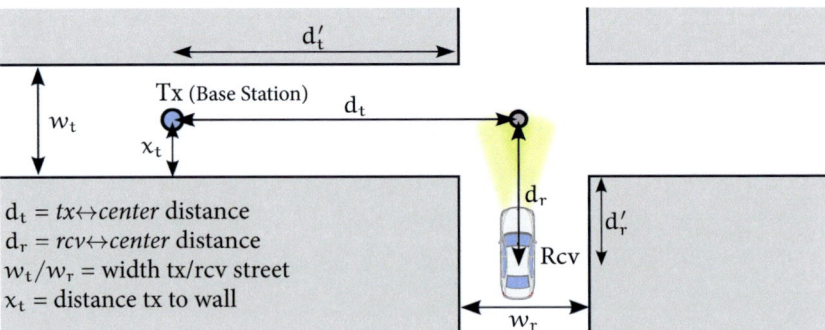

Figure 3.9: The dimensions involved in computing NLOS path loss at intersection in micro-cellular NLOS models in the literature [42; 43; 44; 45; 46; 47]. Not visualized are the tx/rcv-height (h_t, h_r) and wavelength (λ) parameters.

An example NLOS path loss equation for those path loss models is the reflection dominated equation of the VirtualSource [45] model[4]:

$$P_{Loss}(d_t, d_r, w_r, x_t) = 10 \log_{10} \left(\frac{1}{\alpha} \left(\sqrt{\frac{2\pi}{x_t w_r}} \frac{4\pi d_t d_r}{\lambda} \right)^2 \right)$$

where α is a parameter for enabling adaption to individual streets. The formula inherits the intuitive findings on the influence of building positioning. The combination of inter-building distance and the distance from sender to the wall correlates to the amount of field of view into a crossing street. This basic correlation is present in most of those models. As d_t and d_r are multiplied and not summed up, the NLOS path loss will increase more rapidly over distance as compared to LOS conditions.

In order to give a feeling on the influence of inter-building distance on path loss, exemplary reception power values resulting from the given equation parameterized to 5.9 GHz IEEE 802.11p conditions and applied to the example from Figure 3.8 are presented in Table 3.2. The street parameter α was set to 1. The distance from wall to sender is set to 1/2 of the inter-building distance w_r. A situation is assumed where sender and receiver are both 50 m away from the intersection center. It turns out, that increasing the inter-building distance from 20 to 30 m will result in ≈3 dB more signal strength at the receiver.

The predicted absolute power values in NLOS are relatively low. In LOS conditions, the reception power at $d_t + d_r = 100$ m would be ≈-68 dBm according to the FSPL model. Therefore, the power level in the exemplary NLOS conditions is ≈7–13 dB below LOS values according to the VirtualSource model from [45]. In case the model applies to 5.9 GHz conditions, reception ranges in NLOS will be much smaller as in LOS. The strong path loss also implies that transmission power should be as high as possible to enable proper NLOS reception. This will increase radio channel stress in LOS due to high LOS propagation ranges and must be considered in the 5.9 GHz IEEE 802.11p ad-hoc communication evaluation.

---

[4]The complete specification, including break-even distance and diffraction dominated part, and a more detailed discussion of the model is given during the model development in Section 6.3.

Wavelength (λ)	h_r, h_t	P_{tx}	d_t, d_r	w_t, w_r	x_t	Resulting P_r
c/5.9 GHz	1.5 m	20 dBm	50 m	20 m	10 m	-80.8 dBm
c/5.9 GHz	1.5 m	20 dBm	50 m	30 m	15 m	-77.3 dBm
c/5.9 GHz	1.5 m	20 dBm	50 m	40 m	20 m	-74.8 dBm

Table 3.2: Predicted influence of street width on NLOS reception power. Below-rooftop micro-cellular propagation model from [45] parameterized to 5.9 GHz IEEE 802.11p. The factor c represents the speed of light.

3.2 Cellular Communication Systems

Cellular communication always works via infrastructure and uses central coordination, influencing the information delivery of inter-vehicle communication. This section will first describe the general system design and operation principles of cellular networks in Section 3.2.1. Afterwards, it discusses the implications of the system design on the delivery of CAMs in Section 3.2.2—in particular on the information delivery and influence factors on performance. In the following, the radio interface and backbone details of the investigated UMTS and LTE system are described in Section 3.2.3 and 3.2.4 in order to explain technological details. Those sections provide the basis for the technical performance investigation of UMTS and LTE in Section 5.2. Finally, Section 3.2.5 will explain why this thesis focuses on a technical performance analysis of those cellular systems in Section 5.2, rather than performing measurements or simulations.

3.2.1 System Design

Cellular communication systems form a network by covering a geographic area with multiple adjacent cells of limited coverage. Cells are formed by antennas at cell towers (base stations). User Equipment (UE) devices are connected to a base station via the radio interface. Base stations are connected mostly wired to a core (backbone) network. The core network provides management and access to the landline telephone network or the Internet.

The network is formed by a variable amount of antennas at each base station. A typical three-antenna configuration is visualized in Figure 3.10. The area covered by each antenna represents one cell of the network. A UE is connected to one cell. In case it leaves the coverage area, a cell-handover is performed to keep the UE connected to the network and provide a seamless service. The available radio interface resources (capacity) of one cell need to be shared by all connected UEs. The base stations coordinate the radio interface and its resources: For example the monitoring of idle UEs, coordination of the cell-handover process, connection build-up or the assignment of uplink and downlink resources to UEs.

Cellular systems consist in common terminology of the Radio Access Network (RAN) and the core network. The RAN comprises UEs, base stations and radio management functionality. The base stations are to some extent interconnected in the RAN. The core network provides switching, routing and transit of user traffic. It also controls the system in form of databases and network management functions. Traditional core networks contain different elements forming circuit and packet

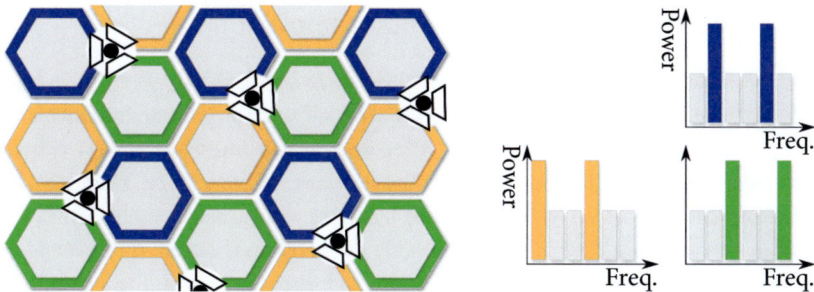

Figure 3.10: 1. A typical three-antenna per tower configuration. 2. Fractional frequency reuse at cell border in LTE to prevent inter-cell interference while operating at a frequency reuse factor of 1. Figure reproduced, adopted from [52].

switched domains. While circuit switching is used to provide voice channels, the packet switched network is dedicated to data traffic such as Internet access.

A cellular system needs a certain frequency bandwidth to be operated. The amount of needed bandwidth is on the one hand determined by the radio interface specification and on the other hand by the frequency reuse factor. Neighboring cells in the Global System for Mobile Communications (GSM) system are for example operated on different frequencies with a reuse factor of 3 to 9. The same frequency is only reused at a certain distance between two cells to prevent inter-cell interference. UMTS and LTE are able to operate at smaller reuse factors; even at a factor of 1, where all cells are operated on the same frequency band by using inter-cell interference coordination mechanisms [52; 53]—an example is given in Figure 3.10. A carrier (network operator) can also operate a system multiple times on different frequency bands in case it owns enough bandwidth.

The operation frequency of cellular networks is typically in the range of 800 MHz to 2.6 GHz. The relatively low frequency—especially in the lower bands of 800–900 MHz—leads to sound propagation conditions due to a low path loss as well as good reflection and diffraction properties. In cities, the antennas of cell towers are normally located above the typical building height, leading to over the rooftop signal propagation conditions.[5] In terms of reception performance, cellular systems further profit from powerful antennas (especially high receive sensitivity) and sophisticated signal post processing capabilities at the base stations due to significantly lower energy consumption restrictions as compared to mobile devices.

---

[5]Radio signal propagation in cellular systems is not further discussed here, as the cellular performance analysis in Section 5.2 of this thesis does not take propagation into account (as argued in Section 3.2.5). Detailed information on cellular signal propagation can be found e.g. in [54].

3.2.2   Inter-Vehicle Communication Implications

The CAM delivery pattern with ad-hoc 5.9 GHz IEEE 802.11p is simple: Each vehicle broadcasts information and overhears all transmissions. In contrast to the decentralized ad-hoc operation, inter-vehicle communication over cellular networks always requires a detour over the network infrastructure. Therefore, the communication pattern looks different: Vehicles will transmit their CAMs to a central server. From there, they are directly delivered to the area of relevance, i.e. all vehicles in the relevant intersection area in terms of cross-traffic assistance.

In case of cellular systems and such a safety use case, message delivery delay is one concern. Delays might occur due to time needed to access the network, management overhead, and the core network detour. However, probably most important, an investigation about the available capacity versus demand is needed. Capacity in cellular systems for information delivery for cross-traffic assistance is determined by a set of basic influence factors:

- **The amount of communicating vehicles per cell.** All communicating clients together create the system load of a cell. In terms of cross-traffic assistance, system load per cell depends on the size of cells, the number of intersections per cell as well as traffic density per intersection. A brief visualization is given on the right in Figure 3.11.

- The cellular system throughput depends on the **frequency bandwidth, the frequency reuse factor and the spectral efficiency of the radio interface.** Possible bandwidth options (channel bandwidth) are defined in network standards. The spectral efficiency describes the maximum throughput that can be achieved within a given frequency bandwidth.

- Cellular systems typically operate with point-to-point connections between backend and UE. However, **broadcast channels might also be available in the downlink**. For certain traffic patterns, this offers opportunities to save network capacity.

- **Multi channel/operator aspects**. A network operator usually runs different technologies on multiple channels with a certain frequency bandwidth. Cross-traffic assistance induced network load can potentially be split up on multiple channels on multiple operators and possibly even multiple technologies.

The overview shows that the CAM delivery induced load per cell, the efficiency of the air interface and the efficient usage of available resources play important roles in answering the question of sufficient capacity. Load demand per cell will be investigated in an environment analysis in Section 5.1.

Due to its inefficient air interface, the GSM standard will not be considered in this thesis. Its spectral efficiency is relatively low in terms of data delivery and

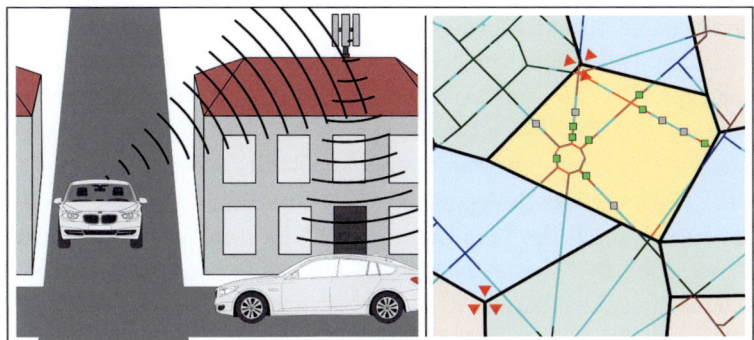

Figure 3.11: Left: Inter-vehicle communication at intersection via cell tower (connection to server not shown). Right: Network capacity demand is influenced by number of vehicles present in a cell (at intersections).

it is operated with high frequency reuse factors of three to nine. UMTS and LTE provide a higher spectral efficiency and can be operated at a frequency reuse factor of one. Their basic air interface properties are described in the next two sections as basis for the cellular performance analysis in Section 5.2.

The efficient usage of the available capacity is especially problematic due to the general connection orientation: In case consequent data transfers are requested by a UE without a certain idle time in between, a managed connection is maintained in the system. This conflicts with the communication characteristic of CAM delivery: Very small, but regular transmissions. If the cellular system would provide a fixed data-rate connection, it would be unused most of the time. While packet-switched connections relieve this fact, maintaining a connection always implies a certain management overhead. Furthermore, the amount of active connections is limited in cellular systems due to limitations of the signaling channels. In consequence, an efficient usage of available resources will be one of the main challenges in the cellular performance analysis in Section 5.2.

3.2.3 The UMTS System

The UMTS network is organized as follows: The UMTS RAN comprises UE, UMTS Base Station (NodeB) and Radio Network Controller (RNC) entities. An RNC node is a control unit between multiple NodeBs and the core network. Those components form a hierarchical structure: An example UMTS network might consist of 30 RNCs, ten thousand NodeBs and five million UEs [55]. The core network comprises a circuit and packet switched domain. The circuit switched domain is formed by a mobile service switching center and a gateway. Packet switching is enabled by a serving General Packet Radio Service (GPRS) support node and gateway GPRS support node. Furthermore, there are a number of common management entities such as a visitor location register, authentication center, identity register and home location register. The UMTS core network is built on top of the existing GSM architecture and allows a parallel operation of both systems.

The UMTS system design introduces a considerable latency. The culprit in particular is the Radio Link Control (RLC) protocol located at NodeB and RNC. According to [56], the protocol and connection delays with respect to the interconnection of NodeB and RNC itself account to a 60 ms delay. The NodeB and RNC account for about 80 % of the total system round trip times of 160 ms in the initial system specification. Round trip times have been reduced to 80–100 ms with the High Speed Packet Access (HSPA) UMTS extension.

The UMTS air interface uses W-CDMA on a 5 MHz channel, consisting of 3.84 MHz data bandwidth and 0.58 MHz guard interval at each side [55]. Up- and downlink are mostly operated in Frequency Division Duplex (FDD) mode. There-fore, in total 10 MHz of spectrum are needed for one symmetric UMTS system. With W-CDMA, multiple connections are transmitted in parallel, identified by orthogonal channelization codes that spread the signal to the full channel data bandwidth of 3.84 MHz. Radio waves from signal components transmitted in parallel overlay at the receiver. In the decoder, the power of a single transmission is virtually increased due to the contained coding gain. This way, it is separated from the other signal components arriving at the receiver. The process is visual-ized in Figure 3.12. All parallel transmissions need to arrive with almost equal power at a NodeB to allow the decomposition of the overlaying signal compo-nents. In consequence, a NodeB signals power adjustment information 1500 times a second to each active UE.

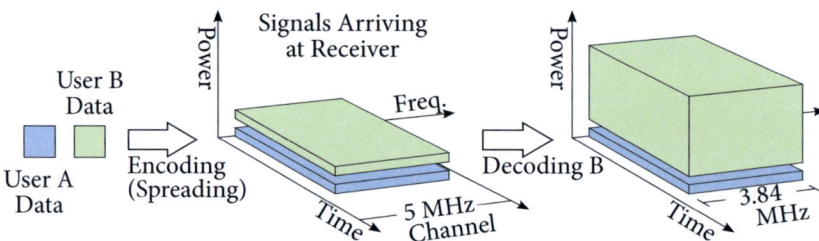

Figure 3.12: The UMTS PHY Architecture – W-CDMA on a 5 MHz channel with 3.84 MHz used. Signals are spread to full 3.84 MHz bandwidth and transmission power is calibrated to get same power levels at receiver. Decoding leads to virtual attenuation of decoded signal from rest of signal components.

In the uplink UMTS uses a 256-node code tree with spreading factors from 2 to 256. The downlink provides factors from 2 to 512. The initial standard uses pure code multiplexing. Some codes are reserved for control channels. This implies that at maximum 256 (minus x) users can be served in parallel. The HSPA extensions to UMTS adopt a packet switched multiple access scheme. Data is transmitted on multiple High Speed Physical Downlink Shared Channel (HS-PDSCH) with spreading factor 16. The packet switching is characterized by distributing user data over those shared channels and a time slotted resource allocation in 2 ms slots. Resources are allocated in time/channel blocks.

The W-CDMA air interface design involves a very short symbol duration of just 260 ns as always the full frequency data bandwidth is used. In consequence, propagation delays of multi-path signal components likely exceed the symbol duration, leading to inter-symbol interference. Inter-symbol interference implies in W-CDMA systems a loss of orthogonality between the multiplexed spread signals: the signals loose parts of their coding induced robustness. In order to mitigate this effect, UMTS applies a strong Forward Error Correction (FEC) via a 1/2 or even 1/3 rate convolutional coding. While the base coding rate is effectively increased due to a final punctuation of the data stream to achieve rate matching, the needed amount of forward error correction overhead is nevertheless reducing the spectral efficiency of the radio interface. Still, UMTS is (subjectively) not very reliable in difficult propagation conditions.

UMTS has a maximum raw throughput of ≈3.84 Mbps, given its Quadrature Phase-Shift Keying (QPSK) modulation and 1/2 coding rate. In consequence, a spreading factor 4 channel is for example able to transport a maximum of 960 kbps. The high data rates of HSPA compared to the initial release of UMTS are achieved by increasing the allowed modulation from QPSK to 16- or even 64-Quadrature Amplitude Modulation (QAM) and an increase of the effective coding rate. The maximum High Speed Downlink Packet Access (HSDPA) data rate for 16-QAM is 14 Mbps and 21.1 Mbps for 64-QAM (without Multiple Input Multiple Output (MIMO)). In those cases, the maximum of 15 factor 16 spreading codes are used as HS-PDSCH. While providing higher data rates, the modulation step-up and less forward error correction will decrease the robustness of the radio transmission.

In addition to higher data rates, one of the biggest advantages of UMTS compared to GSM is the possibility to operate the system with a frequency reuse factor of 1.

3.2.4 The LTE System

The LTE standard is the latest advance in cellular technology and the successor of UMTS. First LTE networks are being operated since 2011. LTE is completely packet switched and Internet Protocol (IP) based. With OFDM it uses a different air interface compared to UMTS.

The LTE core network is based on the UMTS/GSM core network but designed as flat IP-based network architecture. Despite its all IP approach it is able to replace the older UMTS and GSM core networks and take over their responsibility. The biggest advance is a flattened RAN architecture by getting rid of the RNC nodes. In addition to the core network connection, the LTE Base Stations (eNodeBs) are directly interconnected by a new X2 interface now. This new RAN architecture, together with the new air interface, especially leads to a reduced latency and improved connection setup speed compared to UMTS. For example, round trip times will be as low as $\approx$30 ms [56; 57].

The LTE air interface is based on OFDM as carrier modulation method [58]. In the uplink, LTE uses a pre-coded version of OFDM, called Single Carrier Frequency Division Multiple Access (SC-FDMA). SC-FDMA spreads the input bits via a Fourier transformation before applying the OFDM subcarrier modulation. This reduces the peak to average power of the transmitted signal compared to OFDM and helps to keep the power consumption of an UE on a reasonable level.[6]

LTE offers a flexible channel bandwidth of 1.4, 3, 5, 10, 15 or 20 MHz. A channel is subdivided in orthogonal modulated subcarriers of 15 kHz each. Each subcarrier is further subdivided into 0.5 ms time slots, each containing 7 or 6 OFDM symbols. Each symbol of 66.7 µs is preceded by a 4.69 µs Cyclic Prefix (CP) to prevent inter symbol interference due to signal delay spread in multi-path conditions. This leads to a high fading invariance at only 7 % overhead. The combination of OFDM symbol and cyclic prefix is called resource element.

The LTE channel is organized in time and frequency dimension into Resource Blocks (RB) of 12 subcarriers and 0.5 ms length. One RB contains $7 * 12 = 84$ resource elements (OFDM symbols). The Radio Resource Control (RRC) schedules RB to users for transmissions. The LTE channel and resource allocation design is visualized in Figure 3.13.

While the base FEC coding rate is 1/3 in LTE, a less overhead rate of 5/6 is assumed in real applications [60], enabled by the robust OFDM. Furthermore, the LTE link layer is characterized by a fast and effective error correction via Hybrid Automatic Repeat reQest (HARQ). Robust OFDM, lightweight FEC and effective error correction lead to a very good spectral efficiency, outperforming UMTS in realistic conditions by a factor of 1.5 or more—depending on the compared HSDPA release [61]. The LTE spectral efficiency comes close to the Shannon Limit of transmittable information on a noisy channel [62; 63; 61].

---

[6]A detailed explanation why SC-FDMA has been selected for LTE and how it works can be found in [59].

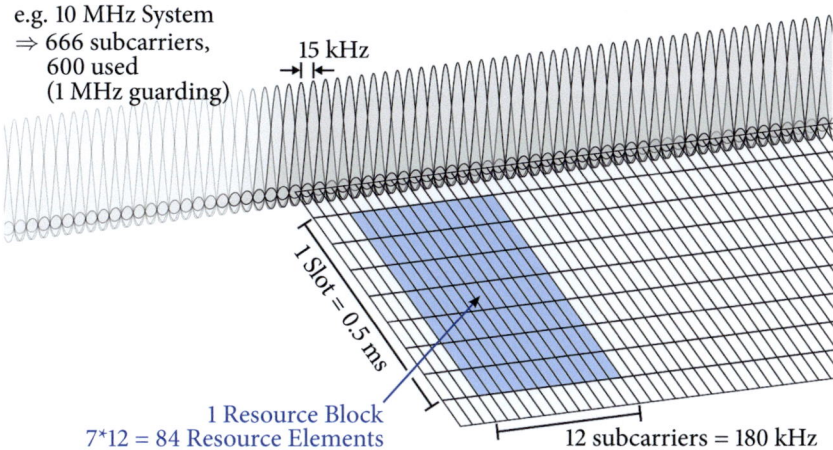

e.g. 10 MHz System
⇒ 666 subcarriers,
600 used
(1 MHz guarding)

15 kHz

1 Slot = 0.5 ms

1 Resource Block
7*12 = 84 Resource Elements

12 subcarriers = 180 kHz

Figure 3.13: The LTE Downlink PHY Architecture – OFDM with 15 kHz subcarriers. Resources are scheduled to users in 0.5 ms long and 180 kHz wide resource blocks.

The major difference between OFDM in LTE and IEEE 802.11p is the subcarrier spacing: LTE uses roughly ten times more subcarriers per MHz compared to IEEE 802.11p, resulting in a much longer symbol duration. In consequence, the overhead due to the cyclic prefix is smaller despite the cyclic prefix being longer, providing a higher inter-symbol interference resistance. The disadvantage of more subcarriers is a higher processing power demand to encode and decode the orthogonal carrier via Fourier transformations. The advances in computer chip power consumption enabled the use of OFDM in LTE, in contrast to UMTS 10 years before.

While LTE delivers peak data rates of up to 300 Mbps, those high rates are only possible under 4x4-MIMO with multi-channel usage. Baseline 2x2-MIMO will enable realistic peak data rates of ≈117 Mbps on the widest 20 MHz channel and 29 Mbps on an UMTS comparable 5 MHz channel. Sector throughput (while serving all subscribers in a cell) will be roughly four times lower than those peak rates [60]—however, the same applies to UMTS.

In conclusion, the biggest advantages of LTE over UMTS are a reduced latency due to RAN advances, a higher spectral efficiency and robustness due to OFDM, as well as more channel bandwidth options (up to 20 MHz). Especially the latter enables significantly increased channel data rates.

3.2.5   Difficulties in Measuring and Simulating Cellular Networks

In general, there are multiple options to assess the ability of a system to handle an envisioned application: Performing measurements, simulation, or a theoretical analysis of its technology. While measurements and simulation can provide detailed results, those techniques also turn out to be difficult to apply in certain cases.

Cellular systems are standardized on the one hand, but highly complex on the other. Also, while the standards are very comprehensive and detailed, they only apply to parts of the systems. The air interface, the UE behavior, the network architecture and its interfaces are all standardized. However, the base station behavior is not; for example the algorithm it uses to schedule resources is completely up to the equipment manufacturer. Furthermore, the systems are highly configurable in their abilities, setup and behavior. Factors like modulation and coding rate will be adapted based on the propagation environment, while factors like channel bandwidth are up to the operators. Even the signaling dimensioning in the air interface is configurable and managed by the base station.

In terms of simulation, the adaptability of cellular systems considerably handicaps the determination of a representative system setup. However, a trusted reference setup is needed to generate results that are representative with regards to deployed systems. Furthermore, the "black box" base station complicates a realistic simulation of base station behavior. This might explain why available open source tools to simulate cellular systems are pretty limited in their level of simulation detail. For example, the ns-2 simulator does not even simulate a shared wireless channel with the EURANE [64] UMTS extension, but point-to-point connections from UE to base station, excluding any scheduler (and air interface) effects. Due to the discussed adaptability and base station induced problems, a simulation of cellular systems was not considered as a feasible approach in this thesis.

Measurements suffer from the same problematic. A change from one network operator to another might imply another base station supplier or a different configuration. Results would be bound to a certain base station supplier, configuration and software version. Even if an own base station would be set up for measurements, the question of finding meaningful parameters remains. Furthermore, the current implementation of base stations does not implement certain parts of the standards such as broadcast channels. Theoretically possible routing schemes of the system could not be tested. It is also impossible to generate realistic interference patterns and signaling load levels without using hundreds of UEs during measurements.

Due to such problems of measuring and/or simulating cellular systems, the cellular performance evaluation in Section 5.2 of this thesis is limited to a theoretic analysis on the ability of UMTS and LTE to handle the investigated use case.

4

State of the Art

Cross-traffic assistance at intersections has been investigated regarding the driver-assistance system design in [20] and [65] at high detail. However, the application relies—as argued in Section 2.2—on a challenging communication exchange that has not been investigated in those works.

This chapter presents the existing knowledge on inter-vehicle communication at intersections and discusses open issues that are addressed in this thesis. The discussion is split by technology: Existing knowledge on cellular inter-vehicle communication will be discussed in Section 4.1, while an analysis on existing knowledge of ad-hoc communication at intersections is given in Section 4.2. Finally, a conclusion on state of the art is given in Section 4.3.

4.1 Inter-Vehicle Communication via Cellular Networks

The performance of cellular networks in terms of delivering information for vehicular ITS safety applications depends on environment factors determining the network load per cell, as well as latency and capacity of the systems. While there is a lot of general information about all three factors available, investigations about the special demands of inter-vehicle communication and the respective impact on performance are rather limited.

This section will firstly discuss existing information on environment factors in Subsection 4.1.1. Following, some general performance investigations related to inter-vehicle communication are presented in Subsection 4.1.2. Finally, the existing research on cellular inter-vehicle communication is discussed in Subsection 4.1.3.

4.1.1 Environment – V2V Induced Network Load

Inter-vehicle communication induced network load per cell is strongly dependent on the number of vehicles per cell. This number depends on the areal coverage of typical cells in cities, the street network, as well as the traffic flow on those streets.

Information about cell sizes in existing cellular networks can be found for example in [66], providing measurement based cell coverage information. A basic estimation of cell sizes via base station position information can be found in [67]. And in [68], cell size information from a network operator is used in a cellular traffic engineering analysis. However, none of these papers is related to vehicular applications or even investigating their network load demand.

In an analysis on a UMTS based vehicular local danger warning system [69], cell shapes used in simulations were approximated based on base station location information via Voronoi diagrams [70]. However, neither an analysis on cell sizes, nor an investigation on realistic vehicle/cell numbers was performed.

To the best of the author's knowledge, there exists no cell topology analysis that incorporates vehicle densities and provides information that allows determining the expected load in cellular networks due to vehicular communication. This motivates the cellular environment analysis in Section 5.1.

4.1.2 V2V Related Performance Investigations

Cellular capacity investigations depend on amount and generation pattern of application induced network traffic as well as the environment. In consequence, existing capacity investigations that are not targeting inter-vehicle communication are of limited benefit. Latency characteristics are to a certain degree independent of traffic amount and message generation pattern. Latency in not over-saturated conditions is determined by the system design and depends on the used communication channel type.

The sensitivity of different data burst sizes in cellular networks to latency is discussed in [56]. More interestingly, the paper also presents round trip times for connections in different HSPA releases and for LTE, including a differentiation between core network, RNC and UE induced latency. Only recently, theoretical assumptions on the induced delay of single components in the LTE and HSPA standards were presented in [57]. Based on these assumptions, the delays of certain operations in different channel states (e.g. call setup from connected) are concluded and compared between the technologies.

The theoretical performance analysis in Section 5.2 proposes to deliver packets in the uplink via the Random Access Channel (RACH). The RACH has special performance characteristics in comparison to established connections. For UMTS, its performance has been e.g. investigated with focus on access priority schemes in [71], concerning delay in [72] and regarding the maximum throughput in [73]. Research on the LTE random access is, so far, rather limited to standardization driven investigations; e.g. regarding the decision on the optimal length of the preamble sequence. Performance figures on such individual design aspects of the LTE random access can be found for example in [58].

None of these investigations were in the context of vehicular networks and therefore do not discuss the influence of results onto the delivery of CAM messages.

4.1.3   Cellular V2V Communication Research

The general feasibility of cooperative traffic safety over different radio systems is discussed in [74]. The demands of three traffic safety application classes and performance factors of radio technologies are analyzed from a high level view.

The CoCar and CoCarX Projects   While the current European and U.S. ITS architecture contains a cellular link and IP based traffic flows[1], the numerous research projects on inter-vehicle communication completely focused on the IEEE 802.11p ad-hoc communication in terms of communication system performance evaluations.

First efforts on evaluating cooperative vehicle applications via cellular networks have been done in the CoCar research project. It was started in 2006 as a sub-project of the German Aktiv research initiative. The list of partners contains network equipment manufacturer Ericsson as well as cellular network operator Vodafone.

The "CoCar Feasibility Study" deliverable [2] discusses different cellular technologies with respect to vehicular safety applications and investigates the commercial feasibility. CoCar proposes a hierarchical architecture consisting of reflector, geocast manager and aggregator components. The aggregator component aggregates information to obtain information such as traffic flow data. The reflector component sends messages from vehicles back to vehicles in proximity, enabling the typical DENM and CAM delivery. The CoCar infrastructure is located outside (on top of) the cellular operator controlled networks, thus providing interoperability between different operators. The technical investigations in CoCar focus on an event message based hazard-warning system via UMTS. In contrast, the delivery of the regular CAMs—investigated in this thesis—results in a much higher network load with a challenging traffic pattern (as discussed in Section 3.2.2).

In the CoCar context, different UMTS releases and transmission options

---

[1]See the ITS communication architecture description in Section 2.1.2.

as well as general capacity aspects for a hazard warning use case were discussed in [75]. In the same context, there exists a simulation-based evaluation [76] of the CoCar car-to-infrastructure traffic information system.

CoCar was followed up by the CoCarX project, intended to refine the found communication architecture, consolidate it with the European Telecommunications Standards Institute (ETSI) ITS architecture, and investigate the benefits of the new LTE standard. LTE latency measurements and load simulations are available in the CoCarX "ITS Services and Communication Architecture" deliverable [77]. The simulations vary the amount of vehicles per cell while assuming a unicast based local dissemination to neighboring vehicles in the downlink, leading to high downlink load demands despite the event driven messages. A discussion on the results of these simulations can be found in Section 5.2.3.

Further Research on Cellular V2V Communication   With "local danger warning", the same use case as in CoCar has been investigated in [69]. The thesis performed simple delay measurements for the UMTS uplink and proposes (opposed to CoCar(X)) to use the UMTS Multimedia Broadcast Multicast Service (MBMS) in the downlink. Same as in CoCar(X), regional dissemination is applied. Simulations show the general feasibility to enable the limited load application.

Not related to CoCar, the propagation of ITS information via the UMTS MBMS was investigated in [78]. An experimental evaluation of UMTS for inter-vehicle communication regarding round trip times and availability can be found in [79].

Conclusion   The research focus regarding cellular intelligent transportation systems so far is targeted at traffic flow information and event driven hazard warnings that produce a limited load. This motivates the analysis of limitations regarding cooperative awareness for vehicular safety with its higher load demand in this thesis; in particular the analysis in Section 5.2 on the technical ability of UMTS and LTE to deliver the required amounts of CAMs.

4.2   Inter-Vehicle Communication via Ad-Hoc Networks at Inner-City Intersections

5.9 GHz IEEE 802.11p based ad-hoc inter-vehicle communication has been heavily researched in the last decade. The communication research focus has been on the usage of communication channels, on measurement and modeling of propagation conditions, on multi-hop dissemination protocols and channel behavior under network load via simulations, as well as pre-requirements such as network simulator enhancements.

This research almost always deals with LOS-dominated propagation conditions. The typically investigated scenario is a straight highway. However, the scenario investigated in this thesis, cross-traffic assistance at inner-city intersection, is prone to NLOS propagation conditions as discussed in the scenario description in Section 2.2.3. Existing research that deals with, or at least involves, NLOS propagation conditions is limited. The following discussion on existing research dealing with NLOS conditions is structured as follows: Firstly, existing information on the environment is discussed in Section 4.2.2. Secondly, the existing knowledge on vehicular 5.9 GHz NLOS propagation is presented in Section 4.2.2. Lastly, existing simulations of the intersection scenario are discussed in Section 4.2.3.

4.2.1 Environment Knowledge

As discussed in Section 3.1.4 about propagation at intersections, the placement of buildings will determine the first LOS while approaching an intersection and likely influence the NLOS signal propagation in terms of path loss. In consequence, knowledge on typical building placement at intersections is needed to achieve representative results in the intended evaluation of communication performance with regards to cross-traffic assistance.

The propagation conditions of real world cities are especially important in the planning of cellular networks. Specialized software such as "ASTRIX" [80] and "Pathloss" [81] compute the expectable coverage of cells in order to determine proper cell tower positions. These programs consider the shape of buildings in order to provide an accurate reception prediction. While these programs internally perform tasks of interest such as LOS/NLOS determination, they are not designed for 5.9 GHz vehicular ad-hoc communication, neither are they able to provide the intended results due to the different problem description.

To the best of the author's knowledge, there has been no work published that analyses the position of buildings at intersections with respect to its influence on ad-hoc vehicular safety communication. This motivates the building position analysis provided in Section 6.1.

4.2.2 NLOS Propagation

A proper understanding of 5.9 GHz vehicular NLOS signal propagation is needed to assess NLOS reception quality. Only a valid NLOS propagation model allows meaningful simulations of NLOS reception under network load in the inner-city intersection scenario.

At the start of this thesis, there existed NLOS propagation models from cellular research and a single measurement of 5.9 GHz NLOS reception [82], both indicating that 5.9 GHz NLOS reception is in general feasible.

While most cellular models deal with over the rooftop propagation, there exist special models [42; 43; 44; 45; 46; 47; 48] for base stations that are located inside a street canyon. Those are often called micro-cellular propagation models. The base stations are for example located at traffic-light posts or at a building wall. In consequence, the environment setup is similar to 5.9 GHz vehicular communication at intersections. However, the models are based on measurements at low frequencies of 0.9–2.1 GHz, without low-profile vehicular ground plate antennas and base station heights of about 2–4 m. Therefore, their claimed validity is by no means a perfect match to vehicular ad-hoc communication at 5.9 GHz.

Nevertheless, those models were used as basis for first attempts to model 5.9 GHz NLOS reception in packet level simulations. In [83], one of the above mentioned cellular models was adopted by using vehicular 5.9 GHz parameters and a V2V NLOS extension to the Qualnet network simulator was proposed. In [84], path loss characteristics of several of these models were evaluated with respect to vehicular communications. A unified model is proposed. Although, the model in [84] was not verified with the new environment parameters. A very brief verification was done in [83].

In course of this thesis, an analysis of the different micro-cellular models showed that the predicted NLOS path loss varies by up to 20 dB between those models when parameterized to 5.9 GHz.[2] This considerable difference of more than two times the required SINR for successful packet decoding questions the usage of those models (at least without adaptations).

First detailed field measurements of vehicular 5.9 GHz NLOS reception were performed with channel sounders in [85]. Channel sounders measure the received energy impulse response over time. This technique potentially allows to identify different propagation paths and provides good insight in low-level characteristics of a received signal. Most recent, measurements with off-the-shelf radios were performed in [86; 87]. While [85] provides detailed channel response results, no path loss model was proposed, as it was in [86; 87]. However, those two models do not take building placement as input dimension into account, albeit inter-building distance is a parameter in all the micro-cellular path loss equations and building placement likely influences 5.9 GHz NLOS reception as it was argued in Section 3.1.4. Furthermore, the testing work performed so far especially lacks a profound scenario selection. For example in [85], different scenarios were specified that were assumed to cover specific multi-path propagation effects.

---

[2]The model comparison, also against measurements, can be found in Section 6.3.2.

However, only one intersection of each type was selected. While building placement is described, the selection of the particular dimensioning is not discussed. Without a statistical decision basis, it is difficult to say whether a representative intersection was tested or not.

In conclusion, a validated NLOS path loss model for 5.9 GHz inter-vehicle communication has not been proposed in literature. This motivated performing the extensive NLOS reception field test described in Section 6.2; with scenario selection based on the building placement analysis in Section 6.1.

4.2.3 Intersection Scenario Simulations

Network simulations are required to evaluate the ability of 5.9 GHz IEEE 802.11p ad-hoc communication to support cross-traffic assistance at intersections. Inter-user interference on the wireless channel will inevitably affect reception rates as discussed in Section 3.1.2. In order to provide valid results, simulations need to accurately model the communication system and must be performed with a representative scenario selection.

A first approach on network simulation for "Intersection Collision Warning" evaluation was done in [88]. Simulations were performed with a center frequency of 200 MHz, a data rate of 1 Mbps, a 20–40 Hz message interval and 12 Byte message size; not matching a current 5.9 GHz V2V setup. NLOS path loss is modeled in a simplified way by an arbitrarily increased loss-exponent (in comparison to LOS conditions) and only one load level is investigated. The evaluation was focused on transmission control scheme performance.

A congestion control algorithm adapting the transmission power with focus on higher power at cross traffic assistance relevant distances was investigated in [49]. An intersection with vehicle movement from the SUMO [89] traffic simulator was used as scenario. One of the micro-cellular NLOS channel models was implemented in ns-2. The model comparison to 5.9 GHz measurements in Section 6.3.2 reveals that the used WINNER-II [42] model underestimates path loss by ≈ 10 dB when parameterized to 5.9 GHz. Given available IEEE 802.11p radio hardware, the paper uses an unrealistically high transmission power range of 24–34 dBm. Only one network load level is simulated. A modified Manhattan grid scenario was used by the same authors in [50]. The simulation environment is unchanged. Evaluation focuses on factors like overall packet detections and geographic distribution of packet collisions.

The overview shows that previous simulation studies investigating NLOS reception conditions of V2V communication under network load lack an accurate simulation of 5.9 GHz V2V communication at intersections as a dedicated NLOS model was not available. Also, an investigation about realistic network load levels in cross-traffic assistance critical situations is missing. In combination, existing knowledge allows no reliable judgment on the question whether cross-traffic assistance is feasible in situations it is needed. The development of a validated 5.9 GHz NLOS path loss model for the vehicular environment in Section 6.3 and the availability of representative building placements from the analysis in Section 6.1 motivate a new investigation. It is provided in Section 6.4.

4.3   Conclusion

The state-of-the-art analysis reveals that the existing knowledge on the required communication exchange in order to enable the investigated cross-traffic assistance application via cellular as well as ad-hoc communication is rather sparse.

Application specific knowledge on the environmental conditions influencing communication is missing for both technologies.

While a communication architecture for cellular inter-vehicle communication has been proposed, the ability of cellular systems to perform the required CAM exchange is an open question. In terms of 5.9 GHz ad-hoc communication, especially knowledge on NLOS propagation is limited. In consequence, the very few existing studies dealing with ad-hoc inter-vehicle communication at intersections lack a proper modeling of NLOS reception. Also, they do not focus on investigating reception conditions in critical phases of cross-traffic assistance.

5

Evaluation of Cellular Communication

The ability of cellular communication systems to enable inter-vehicle communication based cross-traffic assistance is evaluated in this chapter.

The feasibility of cross-traffic assistance is bound to the open question whether cellular systems are able to perform the required regular CAM exchange. Capacity and latency are the obvious two first concerns. The background discussion on inter-vehicle communication implications on cellular systems in Section 3.2.2 showed that capacity in terms of cross-traffic assistance is characterized by a set of basic influence factors: (1) The amount of communicating vehicles per cell, (2) the frequency bandwidth, reuse factor, and spectral efficiency of the air interface, (3) the available communication channels, and (4) multi channel/operator aspects.

The previously identified absence of application specific environment knowledge—manifesting itself in the first influence factor—is tackled in Section 5.1. The analysis combines information about base stations, street layout and vehicle flow data in order to predict the amount of data traffic that will be generated by cellular communication driven cross-traffic assistance.

Following, the technical feasibility of cellular systems to handle the CAM exchange will be discussed in Section 5.2. The analysis investigates methods to efficiently deliver CAMs as well as available overall capacity and system latency. Therefore, it discusses the last three influence factors from the background investigation. The identified available capacity is set into comparison to the identified application demand.

Next, boundary conditions deriving from the technical analysis are discussed in Section 5.3. The discussion presents potential hurdles to realize cellular communication driven cross-traffic assistance. Those are not necessarily of a pure technical nature, but also comprise a fact such as costs.

Finally, a short conclusion on the feasibility and potential performance of cellular inter-vehicle communication is given in Section 5.4.

5.1   Analysis of Expected Data Traffic

Cellular systems provide a certain bandwidth in each cell coverage area. It must be shared by devices. In terms of periodically communicating vehicles, the number of vehicles per cell coverage area is an important factor in determining the expectable data traffic demand. Given a certain CAM transmission rate and size of a CAM, one can predict the resulting network load.

Getting hold of the number of vehicles per cell is a non-trivial task. It depends on the size of a cell, the streets it covers as well as the amount of vehicles driving on those streets. Furthermore, those factors differ from cell to cell and depend for example on the time of the day.

This section analyses cell sizes, street lengths and vehicles per cell under current cellular systems in the City of Munich. An extensive data analysis combines information about base stations, street layout, and vehicle flow data. Cell shapes are approximated from publicly available base station information. Then, the road network is matched to cells. Lastly, street level vehicle flow information is used to obtain the desired number of vehicles per cell information.

Fine grained data from different sources is needed. The data basis is discussed in Section 5.1.1. The analysis of the data regarding cell sizes, street km per cell and vehicles per cell is described in Section 5.1.2. Afterwards, the results are discussed regarding their implications on CAM induced network load in Section 5.1.3. Finally, a conclusion on the analysis is given in Section 5.1.4.

5.1.1   Data Basis

The intended analysis needs to combine data from different domains and sources. This section describes the origin of the data and gives insight about data quality.

5.1.1.1   Cellular Data

The exact configuration and shape of their cellular network is obviously a well-kept secret of cellular network operators. Therefore, cell sizes need to be approximated from publicly available data.

The City of Munich Website provides information about all cell tower (base station) positions in Munich [90]. They are shown in Figure 5.1. Furthermore, for

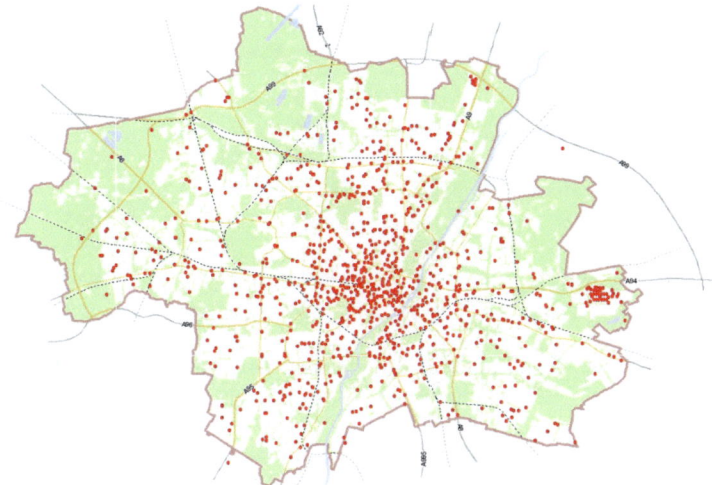

Figure 5.1: City of Munich administrative area with cell tower positions. Source [90].

each tower, the number of antennas for each operator/technology combination is available. The operators are T-Mobile, Vodafone, O2 and E-Plus. Technologies are GSM and UMTS. For each operator/technology combination (one cellular network), the used towers and number of antennas per tower were extracted from the data. Antennas that are below surface (e.g. in the subway system) were discarded. While the performance of GSM is not considered in this thesis[1], it is still worthwhile to analyze the available GSM-data as GSM is operated on frequencies close to parts of the ones that will be used for LTE.

The desired cell shape information for each cellular network was generated via a Voronoi diagram [70] computation. A Voronoi diagram decomposes a space into a discrete set of non-overlapping regions, where the regions are characterized by a minimization of the Euclidean distance of all points in the regions to a set of input points in space. Artificially generated "antenna positions" were used as input points. For each base station, they were placed uniformly distributed on a circle with 20 m radius around the base station location. An example output can be seen in Figure 5.4 in Section 5.1.2.2. Keyhole Markup Language (KML) representations of all diagrams are available via the thesis website [10]; see Appendix A.1.

In order to get a sound data basis, a few things had to be taken care of: the direction of antennas is not known, it is therefore determined randomly. In consequence, the Voronoi algorithm might determine "very small" cells if towers

---

[1]As argued in the background discussion in Section 3.2.2.

Technology	Operator	Tower Number	All Antennas		3 per Tower	
			Number	Evaluated	Number	Evaluat.
UMTS	E-Plus	118	380	87.1 %	354	87.9 %
UMTS	O2	229	694	92.5 %	687	93.2 %
UMTS	T-Mobile	254	764	93.3 %	762	92.8 %
UMTS	Vodafone	260	787	93.0 %	780	92.9 %
GSM	E-Plus	165	799	90.6 %	495	90.3 %
GSM	O2	216	1208	88.5 %	648	90.6 %
GSM	T-Mobile	269	903	92.0 %	807	93.6 %
GSM	Vodafone	277	1182	86.9 %	831	92.7 %

Table 5.1: Cell tower and antenna number data basis. Results of data filtering.

are close to each other and the angles are unfortunate. In effect, exceptionally small cells were discarded. The randomness also imposes that there does not exist "one network". Therefore, ten Voronoi diagrams for each network were produced and the results were averaged.

A rectangle including all cell tower points was used as border for the algorithm. All cells touching the border were excluded from evaluation. There might still exist cells that are too big due to the border setup. Therefore, cells being unrealistically big were discarded. The exclusion thresholds were determined by visual inspection of the diagrams and resulted in discarding cells smaller than $0.025 \, \mathrm{km}^2$ and greater $3.0 \, \mathrm{km}^2$.

Another problem of the input data is base stations with more than three antennas. The question was, if this is the real antenna configuration, or if the operator operates two networks on different frequency bands with overlapping cell borders (two shifted 3 antenna configurations). As it is not possible to answer this, two networks are analyzed, one with all antennas, and one with a typical 3 antenna configuration for each operator/technology combination. Table 5.1 shows the investigated networks with the respective numbers of towers and antennas and the percentage of not discarded cells. The average evaluated area is $243 \, \mathrm{km}^2$, covering 78 % of the total Munich administrative area of $310 \, \mathrm{km}^2$.

5.1.1.2 Street Map and Vehicle Frequency Data

The map data stems from NAVTEQ. The data does not include lane number information and middle separated streets are represented by two distinct segments. Street segments are classified into six different types (bottom part in Table 5.2).

In order to get hold of the vehicle number per street stretch, the analysis has to rely on vehicle frequency information. Such vehicle frequency measurements are unfortunately only available for selected important intersections from local administrations. However, information for the complete street net is needed for the intended analysis. An appropriate data set was found in the FAW-FREQUENZATLAS 5.0 [91] from the DDS Digital Data Services GmbH. It was developed for determining advertising impact. It provides person-frequency data for vehicles, pedestrians and public transportation for all major cities in Germany. The data description comprises that vehicle person frequencies were computed as VehicleFreq ∗ 1.16. Vehicle frequencies were deduced from big amounts of frequency countings from different sources (local administration, service providers, German ministry of transportation, >90.0000 dedicated countings), population density, street network and category, and point of interest accumulations. The best data quality is available for big cities (such as Munich). The frequency numbers reflect an average daytime hour on a workday. Unfortunately, the data provides no worst-case condition numbers (rush hour).

A false-color visualization of the flow data is shown in Figure 5.2. The flow information is given in twelve categories, as shown in Table 5.2. For each category, the mean value was used. The table also shows the street length per category.

As vehicle density (vehicles/km) is needed to be able to compute the number of vehicles per cell, a conversion from vehicle frequency to vehicle density was needed. The equation to do so is Freq(Veh/h)/Speed(km/h) = Density(Veh/km). In consequence, average speed is an important factor. Example numbers showing the impact are given in the frequency category table. Average speed was set to values as they are often assumed in navigation systems. Selected values are given in the street category table. Note that 30 km/h for city streets is probably on the high side and a lower number (rush hour!) would increase the vehicle density.

Figure 5.2: Color-coded visualization of vehicle flow data. Center of presented map excerpt is roughly at 48.131 Lat, 11.560 Lon. Google Earth™[92] screenshot.

ID	Frequency Vehicles/Hour	Street km with Freq.	Vehicles/km at Speed 30 km/h	80 km/h	120 km/h
1	1 - 172	1670.8	2.9	1.1	0.7
2	173 - 344	243.2	8.6	3.2	2.2
3	345 - 517	116.7	14.4	5.4	3.6
4	518 - 689	199.3	20.1	7.5	5.0
5	690 - 862	214.8	25.8	9.7	6.5
6	863 - 1077	141.8	32.3	12.1	8.1
7	1078 - 1293	152.9	39.5	14.8	9.9
8	1294 - 1508	116.1	46.7	17.5	11.7
9	1509 - 1724	49.0	53.9	20.2	13.5
10	1725 - 2586	88.0	71.8	26.9	18.0
11	2587 - 3448	71.0	100.6	37.7	25.1
12	3449 - Infinity	2.3	143.7	53.9	35.9

ID	Street Category	Street km	Used Avg. Speed
1	Autobahn	126.2	120
2	Multi-Lane Freew.	158.7	80
3	Freeway	35.2	80
4	Country Road	131.2	80
5	City Street	634.7	30
6	Other Street	1981.3	30

Table 5.2: Vehicle flow and street data – frequency and street categories.

5.1.2 Data Analysis

The analysis is based on the data as described in Section 5.1.1. The ultimate goal is knowledge about typical numbers of vehicles per cell coverage area. Intermediate results of interest are typical cell sizes and street km per cell.

The presented statistics were separately computed for each Voronoi diagram. Results were averaged over the different random number seeded Voronoi diagram generations in order to obtain results for one network (Operator/ Technology/ AntennaConfig). Afterwards, the resulting numbers were further averaged for a certain technology. The averaging over averages ensures a fair weighting.

5.1.2.1 Cell Sizes

Cell sizes are certainly a major influence factor on any further results. For every cell, the size in km^2 was computed. As described in Subsection 5.1.1.2, a visual inspection of the computed Voronoi diagrams showed that the biggest cells not suffering from the border problematic have a size of $\approx 3\,\text{km}^2$.

It also revealed that cell sizes are—as expected—the smaller the more they are located in the city center. Note that a potential overlapping of cells—leading to slightly larger cells—is not taken into account.

Most cells have sizes of 0.1–0.4 km^2 as the cell size histograms in Figure 5.3 show. But, the histograms also reveal that there exists a not negligible amount of cells with a size of more than 0.6 km^2. Those cells might impose load problems, depending on the question if bigger cells cover a similar dense and heavily used street network as the small ones.

Average size and corresponding standard deviation for both technologies and antenna configurations are given in Table 5.3. The numbers show that for UMTS, it is irrelevant whether the number of antennas per base station is limited to three or not. This could be expected, as the network wide average number of antennas per cell tower is only slightly larger than 3.0 for all four network operators (deducible from Table 5.1). In consequence, only the UMTS/3Antenna configuration is shown in the following. For GSM, the influence of the limitation becomes obvious: results with limitation are close to UMTS ones.

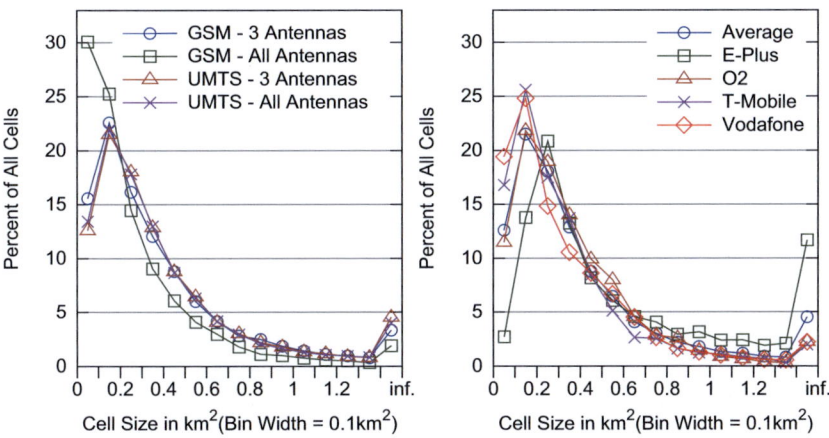

Figure 5.3: Histogram of cell sizes – Left: comparison of technology/antenna-configuration averages – Right: UMTS numbers for different operators.

Technology	Antenna configuration	Avg in km^2	Std.-Dev.	Max
UMTS	All Antennas	0.41	0.40	2.74
UMTS	3 Antennas	0.43	0.40	2.78
GSM	All Antennas	0.29	0.33	2.78
GSM	3 Antennas	0.40	0.39	2.76

Table 5.3: Cell sizes – operator averaged.

Three out of four configurations show an average cell size of $\approx$0.41 km^2, corresponding to a diameter of 720 m if cells would cover a circle. These numbers correspond well to measured numbers via Cell-IDs for a WiMAX network in the city of Brussels in [66].

A comparison between operators for UMTS reveals that T-Mobile and Vodafone have a small cell size advantage compared to O2. The E-Plus network has a notable amount of big cells. As the numbers are very similar for three out of four operators, it seems justifiable to concentrate on technology averages in the following.

5.1.2.2 Street Km per Cell

The number of street km per cell provides a more detailed look at potential system load due to communicating vehicles.

Here, intersection assistance only needs to exchange CAMs in intersections areas. In order to save bandwidth, it might be wise to restrict CAM delivery to situations where vehicles are in a certain radius of an intersection. In order to reflect this correlation, not only the total number of street km per cell was computed, but also the amount that is close to intersections.

The application discussion in Section 2.2.2 showed that a warning will be triggered $\approx$3 s before a collision might occur. The last point of interception will be $\approx$1 s before impact. Due to potential delays of cellular systems and the short time frame, the second number was considered as 1.5 s in this analysis. This corresponds to 42 and 21 m at a speed of 50 km/h. In addition to the normal street network, street stretches with a maximum travel distance of these two distances to any intersection were identified.

Figure 5.4: Visualization of streets per cell computation. Streets within 42 m to intersection are highlighted. Voronoi diagram for Vodafone UMTS network. Center of presented map excerpt is approximately at 48.129 Lat, 11.567 Lon.

For all three cases, the identified street stretches were matched to the cells to compute street length per cell numbers. The resulting metric is km/cell. A visualization of the matching result in case of 42 m of interest can be seen in Figure 5.4. Segments of interest are colored in one of the three cell colors, instead of the standard street color.

The histogram in Figure 5.5 shows that in case of no pre-filtering, the percentage of cells only slowly decreases from its maximum at 1 km towards higher numbers of 6 to 8 km. Also, 10 % of all cells have >9.5 km of streets. If only streets close to intersections are of interest, most cells cover less than 3 km (21 m to intersection) or 4–5 km (42 m) of those streets stretches.

Average and maximum numbers can be found in Table 5.4. In average, 4.4 km of streets are located in one cell for UMTS and GSM with three antennas per tower

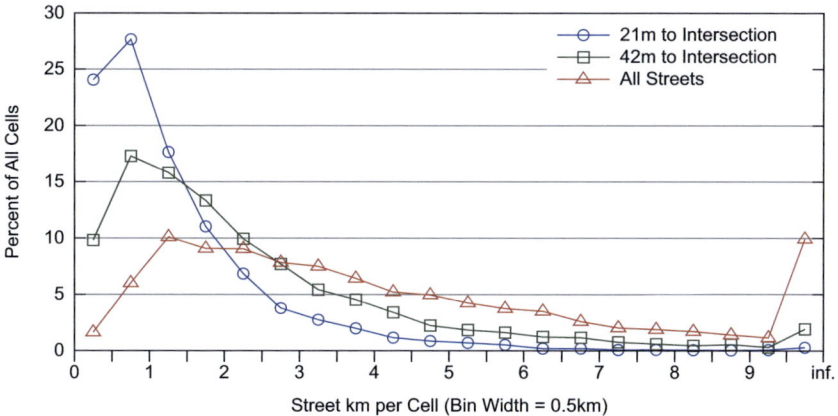

Figure 5.5: Relative histogram of average street km per cell – comparison of classification for UMTS – operator averaged.

Street Interest	Tech.	Antenna config	Avg (km)	Std.-Dev.	Max
All Streets	UMTS	3 Antennas	4.6	3.7	24.6
	GSM	3 Antennas	4.2	3.4	23.2
(3068 km)	GSM	All Antennas	3.0	2.8	22.6
42 m to	UMTS	3 Antennas	2.4	2.0	13.3
Intersection	GSM	3 Antennas	2.2	1.9	13.0
(1495 km)	GSM	All Antennas	1.5	1.5	12.3
21 m to	UMTS	3 Antennas	1.3	1.1	7.4
Intersection	GSM	3 Antennas	1.2	1.0	7.1
(823 km)	GSM	All Antennas	0.8	0.8	6.8

Table 5.4: Street km per cell – operator averaged.

configuration. The maximum value is 24.6 km per cell, corresponding to more than five times the average. Taking only street stretches within 42 and 21 m to intersections into account, values turn out ≈50 % and ≈70 % lower. This corresponds to the total correlation in Munich: for example, 1495 km out of 3068 km streets, or 48.7 %, are within 42 m to an intersection.

5.1.2.3 Vehicles per Cell

For each street segment per cell, the vehicle number was computed by combining its vehicle frequency information and average speed (based on street category) with its length. The sum over all segments in a cell leads to the desired vehicles/cell number.

The relative histogram of vehicles/cell for UMTS networks in Figure 5.6 reveals that the incorporation of the varying vehicle densities into the results does not significantly reduce result deviation, as it might be suspected due to the fact that bigger cells are more likely in suburban areas with probably less vehicle density. Considering the complete street network, the average amount of vehicles per cell on a workday is between 10 and 100 vehicles. A small percentage of cells comprise more vehicles.

The average number is ≈50 vehicles for UMTS and GSM/3Antenna as can be seen in Table 5.5. A maximum of more than 350 vehicles/cell is reached. Interestingly, UMTS in all three cases (Full/ 42 m/ 21 m) has a considerably higher maximum value compared to the GSM/3Antenna case, which is comparable in its tower and antenna numbers. Still, the maximum turns out to be as more than six times the average.

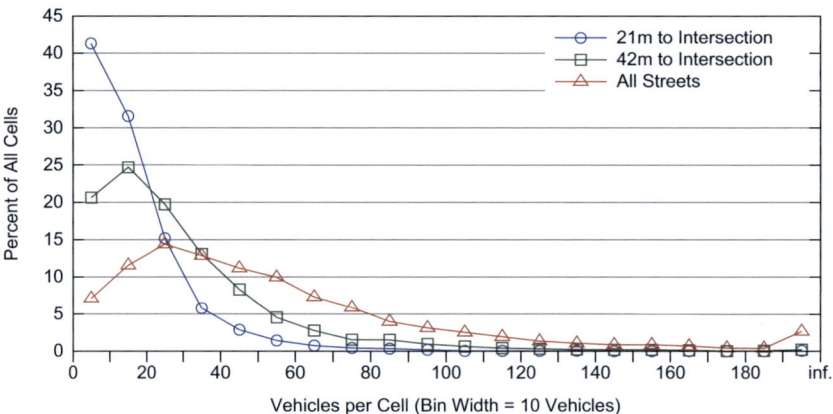

Figure 5.6: Relative histogram of average amount of vehicles per cell – UMTS and operator averaged.

Street Interest	Tech.	Antenna config	Avg	Std.-Dev.	Max
All Streets	UMTS	3 Antennas	56.0	43.1	362.5
	GSM	3 Antennas	50.6	38.6	297.5
	GSM	All Antennas	35.2	31.6	286.1
42 m to	UMTS	3 Antennas	28.7	22.8	171.5
Intersection	GSM	3 Antennas	25.6	20.3	137.7
	GSM	All Antennas	17.7	16.4	128.3
21 m to	UMTS	3 Antennas	16.0	13.1	98.9
Intersection	GSM	3 Antennas	14.3	11.6	77.6
	GSM	All Antennas	9.9	9.3	73.6

Table 5.5: Vehicles per cell – operator averaged.

This evaluation naturally provides selected plots only. The complete set of all plots—showing results for each single network operator at a certain technology or antenna configuration—is available at the thesis website [10].

5.1.3 Result Discussion – Implications

It is important to be aware of the sensitivity of the provided vehicle per cell numbers to changes of the input data. The number of vehicles per cell is dependent on cell shape (implying streets/cell), vehicle frequency and average speed. The cell shape approximation can be considered as rather reliable and the street network is a non-changing parameter. Of course, operators could split big cells for handling future vehicle connectivity demand. This would reduce the maximum numbers. In relation to cell size, vehicle frequency and average speed inherit a higher uncertainty. Dividing the average speed in half will double the vehicle per cell number. A doubled frequency would also double the number.

In consequence, if a worst-case for cell load by vehicular communication is of interest, the vehicle/cell numbers from Section 5.1.2.3 might easily double in rush hour conditions due to a higher vehicle flow than the used daytime average and lower average speeds. Therefore, a cellular communication based exchange of CAMs for cross traffic assistance might introduce $\sim 171.5 * 2 \approx 343$ communication nodes to a cell if vehicles only start communicating at warning distance. At an exemplary 5 Hz CAM transmission rate, this would lead to 1715 CAM/Cell/s. For average conditions, the same computation leads to a much lower number of 287 CAM/Cell/s.

Table 5.6 shows how load varies depending if CAMs are only transmitted in intersection vicinity or on all streets, daytime average or rush hour conditions are assumed and a transmission frequency of 5 or 10 Hz is selected. In case of a total

Traffic Condition	Cell Size	CAM-Tx-Area	Vehicles per Cell	CAM/Cell/s at 10 Hz	CAM/Cell/s at 5 Hz
Rush Hour	Max	All Streets	720	7200	3600
		42 m to ISect.	340	3400	1700
Rush Hour	Avg	All Streets	110	1100	550
		42 m to ISect.	60	600	300
Daytime Avg.	Max	All Streets	360	3600	1800
		42 m to ISect.	170	1700	850
Daytime Avg.	Avg	All Streets	55	550	225
		42 m to ISect.	30	300	150

Table 5.6: Exemplary load per cell – UMTS base station data with 3 antennas per base station – Rush hour assumed as two times daytime average.

worst-case scenario with no intersection vicinity limitation, often assumed 10 Hz transmission frequency, and at rush hour, a number of 7200 CAMs might be needed to be delivered per cell and second in an average 2011 Munich UMTS network.

In general, the found vehicles per cell numbers show that constantly communicating vehicles might introduce a lot of additional load to cellular networks. For example, UMTS is operated on a total bandwidth of 2*60 MHz in Germany, resulting in a combined theoretic peak downlink data rate of $12 * 21.1$ Mbps ≈ 250 Mbps, assuming the fastest available HSDPA data rate. As discussed in the cellular background Section 3.2, roughly 1/4 of the peak number remains as average sector throughput, resulting in roughly 65 Mbps. If it is assumed that 1/3 of all vehicles would receive data with 128 kbps (e.g. an mp3 radio-stream), one gets at rush hour: $2 * 362 * 1/3 * 128$ kbps $= 30.2$ Mbps. Of course, this is under rush hour conditions in a big cell, but it corresponds to almost 1/2 of the totally available bandwidth. While the introduction of LTE will introduce additional bandwidth, communicating vehicles might nevertheless use a not negligible amount of available cellular bandwidth in the future.

5.1.4 Conclusion

This environment analysis investigated the expected number of vehicles in the coverage area of cells in cellular networks. On this basis, network load implications of a cellular network based cross-traffic assistance system at intersections are discussed.

The analysis shows that the average cell size in Munich is roughly 0.41 km² for GSM and UMTS networks if a three antennas per base station configuration is assumed. The average length of streets per cell turns out at roughly 4.4 km. Finally, the average expected amount of vehicles per cell is ≈50. However, maximum values turn out five to six times higher. Rush hour values will be even higher, as the given numbers are based on the daytime average vehicle flow.

While it is important to keep potential uncertainty factors of the data basis in mind, data quality and results seem valid enough to do a meaningful prediction of expected network load under different conditions. In case CAMs are transmitted only in warning distance to an intersection and at a limited transmission frequency of 5 Hz, the number of ≈1700 CAM/Cell/s might need to be handled in worst-case conditions. In case of no such limitations, the maximum number raises to 7200 CAM/Cell/s.

In general, the application independent nature of most results provided in this section allows using them beyond the cross-traffic assistance use case. The results might help to assess network load as introduced by the envisioned raising number of constantly connected vehicles that obtain data such as traffic information, map updates or audio and video streams from the World Wide Web.

5.2   UMTS / LTE Performance Analysis

The analysis in Section 5.1 investigated the capacity demand of cellular CAM exchange based cross-traffic assistance. This section is on the one hand intended to evaluate if UMTS and LTE are able to handle the found capacity demand, and on the other hand to investigate if the systems can meet the latency requirements of the application. Because of the methodic limitations of measurement and simulation of cellular systems as discussed in Section 3.2.5, the investigation in this chapter will be performed as a theoretic analysis.

In a first step, possibilities of delivering CAMs in an efficient way are discussed in Section 5.2.1. Following, the performance of the systems is investigated regarding uplink delivery in Section 5.2.2 and downlink delivery in Section 5.2.3. Finally, the found performance values of UMTS and LTE are compared in Section 5.2.4.

5.2.1   CAM Delivery via Cellular Systems: System Usage

CAM Delivery Design   The general pattern of delivering CAMs in cellular systems is assumed to be the same as proposed in the German CoCar and CoCarX research projects [2; 77]. CAMs are transmitted from a vehicle to a base station, from where they are directly forwarded to a server in the backend. This server is located on top the different network operators, therefore enabling interoperability between different networks. The backend comprises a reflector component that delivers a received CAM to all vehicles of relevance—the surrounding vehicles in the intersection in terms of cross-traffic assistance. Specifics of such components will not be investigated here, as this thesis compares wireless communication performance rather than defining or evaluating backend designs. Given the performance of the existing Internet backend infrastructure, it is assumed in this thesis that it is feasible to realize the needed high throughput / low latency backend.

System Usage   Section 3.2.2 discussed implications of inter-vehicle communication in context of cellular communication systems. It showed that the question of whether cellular systems provide sufficient capacity or not depends not only on air interface efficiency, but also on an efficient usage of available resources. A cellular system typically provides managed point-to-point connections. However, cell broadcast is for example also defined in UMTS and LTE. Furthermore, the communication channels provided by the systems inherit different performance characteristics and restrictions.

In addition, Section 3.2.2 showed a general conflict between connection driven point-to-point connections and the message pattern of CAM delivery— short but regular messages. In order to prevent an under-saturation of managed connections, a discussion on an efficient delivery of CAMs via the communication mechanisms in the systems is even more important. A discussion on possibilities to deliver CAMs efficiently is performed regarding the downlink in the next Section 5.2.1.1 and concerning the uplink in Section 5.2.1.2.

A remaining question regarding the transmission of CAMs via cellular networks is the message size. It is assumed in the following analysis that the CAM format as specified by the German sim^{TD} project [93] is being used. The format is close to the ETSI CAM and DENM message standards [94; 95]. Such a CAM contains roughly 80 Byte content plus a $\approx$120 Byte security certificate. Same as in the CoCar research project, it is assumed in this work that no security payload is needed in case of a cellular system as it should be possible to provide access control via Subscriber Identity Module (SIM)-cards [2]. However, it is up to future research if SIM card based security is really sufficient.

5.2.1.1   Downlink Operation

Downlink transmission of CAMs can be accomplished by unicast or cellular broadcast. Previous work, such as the German CoCar and CoCarX project assumed to leverage normal unicast transmissions to deliver CAMs. In consequence, each single CAM delivered in the uplink needs to be reflected to several vehicles via separate transmissions in the downlink. The disadvantage of this approach is the strong duplication overhead. In case a message is intended to be forwarded to the ten next neighboring vehicles, ten times the amount of CAM data received in the uplink has to be delivered in the downlink.

Cellular broadcast technology, such as Cell Broadcast or MBMS, offers the possibility of sending a received CAM only once in the downlink. MBMS is standardized for both UMTS and LTE. Due to no duplication overhead, broadcasts can decrease the overall network load of the intersection assistance application. Especially if there are many vehicles in the same intersection area, broadcast transmission can be much more resource efficient than unicast. The difference in resource consumption between unicast and broadcast is visualized in Figure 5.7.

Furthermore, no connection is needed in case of broadcasts. In UMTS, a fixed data rate connection assigned by the system would be under-utilized if it is used to transmit CAMs. While the packet switched HSPA and LTE will not suffer from underutilized connections in the downlink as the downlink resources to deliver CAMs can be perfectly scheduled by the base station, acknowledgments will nevertheless lead to a certain management overhead. This overhead inherits on the other hand a certain advantage, as transmission errors can be corrected.

In case of broadcasts, a more robust modulation and coding than unicast is required as no acknowledgment based correction of packet losses exists. Furthermore, broadcasts inherit three other limitations: Firstly, using the whole channel capacity for broadcasting in a frequency reuse one configuration will prevent or complicate certain inter-cell interference mitigation techniques. For example, the partitioned usage of frequency sub-carriers—coordinated between cells—as performed in LTE (compare Figure 3.10) will be complicated. The likelihood that a designated receiver of a broadcast is located at the cell edge is high, resulting in high power requirement for most CAMs. This conflicts with the concept of a reduced transmission power for users located close to the base station that is needed to allow the partitioning of frequencies between cells at the cell border. In consequence, inter-cell interference raises and might lead to increasing non-receptions

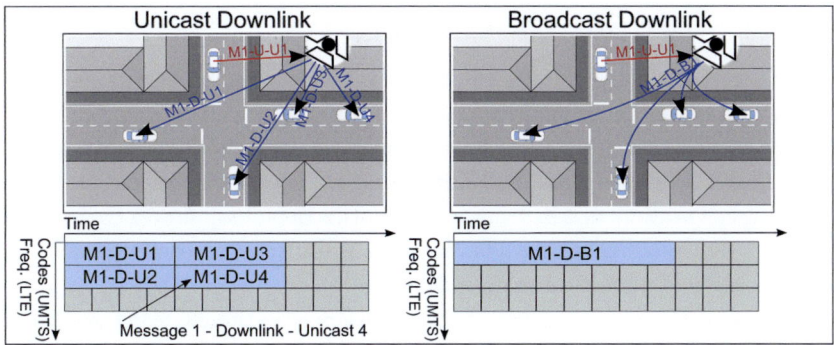

Figure 5.7: Unicast vs. broadcast based CAM delivery: Efficient but multiple individual transmissions vs. robust single transmission covering a complete cell.

	Unicast	Broadcast
Advantages	- Frequency efficiency (modulation & coding) - Error correction	- Efficiency: Single transmission per CAM
Dis-advantages	- High overhead by multiple transmissions of single CAM - Connection management overhead (error correction) - Limited range of delivery (delivery range vs. overhead)	- Reduced efficiency due to robust encoding need - Packet loss possible (no error correction) - Inter-cell interference? - Limited to capacity of single system, Single operator for optimal efficiency

Table 5.7: Downlink via unicast or broadcast: advantages and disadvantages.

of broadcasted CAMs. Secondly, to keep the broadcast efficiency advantage, it is needed that all broadcasts are transmittable in a single system. A standard cellular radio is able to lock onto one channel in downlink. If the load is split, the radio would need to be able to monitor two or more channels to receive all CAMs. Thirdly, as every CAM has to be delivered to all surrounding vehicles, a single network operator should be used. Otherwise, all broadcast data has to be transmitted via every operator resulting in duplication overhead.

It becomes obvious that both techniques, a broadcast and unicast based delivery, provide certain advantages and disadvantages. An overview about the advantages and disadvantages of both techniques can be found in Table 5.7. In order to enable a founded decision, the performance of both techniques will be investigated later on in Section 5.2.3.

5.2.1.2 Uplink Operation

Uplink transmission will use a point-to-point connection via a base station to the central reflection entity. In case of UMTS, messages can either be delivered via dedicated connections with closed loop power control—Dedicated Channel (DCH) and Enhanced Dedicated Channel (E-DCH)—or via the RACH. In the latter case, a random access procedure performs open loop power control and signals a transmission wish to a base station. If the transmission is granted, the device can send a small amount of data.

While dedicated connections have an advantage in latency, using the RACH inherits a capacity advantage in case only small amounts of user data—such as small CAMs—are transmitted. The transmission pattern, very small but regular messages, can imply an underutilization of dedicated connections. Utilizing the

RACH allows transmitting data without such a dedicated, managed connection. LTE transmits all uplink data on the Uplink Shared Channel (UL-SCH). Similar to UMTS, it might perform a random access approach to get re-synchronized with the system or request an uplink grant.

In case a fully periodic traffic pattern for uplink CAMs is assumed, a dedicated bearer with pre-scheduled transmission slots for CAMs could be useful in HSPA or LTE. The base station would schedule short uplink slots on a fixed regular basis for each vehicle in an intersection area, depending on the desired delivery rate and CAM size. In LTE, such a technique (called semi-persistent scheduling [96]) is used to enable efficient voice over IP transmissions.

However, an important aspect regarding the decision between a connection based or random access driven uplink approach is the ability to support certain data traffic optimization. "Adaptive Beaconing" allows to reduce the amount of transmitted CAMs. It follows the idea that the need for a status update correlates with amount of state (direction, speed, ...) change over time. A vehicle waiting at a red light might not need to send status updates at 10 Hz. A discussion on situation-adaptive beaconing strategies and their potential can be found e.g. in [97].

Event-driven adaptive beaconing motivates using a random access based CAM delivery as it has the potential to reduce the total amount of uplink messages significantly. The proposed optimization of pre-scheduled transmissions can however not be applied, because the base station does not know when the vehicle state might change. Therefore, it is not able to schedule a resource slot in the right moment.

Because of these considerations, this work concentrates on an investigation of RACH performance in UMTS and LTE. The goal of the uplink analysis in Section 5.2.2 is to understand the performance characteristics of UMTS and LTE in case their RACH is used for the transmission of CAMs in the uplink; namely the theoretically possible throughput and latency.

5.2.1.3 Discussion on Assumptions

One should be aware that the assumption of a purely random access driven uplink delivery of CAM messages in UMTS and LTE is of academic nature. Cellular systems comprise a state machine. UEs can (simplified) either be in idle or in connected state. In idle state, they only occasionally monitor signaling in downlink and perform cell changes. In connected state, a base station actively controls the UE, resources are assigned to it and the UE provides information such as Channel Quality Indications (CQI) to the base station.

This work assumes that UEs stay in idle state, and leverage the RACH for every CAM transmission. However, with today's schedulers, this is not the case.

In UMTS, more than two subsequent RACH transmissions will lead to a connection setup. A dedicated channel is assigned to the UE in that process. The connection is not closed as long as there are regular transmissions, such as CAMs with a rate of 1–10 Hz. UMTS is code limited in this case rather than limited by the random access design and its configuration.

In LTE, the scheduler will keep an UE in connected state as long as there is no certain idle time. CAM transmissions will likely keep an UE connected. In contrast to UMTS, an UE will not get fixed dedicated transmission resources though. In case of no assigned uplink resources, 1 Bit slots on the Physical Uplink Control Channel (PUCCH) are scheduled to UEs to enable the delivery of Scheduling Request (SRs). This way, an UE could acquire on demand uplink resources for CAMs. The PUCCH is also used for CQI reports and MAC layer acknowledgments in case of no scheduled resources on the UL-SCH. The supported amount of CAM transmissions via scheduling requests is up to further research. Such an investigation also needs to cover additional load on the PUCCH and Physical Downlink Control Channel (PDCCH) by vehicles transmitting CAMs. This is beyond the scope of this thesis.

The assumed completely random access driven transmission of CAMs can be enabled by a context aware scheduler. LTE for example already uses a kind of context aware scheduling for fixed rate data streams like voice over IP.

5.2.2   Uplink Analysis: Random Access in UMTS and LTE

The performance investigation of a random access driven uplink delivery is performed separately for UMTS and LTE (Section 5.2.2.1 and 5.2.2.2). Afterwards, the found key facts of both RACH designs are compared in Section 5.2.2.3.

For each technology, the particular physical and logical RACH design is explained and resulting performance implications with respect to CAM transmission are discussed.

5.2.2.1   UMTS Random Access

This section will first describe the RACH design in UMTS before investigating the resulting performance characteristics.

UMTS Random Access Design   Random access is the process of getting access to a shared medium. In UMTS, the RACH is used each time a not yet connected mobile sets up a connection in order to make a call, transmit, or receive data. Furthermore, this channel is also used for transmission of small amounts of data such as a text message via the Short Message Service (SMS).

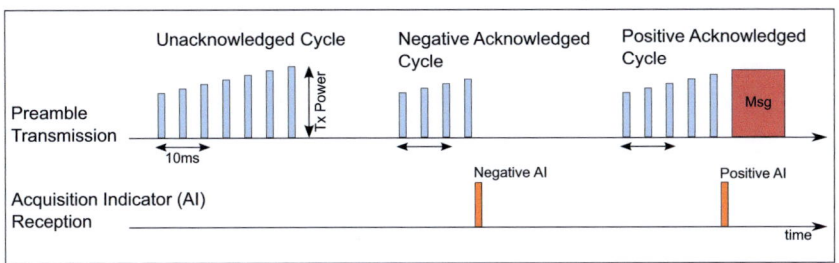

Figure 5.8: UMTS random access procedure: Preamble power ramping, acquisition indication and message transmission. Adopted from [55].

The UMTS random access procedure consists of preamble transmission, acquisition indication response, and message transmission. The requirement of equally powered signals at a NodeB implies that preamble transmission power has to be selected carefully to prevent disturbance of other signals by overpowering. As guessing accurate uplink path loss from downlink status indicators is not accurate enough, power ramping is used for open-loop power control: the transmission power of the preamble is increased step-wise. If power is sufficient to allow successful preamble decoding in the NodeB, it replies with an acquisition indicator (last part in Figure 5.8).

During this access procedure, preambles as well as the data message can get lost by collisions due to parallel access attempts. Data part collisions can arise if two UEs used the same preamble ID in the same access slot.

The random access procedure uses the Physical Random Access Channel (PRACH) for preamble transmissions on the uplink and the Acquisition Indicator Channel (AICH) for feedback [55; 98; 99]. PRACH and AICH are both transmitted with a Spreading Factor (SF) of 256. Both are slotted by 15 slots in 20 ms time frames. A preamble consists of a 16-chip sequence that is repeated 256 times. This leads to 16 different preambles. The repetition potentially allows successful decoding of multiple preambles transmitted in the same slot. An AICH slot can contain 16 symbols, each encoding three states: positive, negative and not received. Therefore, all 16 possible preambles can be addressed in one AICH slot. PRACH and AICH design is visualized in Figure 5.9.

After receiving an acquisition indicator, the data transmission is continued on a data channel correlated to the preamble. In total, up to 16 data channels can be used. However, only one is used in today's networks since such a big RACH capacity is currently not needed. An SF code from 32 to 256 can be configured for each channel. Random access can be configured to use 10 or 20 ms data transmissions. Typical current systems use one data channel with SF 32 channelization code and

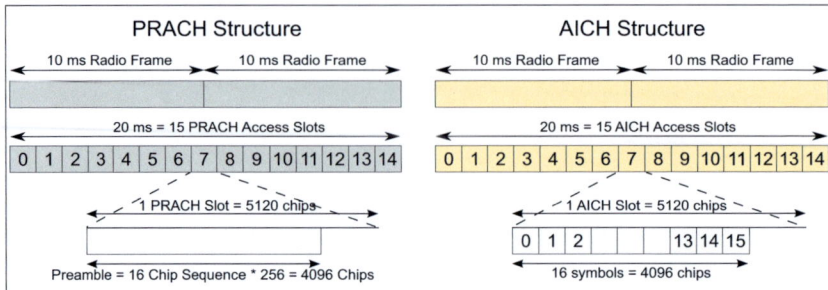

Figure 5.9: Structure of the UMTS physical random access and response channel. Adopted from [55].

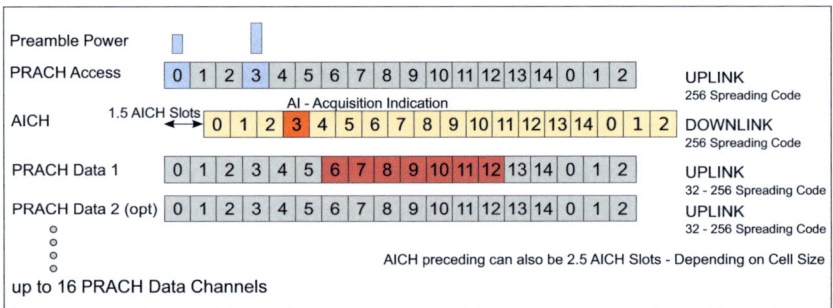

Figure 5.10: Interaction of PRACH/AICH and data transmission channels in the UMTS random access procedure. Adopted from [55].

10 ms slot length. With an SF 32 code, 40 Byte of payload can be transmitted in a 10 ms radio frame.

The transmission and processing delays in the UMTS system imply that the AICH follows the PRACH by 1.5 slots. This means that the shortest delay between two preamble transmissions is 2 slots, i.e. 2.67 ms. Figure 5.10 shows the complete UMTS RACH with timing and dedicated data channels.

UMTS Random Access Performance Analysis   Given the shortest delay of 2 slots, a random access procedure with one power ramping step requires a minimum of $2*3*1.34 = 8.04$ ms for the access. It would increase to 20.1 ms in case of five preamble transmissions. In reality, a value somewhere in between is realistic. The message transmission needs additional 10 ms. Simulation and measurements indicate that roughly 45 ms are needed to transmit a 40 Byte message [75; 76]. Reasons for this high number are preamble collisions and a configurable assignment of PRACH slots to UEs. This can limit the number of available slots, thus increasing inter-preamble times.

Summarized, there are the following performance characteristics and dependencies. The theoretical maximum number of preamble transmissions per second is given by:

$$\frac{1000 \text{ ms}}{20 \frac{\text{ms}}{\text{Frame}}} * 15 \frac{\text{Slots}}{\text{Frame}} * 16 \frac{\text{Preambles}}{\text{Slot}} = 12000 \frac{\text{Preambles}}{\text{s}}$$

If an average of two power ramping steps and a certain loss by signal degradation and collision is incorporated, the following maximal amount of successful random accesses remains:

$$\frac{\frac{\text{TheoreticPreamble}_{\text{Rcv}}}{\text{s}}}{\text{RampingSteps}} * (1 - \text{DecodingErrorRate})$$
$$* (1 - \text{CollisionFactor})$$
$$\approx \frac{12000}{3} * 0.7 * 0.7 = 1960 \frac{\text{Accesses}}{\text{s}}$$

The 0.7 values reflect an estimated 30% slot collision probability and 30% reception loss. If only one data channel is configured as it is common in current systems, only 1/16 of 1960 remain, equaling roughly 122 accesses per second. Assuming such a configuration, the number of deliverable 40 Byte chunks per second is limited by the capacity of an SF 32 code channel configured for RACH transmissions to:

$$\frac{1000 \text{ ms}}{10 \text{ ms Slot Size}} * \text{UtilizationFactor}(0.7)$$
$$= 70 \text{ Chunks of } 40 \text{ Byte}$$

The utilization factor incorporates the fact that not all slots will be occupied due to the randomness of successful preamble reception. A value of 0.7 is consistent with the maximum throughput findings in [73]. Comparing 122 Accesses/s to 70 DataChunks/s, it becomes obvious that the number of RACH data channels and their capacity are the limiting factor, and not the amount of resolvable accesses. This also implies that even if the loss factors in the previous formula are selected higher (up to 0.45), the resulting maximum resolvable access number would still cover the data channel transmission number of 70.

Lastly, latency for an arbitrary sized packet is given by:

$$\text{Latency}_{\text{tx}} = \left\lceil \frac{\text{Payload(Byte)}}{\frac{40\,\text{Byte}}{\text{RandomAccess}}} \right\rceil \frac{t_{\text{access}} + t_{\text{chunk-tx}}}{\text{RandomAccess}}$$

$$\approx \left\lceil \frac{\text{Payload(Byte)}}{40} \right\rceil * (35 + 10)\,\text{ms}$$

As summary, the number of possible transmissions per second per cell over the UMTS random access is configurable via the number of RACH data channels. One random access procedure is needed for each 40 Byte payload. Longer packets need to be split up, resulting in increased latency.

5.2.2.2 LTE Random Access

Same as for UMTS, this section will first describe the RACH design in LTE before investigating the resulting performance.

LTE Random Access Design   As discussed in background Section 3.2.4, LTE utilizes a completely different radio interface design as compared to UMTS. OFDM is used as modulation scheme and resources are scheduled in time/frequency resource blocks. The radio design of LTE has implications on the LTE RACH: Firstly, the random access system needs to fit into the resource blocks. Secondly, the fading invariance advantages need to remain. Lastly, the RACH needs to be bigger dimensioned compared to UMTS as random accesses might be needed in case a UE needs to perform Hybrid Automatic Repeat reQest (HARQ), TCP ACK or scheduling request transmissions and is out of scheduled uplink resources on UL-SCH and PUCCH.

The LTE RACH has a four-phase design [58; 100; 101] with contention resolution in contrast to the two-phase design in UMTS. The basic procedure is visualized in Figure 5.11. In phase one, the preamble is transmitted. This transmission is not uplink synchronized. An LTE base station (eNodeB) answers with a message containing information identifying message one, a timing adjustment indication, and an uplink grant for message three. Message two enables the UE to identify if its own preamble transmission is addressed. However, when two UEs transmitted the same preamble, they both conclude a positive response. Phase three and four resolve such situations and ensure that only one UE is transmitting data. Message three contains an ID of the UE and the requested type of resources. If two UEs answer due to a collision in phase one, the eNodeB will at maximum decode one of them successfully and signal this to the corresponding UE in phase four. When the UE acknowledges this message, the eNodeB will schedule the required uplink resources to the UE to enable it to transmit its data. Message three is already uplink synchronized due to the timing information in message two. Except for the preamble transmission, the resources for all messages are not predetermined but scheduled by the eNodeB. Message two and four are advertised by downlink resource allocation indicators.

There are 64 preamble signatures. All of them are used at any time. The RRC can reserve a subset of these to dedicated UEs for contention free access. Preambles are transmitted in a 1 ms time slot. They are preceded by a cyclic prefix to compensate unknown propagation delay. A preamble is shorter than 1 ms to ensure that its signal remains in the slot despite up- and downlink propagation delays and fading. In consequence, the need for power ramping is reduced as overpowering will likely not affect other uplink resource blocks.

The timing of the different messages is visualized in Figure 5.12. A response detection window for message one and a processing delay window for message three lead to certain delays. The whole access procedure takes roughly 10–20 ms.

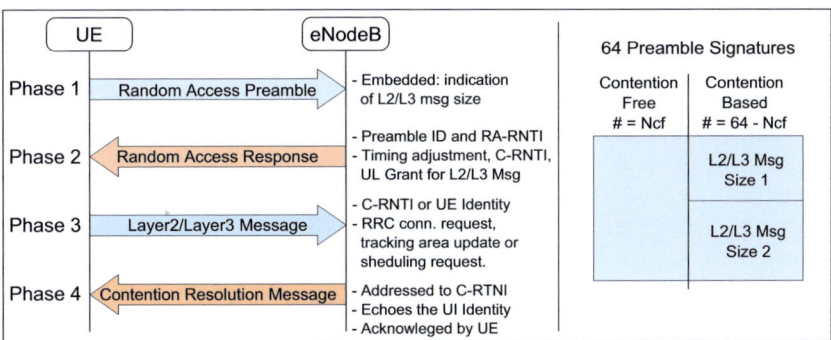

Figure 5.11: Basic design of the LTE random access procedure. Adopted from [58].

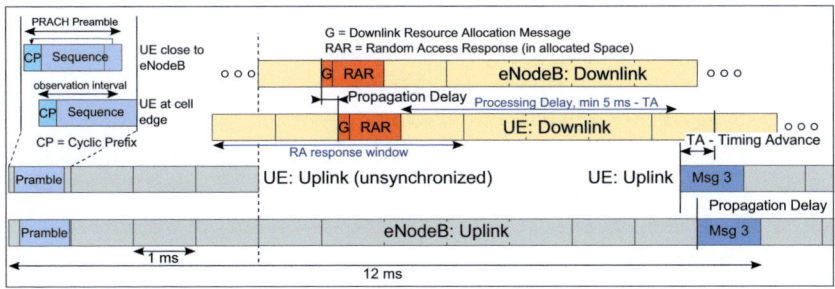

Figure 5.12: Timing and interaction on the LTE physical random access. Adopted from [58].

In case of no success, another cycle is needed just as in UMTS.

The predetermined preamble resources are dimensioned as follows: In cells of up to 14 km radius, the 1 ms preamble slot occupies 1.08 MHz, corresponding to 6 RB. One slot (1 ms) is used per 10 ms per cell on a 5 MHz channel, two slots on a 10 MHz channel and three slots for 20 MHz. This corresponds to roughly 1/50 of the available uplink resources on a 10 MHz channel. However, it has to be considered that the level two, three, and four messages need additional resources. In case of UMTS, the access part is completely covered by two reserved 256 SF codes, representing 1/64 of the available resources.

LTE Random Access Performance Analysis   In case of the LTE random access, there are the following performance characteristics and dependencies on a UMTS comparable 5 MHz channel. The theoretical maximum number of preamble transmissions per cell is given by:

$$\frac{1000\,\text{ms}}{10\frac{\text{ms}}{\text{Frame}}} * 1\frac{\text{Slot}}{\text{Frame}} * 64\frac{\text{Preambles}}{\text{Slot}} = 6400\frac{\text{Preambles}}{\text{s}}$$

Incorporating one power ramping step and loss due to collisions and reception problems (expressed by the artificially selected 0.7 factors) leads to the following approximate maximum number of successful accesses per second:

$$\frac{\frac{\text{TheoreticPreamble}_{\text{Rcv}}}{\text{s}}}{\text{RampingSteps}} * (1 - \text{DecodingErrorRate})$$
$$* (1 - \text{CollisionFactor})$$
$$\approx \frac{6400}{2} * 0.7 * 0.7 = 1568\frac{\text{Accesses}}{\text{s}}$$

While the preamble collision factor is probably the same as in UMTS here, the contention resolution will prevent colliding packet transmissions. The values for collision factor and decoding error are of course an estimated assumption here and might need to be changed when more knowledge is available. However, the complete UMTS vs. LTE performance comparison in Section 5.2.4 will show that other, high-level factors seem to be more important for overall performance anyway.

The number of deliverable packets per second—in case the number of accesses is artificially assumed not limiting—depends on the available UL-SCH resources. Therefore, with small packet sizes, the number of possible accesses is likely the limiting factor.

The latency for a random access initiated packet transmission is given by:

$$\text{Latency}_{\text{tx}} = t_{\text{access}} + t_{\text{data-tx}} \approx 15\,\text{ms} + t_{\text{data-tx}}$$

The analysis shows that the capacity limiting factors are different compared to UMTS and latency is considerably smaller. The amount of possible random access driven CAM transmissions is higher than in UMTS (at least as long as an UMTS system configuration is assumed with one random access data channel). However, the RACH will be more utilized in the completely packet switched LTE compared to UMTS. Random access requests have to be performed even in connected state, for example when a UE uses Discontinuous Reception (DRX) or in case it has no resources to transmit a scheduling request.

5.2.2.3   UMTS / LTE RACH Comparison

A comparison of the UMTS and LTE RACH based on the analyses in Section 5.2.2.1 and 5.2.2.2 is given in Table 5.8. It shows differences in the RACH design, factors that influence performance, and resulting theoretical performance limitations.

UMTS and LTE have a comparable dimensioning of the preamble part. However, UMTS is limited by the number of random access data channels. As previously mentioned, it is restricted to one channel in today's systems. The LTE RACH does not work with dedicated data transmission resources. This increases the amount of ad-hoc transmittable data, as big packets do not have to be split into small chunks, each needing a random access. Furthermore, this also leads to an increasing latency advantage of LTE as soon as packets need to be split in order to enable the delivery via the UMTS RACH. Finally, LTE has advantages due to its less fading variant design.

In conclusion, the LTE RACH has several advantages against the UMTS RACH. It enables more accesses by default, is more robust, has a latency advantage, and contains no packet size limitation.

5.2.3   Downlink Analysis: Broadcast vs. Unicast in UMTS/LTE

As discussed in Section 5.2.1.1, a broadcast based CAM downlink delivery inherits a "transmit once" advantage compared to a unicast driven approach. However, the discussion also revealed that the broadcast approach suffers from multiple problems, motivating to still investigate unicast despite the involved duplication overhead.

Unicast Based Downlink   Performance numbers for a unicast based downlink can be found in the CoCarX "ITS SERVICES AND COMMUNICATION ARCHITECTURE" deliverable [77]. The study reveals that a 5 MHz LTE cell reaches its capacity at ≈ 60 vehicles/cell given vehicles transmit 10 CAM/s, under the assumption that CAMs are forwarded to the next 10 neighbors. The total packet size in the study was 120 Byte, covering the assumed payload in this thesis of 80 Byte. In consequence, such a cell can handle $\approx$6000 CAM/s given a unicast downlink.

The numbers represent a user data throughput (sector throughput) of 6000 CAM/s $*$ 120 Byte/CAM $=$ 5.49 Mbps. As sector throughput is often assumed roughly four times lower as peak rates [60], a peak data rate equivalent of $\approx$22 Mbps can be concluded. Given that the cell "reaches capacity" at $\approx$6000 CAM/s, the equiv-

	UMTS	LTE
Number of preamble sequences per channel	1 per data channel, max 16	64
Access Slots per 5 MHz channel	15 every 20 ms	Configurable: 1 slot each [1..20] ms. 1 each 10 ms assumed in 3 cells per tower config
Max preambles receivable per cell per second	$15 * 16 * 50 = 12.000$	$1 * 64 * 100 = 6.400$
Power ramping	Yes, ~2–3 steps	Sparsely needed: < 1–2 steps
Max resolvable accesses (under power ramping)	$12.000/3 \approx 4000$ (assumption: 2 steps)	6.400 (no power ramping) 3.200 (with 1 step)
Contention resolution	No	Yes
Fading invariance	No	Yes
Disturbance of other channels by RACH	Yes (by overpowering)	No
Delay to data transmission	~45 ms (more if unsuccessful cycle)	~10-30 ms (depends on power ramping need)
Payload per access	40 Byte with SF 32 code	No strict limit due to resource request for delivery during access
Resource consumption	Fixed, # PRACH data channels	Variable, as requested for payload delivery
Limiting factor for transmission number	Data channels, their assigned number	Achievable number of successful accesses
Standard RACH load	Connection setup, cell change info, small user packets	Connection setup, cell change information, scheduling requests

Table 5.8: Comparison of the RACH in UMTS and LTE.

alent peak number—and therefore the CAM/s number—seems theoretically sound considering the theoretic LTE peak data rate of 29 Mbps on a 5 MHz channel [60].

Given a maximum frequency bandwidth of 20 MHz, LTE could provide a maximum of $\approx$24000 CAM/s via unicast in a single system in the downlink. Given this number, the maximum number of supported vehicles per cell can be derived from:

$$\frac{1200\,\text{CAM/MHz/s} * \text{CFW}}{\text{NBF} * \text{tx}_{\text{Freq}}}$$

where CFW is the channel frequency width (5, 10 or 20 MHz), NBF the number of neighbors the message is forwarded to and tx_{Freq} the transmission frequency in CAM/s. As an example, if vehicles transmit CAMs five times a second, the CAMs are forwarded to the next 20 vehicles and a 20 MHz channel is used, a single cell can support up to 210 vehicles. This number does not cover the worst-case rush hour number of 340 vehicles within 42 m to an intersection as given in Table 5.6.

The resulting capacity numbers for UMTS will be lower. On the one hand, UMTS is limited to a 5 MHz channel. On the other hand, LTE is at least 50% more spectrally efficient than a current HSPA UMTS system [61]. Taking the LTE numbers and applying this, one UMTS system should be able to handle a maximum of 4000 CAM/s.

Of course, it's an open question how many vehicles must be covered in the neighborhood. Delivering each CAM to 10 vehicles might be enough for cross-traffic assistance in suburban intersections: It might be sufficient to deliver information to vehicles located between one and three seconds away on the crossing street only. However, certain use cases such as "Future Speed Profile" that need a longer information horizon would not be feasible in such a configuration.

Broadcast Based Downlink   In contrast to unicast messages, broadcasts are not error corrected. This implies the need for a robust encoding of broadcasts in order to enable robust cell edge reception, thus reducing the available capacity.

The RACH needs a robust encoding, too. Given the UMTS RACH capacity per channelization code numbers from Section 5.2.2.1, it is possible to deduce the maximum number of CAMs that can be delivered via UMTS cell broadcast. Assuming the same robust coding used for the RACH messages, it is possible to transmit 50 messages per second per 32 SF channelization code (80 Bytes per CAM = 2 slots = 100/2). As a maximum of 31 of these codes could be used for cell broadcast (one 32 SF code is blocked by cell management), transmitting $50 * 31 = 1550$ CAM/s would be possible. However, it should be noted, that the current standard only allows to use four 32 SF codes for MBMS operation on the common Forward Access Channel (FACH).

System usage	UMTS (HSDPA)	LTE (5 MHz)	LTE (20 MHz)
Unicast capacity (CAM/Cell/s)	≈4000	≈6000	≈24000
Unicast capacity under forwarding to 10 vehicles (e.g.)	≈400	≈600	≈2400
Broadcast capacity (CAM/Cell/s)	≈1500	≈2300	≈9000

Table 5.9: Downlink via unicast or broadcast: Performance comparison.

Based on the 50% spectral efficiency advantage as given in the unicast evaluation, a number of ≈2300 CAM/s can be assumed on an UMTS comparable 5 MHz LTE channel. In case it is operated on the maximum 20 MHz bandwidth, LTE should be able to deliver ≈9000 CAM/Cell/s via broadcast.

This number covers the highest number of 7200 CAM/Cell/s given in Table 5.6, representing a worst-case cell (big cell with rush hour traffic and every vehicle transmitting CAMs at 10 Hz) in the city of Munich.

Broadcast or Unicast   The approximated capacity numbers for a unicast and broadcast based downlink delivery of CAMs are compared in Table 5.9. A unicast based delivery allows to transmit ≈2.5 times the number of broadcast messages. However, the duplication overhead to notify all vehicles in vicinity separately easily turns this advantage into a disadvantage.

Even a 20 MHz LTE frequency channel is not able to distribute the maximum number of 7200 CAM/Cell/s as found in the environment analysis in Section 5.1 via unicast (ten addressed neighbors). Of course, it is possible to deliver the unicast CAMs via several frequency channels (and therefore also network operators). This allows to increase the available capacity to deliver the required amounts of CAMs.

A broadcast based delivery can be realized with a single system, however. Therefore, broadcasts inherit an advantage in terms of consumed capacity. Unicasts would be "number of neighbors delivered to" divided by the broadcast robustness overhead times more expensive. In the above configuration, this would lead to a cost advantage of factor $10/2.5 = 4$.

In consequence, this thesis proposes to deliver CAMs via broadcasts in the downlink. However, one should be aware that inter-cell interference due to high amounts of broadcasts might be an issue.

5.2.4   UMTS / LTE Performance Comparison

This section uses the findings from the uplink investigation in Section 5.2.2 and downlink investigation in Section 5.2.3 to compare the ability of UMTS and LTE to deliver CAMs. The investigation results as well as performance numbers based upon those results are given Table 5.10.

As uplink load might be split on multiple frequency channels / operators, the table starts with an overview over the maximal available frequency resources for each technology. In Germany, there are 120 MHz reserved for UMTS for example. Approximately 60 of these are used in the uplink. The German 2010 frequency auction [102] provided around 170 MHz of uplink frequency for LTE based systems. However, only 2 * 30 MHz of those are located in the more robust 800 MHz band,

	UMTS	LTE
Available spectrum in Germany	120 MHz Total $\approx$60 MHz Uplink	$\approx$340 MHz Total $\approx$170 MHz Uplink
Channel bandwidth	5 MHz (3.84 MHz used)	1.4/ 3/ 5/ 10/ 15 or 20 MHz (90 % used)
Uplink: Number of channels	12	34 (in case of 5 MHz channels)
Uplink: RACH transmittable CAM/Cell/s	$\approx$35 per RACH data channel (32 SF code) Max: $\approx 31 * 35 \approx 1000$ Today: ≈ 25	Limited by access number Max on 5 MHz: $\approx$1200 Max on 20MHz: $\approx$3600
Uplink: Used channels for CAM transmissions	Configurable, 6 in the following (30 MHz in total)	Configurable, all 6 available 5 MHz channels @ 800 MHz in the following (30 MHz)
Uplink: Total RACH transmittable CAM/Cell/s	Max: $\approx 6 * 1000 \approx 6000$ Today: $\approx 6 * 25 = 300$	$\approx 6 * 1200 = 7200$
Downlink: Broadcast transmittable CAM/Cell/s (1 channel)	$\approx$1500	$\approx$2300 (5 MHz) $\approx$9000 (20 MHz)
Uplink: uplink delay to packet size correlation	$\approx$55 ms per $\approx$40 Byte	$\approx$10–50 ms per packet (independent of size)
Round trip time for CAM transmission	$\approx$350 ms	$\approx$50–100 ms
Costs of operation (without maintenance)	Bandwidth in up- (reserved) and down-link, degraded uplink performance	Bandwidth usage up- and down-link

Table 5.10: Comparison of UMTS and LTE based CAM delivery performance: Number of transmittable CAMs per cell, latency characteristics, and cost factors.

while most of the rest resides in the much higher 2.6 GHz band.

In order to transmit an 80 Byte CAM, two random access procedures are needed in UMTS. This leads to a maximum of 35 CAM/s, as one data channel can handle circa 70 chunks of 40 Byte per second. In case all capacity is reserved for random access driven operation, this leads to a conservative number of ≈1000 CAM/Cell/s. However, in today's systems only 1 RACH data channel will be used. In such a configuration some of the accesses have to be reserved for normal operation—a capacity of 25 CAM/s on the one RACH data channel seems to be reasonable.

The LTE RACH performance investigation found that ≈1500 accesses/s should be possible on a 5 MHz channel. [103] states that the uplink air interface sector throughput will be ≈0.63 Mbps/MHz, leading to 3.15 Mbps on a 5 MHz channel. This represents sufficient capacity to transmit ≈5000 CAM/s. Therefore, the access number is the limiting factor here. It should be noted, that it remains an open question how many of those accesses would be needed (e.g. for HARQs) in order to serve normal traffic within the rest of the available capacity. In order to remain conservative, a maximum number of 1200 CAM/s in a 5 MHz cell is assumed. Given a three times higher RACH dimensioning in a 20 MHz cell, a maximum number of 3600 CAM/Cell/s results.

Based on those uplink numbers, it is exemplary assumed that the complete 30 MHz of uplink spectrum in the 800 MHz LTE band is available for uplink CAM delivery. The same six 5 MHz channels are assumed for UMTS. UMTS would allow for transmitting roughly 6000 CAM/Cell/s at maximum, while being limited to a very low number of 300 CAM/Cell/s with today's base station software configuration. LTE is able to deliver 7200 CAM/Cell/s, despite only using 25% of the available capacity on the assumed frequency channels for CAM delivery.

In the downlink, the usage of broadcasts as argued in Section 5.2.3 leads to the limitation that a single frequency channel must be used. Today's radios will not be able to monitor several frequency channels in parallel. In consequence, the single system capacity numbers from the broadcast analysis in Section 5.2.3 represent the downlink limit. As uplink capacity can be increased by distributing vehicles onto additional frequency channels, the downlink broadcast capacity is the overall capacity limiting factor in terms of delivering CAMs.

Capacity The analysis on expected data traffic per cell in Section 5.1 presented CAM/Cell/s demand numbers for different conditions in Table 5.6. A worst-case number of 3400 CAM/Cell/s was given in case only cross-traffic assistance is of interest. In case CAMs are intended to be transmitted also on roads that are not in intersection vicinity, an even higher number of 7200 CAM/Cell/s results. Those numbers cannot be handled by UMTS. LTE is able to handle such numbers with its capacity of 9000 CAM/Cell/s on the widest 20 MHz channel.

A 10 MHz channel will only provide enough capacity for the intersection-limited case or in case of a reduction of CAM frequency from 10 Hz to 5 Hz. This is important in Germany for example, as no network operator got hold of more than 10 MHz spectrum in the 800 MHz band [104]. In case an average cell size is considered, worst-case numbers in big cells of 600–1100 CAM/Cell/s were found. The available capacity of both systems is high enough in such conditions.

Latency   LTE has a latency benefit compared to UMTS due to less need for power ramping and only one random access per packet instead one per 40 Byte payload. Furthermore, the RAN is faster as discussed in background Section 3.2.4. Resulting round trip times of 50–100 ms are most likely tolerable. 350 ms in case of UMTS seem questionable in case of safety relevant use cases. Potential delays in the backend by needed data fusion between different operators are not incorporated here and are up to future research.

The costs of operation are a question of the consumed resources and their cost rate. CAM transmissions reduce the available bandwidth for regular carrier services. In contrast to LTE, the UMTS resource consumption is static in the uplink. Also, one should be aware that it is doubtable that cellular carriers allow such a high additional CAM load on all of their channels. This would reduce the deliverable number of CAM per cell compared to the given amount. A more detailed cost evaluation is given later on in Section 5.3.3.

The numbers in Table 5.10 are of course region specific (available frequency) as well as system configuration dependent (e.g. the amount of used uplink channels). The analysis is intended to give an impression of the technical potential and influence factors in case UMTS/LTE is used to deliver CAMs in intersection areas.

5.2.5   Conclusion

This performance analysis investigated system usage, capacity and latency of UMTS and the forthcoming LTE when used to deliver CAMs. Capacity results were compared to the demand numbers found in Section 5.1.

It was proposed to use random access driven transmissions in the uplink to deliver CAMs efficiently. The investigation shows that the random access design in LTE is more advanced than the UMTS one. LTE especially profits from its load adaptive RACH design. Random access driven packet transmissions are size invariant and do not need pre-allocated resources, as it is the case in UMTS.

A comparison between unicast and broadcast downlink delivery revealed that a broadcast of CAMs is advantageous due to higher efficiency and greater coverage. However, a single frequency channel must be used. LTE profits from its increased spectral efficiency compared to UMTS HSPA and the option to be operated on frequency channels of 10 and 20 MHz. Both facts increase the broadcast capacity in a single system.

The analysis revealed that the capacity limiting factor is the downlink, due to the inability to split broadcast load on several frequency channels with common radios. LTE should be able to meet even the worst-case CAM capacity demand, while UMTS is only able to meet average conditions. In general, the analysis also shows that the particular capacity of UMTS and LTE networks for CAM transmissions is very configuration dependent. Therefore, the resulting final per technology numbers should be taken with care—it is important to understand the different influence factors on performance.

Absolute round trip times of below 100 ms in case of LTE seem reasonable for the desired use case. An UMTS number of 350 ms seems too high. Here, the UMTS RACH accounts for more than 100 ms just to transmit CAMs to the base station.

Although this analysis does not investigate all system options in detail and some rather academic assumptions are made, it shows important performance relations and influence factors when a cellular system is used for cross-traffic assistance, instead of decentralized 5.9 GHz IEEE 802.11p communication.

5.3 Boundary Conditions

The feasibility to use cellular systems for CAM delivery is certainly not decidable based on their theoretic ability to handle the required load and latency demands alone. The performance analysis in Section 5.2 already revealed some requirements and problems. This section discusses boundary conditions that need to be considered in detail.

Firstly, constraints are discussed in Section 5.3.1 that could potentially complicate a rollout. Secondly, the reliability of cellular based V2V communication system is briefly discussed in Section 5.3.2. Lastly, the issue of operating costs is discussed on a high level basis in Section 5.3.3.

5.3.1 Rollout Constraints

The performance analysis in Section 5.2 proposed an efficient transmission via a RACH driven uplink and broadcast based downlink to reduce capacity consumption. The analysis revealed several boundary conditions that might hinder a rollout. These will be discussed in the following in more detail to shed light on the general feasibility of such an efficient cellular CAM delivery to enable vehicular active safety applications.

Broadcast Downlink Implications

- *One frequency channel / operator limitation* – The CAMs needed to enable cooperative safety applications such as cross-traffic assistance are optimally delivered by and to every vehicle. In such scenario, it would be natural to operate the system via multiple network operators to gain benefit from competition. In consequence, a vehicle would be connected to the backend via a certain operator. However, the broadcast delivery implies that all data must be delivered via every operator to inform all vehicles. This results in a costly duplication overhead. The only way to prevent such overhead would be to operate all vehicles in a single broadcast downlink channel. Unfortunately, this implies the need to use a single operator.

- *High frequency channel bandwidth requirement* – As current radios are only able to monitor a single frequency channel, a broadcast driven downlink is limited to the capacity of a single channel. The analysis in Section 5.2.4 revealed that a 10 MHz LTE channel is needed at least. 10 MHz represent the complete bandwidth a single operator in Germany possesses in the 800 MHz band (Three operators got hold of 10 MHz each) [104]. It is assumed here that the 800 MHz band is favored as its superior propagation properties (compared to rest of the LTE spectrum at 2.6 GHz) match the requirements of a safety application. Therefore, operating the system on a 20 MHz channel to gain enough broadcast capacity to support the highest found capacity demand would not be possible in the 800 MHz band. Also, taking the single operator limitation into consideration, a single operator would need to dedicate a lot of his available capacity in the valuable[2] low frequency band to vehicular safety.

- *Base station updates* – While MBMS is standardized in UMTS and LTE, it is not rolled out in today's cellular networks. A base station software update would be needed.

RACH Uplink Implications

- *Base station updates / standardization requirement* – The assumption of a pure RACH driven uplink is academic in terms of today's networks: The scheduler in base stations would open a dedicated connection as soon as several RACH

---

[2]≈590 Mio € were paid in the 2010 German frequency auction for 2×5 MHz paired spectrum in the 800 MHz band. In the 2.6 GHz band, only ≈19 Mio € were paid for the same bandwidth [104].

transmissions happen in a short time frame. A context aware scheduler would be needed that does not open a connection in case a random access containing a CAM happens. Therefore, existing base stations would need to be updated. Furthermore, the scheduler behavior would need to be standardized in order to allow interoperability. However, standardization takes its time. This would delay the rollout of such a cellular communication driven vehicular safety system. In contrast, the 5.9 GHz IEEE 802.11p standards are already finalized or in their final phases.

- *UE hardware limitations* – Section 5.2.4 showed that even with LTE, one uplink frequency channel is not sufficient to handle the CAM load; at least not RACH driven. In consequence, vehicles would be operated on different uplink channels. A single cellular system is operated on a certain symmetric uplink / downlink channel pair. In order to retrieve uplink grants and similar information, a UE has to monitor the downlink channel that is assigned to the uplink one. However, broadcasting implies that all vehicles should be logged into a single downlink channel. In consequence, a vehicle potentially needs to monitor two downlink channels. UEs are not designed to monitor several downlink frequency channels in parallel. Even if they were, they might be on different operators and in consequence a single SIM might be not sufficient. A possible solution might be two radios with one SIM each. One to transmit CAMs in the uplink, the second to monitor the broadcast downlink. However, this would raise hardware costs, eventually reducing the often seen cost advantage against 5.9 GHz IEEE 802.11p of cellular hardware being more and more common—and therefore being eventually existent—in vehicles.

5.3.2 System Reliability

Cross-traffic assistance is an active safety application. In consequence, a reliable information delivery is required.

From a communication perspective, the radio, the antenna, the antenna cable as well as the transmission over the air interface itself might fail. Hereby, antenna, cable, and air interface delivery are failure points that apply to both technologies, ad-hoc as well as cellular communication. Removing low complexity hardware such as antenna and cable from the list, 5.9 GHz IEEE 802.11p inherits a single point of potential hardware failure, which is the radio. In contrast, a cellular based system introduces additional ones: The base station, the core network as well as the V2V backend that reflects the CAMs could fail.

In terms of the air interface, channel stress and severe fading in terms of 5.9 GHz IEEE 802.11p inevitably lead to some packet loss. However, broadcasts in a cellular system, being not corrected based on acknowledgments, might also get lost due to fading and inter-cell interference. Channel fading can, especially in an urban environment, lead to areas without reliable reception. Furthermore, there still exist white spots in rural areas that are not properly covered by the different network operators. This is especially true in the U.S. Cellular coverage can also be affected by outages in the power grid as electricity is needed in order to operate a base station.

Finally, cells might be over-saturated. For example at New Year's Eve, the number of text messages delivered per time raises by several orders of magnitude above average just after midnight [105]. While prioritization mechanisms exist, it still seems to be a legitimate question if a delay-free CAM delivery can be guaranteed in such situations of unusual high load in the network.

5.3.3 Costs

5.9 GHz IEEE 802.11p ad-hoc communication does not require infrastructure in order to enable cross-traffic assistance. This is a cost advantage over cellular communication, where network operators need to pass on infrastructure and operational costs to customers.

A reliable assessment of the monetary costs per vehicle for a cellular communication based vehicular safety system is difficult given several variable factors influencing data consumption and other operation expenses. Therefore, this section focuses on investigating cost factors and dependencies.

The costs in order to realize a cellular V2V communication system would be on the one hand investments in cellular hardware / infrastructure and on the other hand operational costs.

Hardware / infrastructure investments will manifest themselves as follows: While it is often argued that a cellular radio is more and more common in vehicles and does not represent a cost factor, the constraint analysis in Section 5.3.1 revealed that an existing, single off-the-shelf radio might not be sufficient. The likely need for a second radio represents vehicle-bound hardware costs. Furthermore, the analysis showed that the software running in the base stations needs to be updated to deliver CAMs efficiently. The functionality needs to be standardized and the software update must be rolled out, representing costs for the network operators. Lastly, the V2V backend infrastructure to reflect CAMs needs to be installed.

Operational costs will manifest themselves in operating the backend and data consumption in the cellular networks. The latter is probably the more important factor, since wireless spectrum is a limited resource and a lot of infrastructure is needed in order to operate a wireless network. For example, the data given in Table 5.1 reveals that most operators are running >200 base stations to cover the city area of Munich only. In the following, a very basic calculation is presented to estimate monetary costs to deliver CAMs via a cellular network:

$$CAM_{km} = \frac{tx_{rate}}{speed_{avg}}$$

$$UL_{Data/km} = CAM_{km} * Size_{CAM}$$

$$DL_{Data/km} = UL_{Data/km} * (100\% + MultiCellDeliveryOverhead)$$

$$UserEquivalent_{Data/km} = UL_{Data/km} * (100\% + UL_{RobustnessOverhead})$$

$$+ DL_{Data/km} * (100\% + DL_{RobustnessOverhead})$$

$$Cost_{km} = UserEquivalent_{Data/km} * Cost_{Data}$$

$$Cost_{Function} = Cost_{km} * km_{year} * Years$$

Firstly, the amount of CAM to be transmitted per km is derived from the CAM transmission rate and the average speed of the vehicle. Next, the net data amount to deliver those CAMs is computed. In the downlink, it has to be considered here that some CAMs need to be delivered into more than one cell to reach all vehicles in proximity of the sending vehicle. Based on those net data, the user billed equivalent data amount is judged. This is needed, as data delivered via broadcast and RACH consumes—due to the robust encoding—more resources than regular cellular data traffic currently billed. Given a certain price per data unit, it is now possible to derive the costs per km to send and receive CAMs. In case the system is intended to be sold to the consumer as a special equipment function, the costs over the live time of the vehicle might be accumulated, expressed by the last equation.

In order to provide a more concrete impression on the potentially resulting numbers, the equations are exemplarily filled with values in the following. The selection of those values will be discussed subsequently.

$$CAM_{km} = \frac{10 \frac{CAM}{s} * 3600 \frac{s}{h}}{25 \, km/h} = 1440 \, CAM/km$$

$$UL_{Data/km} = 1440 \, CAM/km * 80 \, Byte/CAM \approx 115 \, KByte/km$$

$$DL_{Data/km} = UL_{Data/km} * (100\% + 30\%) \approx 150 \, KByte/km$$

$$UserEquivalent_{Data/km} = UL_{Data/km} * (100\% + 20\%)$$

$$+ DL_{Data/km} * (100\% + 150\%) = 510 \, KByte/km$$

$$Cost_{km} = UserEquivalent_{Data/km} * 2 \, Cent/MB = 1.0 \, Cent/km$$

$$Cost_{Function} = Cost_{km} * 4300 \, km/Year * 10 \, Years \approx 430 \, Euro$$

As the investigated scenario in this thesis is cross-traffic assistance at urban intersections, urban traffic is assumed as an example. An assumed average urban speed of 25 km/h and a CAM transmission rate of 10 Hz result in 1440 CAM/km. The overhead of CAMs being delivered to multiple cells is set arbitrarily to 30 %. A combined net data consumption of 265 KByte/km results. Broadcast robustness overhead in the downlink is set to 150 % based on the LTE unicast to broadcast relation of 24000 to 9000 CAM/Cell/s as found in Section 5.2.3. As RACH driven messages are transmitted on the regular shared uplink resources in LTE, only a small overhead of 20 % is assumed to account for the increased RACH resource consumption compared to normal network operation. Subsequently, the resulting user equivalent data rate of 510 KByte/km is not simply multiplied by the cost per data unit a normal user pays: In Germany, a common 2011 price for 1 GB traffic per month is 10 €. This leads to a price of 0.01 €/MB. However, those data packages are calculated based on the average consumed traffic per user per month. If an average actual consumption of 50 % is assumed, the real price would be 0.02 €/MB. Multiplying the user equivalent data rate with this price, a cost of 1 Eurocent per km results. In case of an average annual driving distance of 13000 km [106], and as-sumed 1/3 of those are city traffic, the costs for a 10 year lifetime would be ≈430 €. If also highway km (1/3, 120 km/h) and rural road km (1/3, 80 km/h) are incor-porated, the total sum would be at ≈650 €.

Of course, the uplink overhead value as well as the average consumed MB per month to derive real costs per MB are purely artificial assumptions. In general, pricing knowledge from operators and further investigations on overhead would be needed to assess a realistic cost structure of a broadcast/RACH based CAM delivery. Furthermore, the average driven distance number of 4300 km/year as well as a ten-year lifetime might also be debatable.

Also, one should keep in mind that the resulting costs per km and equipment are pure expenses to deliver the data via the cellular network. While the profit margin of the network operator is incorporated in the example, the profit margin of the vehicle manufacturer is not. Also, the backend operation costs, infrastructure investments, cellular hardware costs in the vehicle, and components running the assistance system are not accounted for. Therefore, the net costs for the vehicle manufacturer are considerably higher. In conclusion, even if it is not possible to derive a reliable cost number based on the available information, it is rather obvious that a special equipment package enabling cellular communication driven cross-traffic assistance would be not quite cheap.

5.3.4   Conclusion

This boundary condition analysis investigated potential issues that might impact the application of a cellular V2V communication system for active safety applica-tions. Potential rollout constraints, reliability concerns, and costs were discussed.

The constraint analysis discussed rollout related complications of the proposed information delivery. A broadcast based downlink delivery implies a need for base station updates and high resource consumption in a single operator's network. Also, the required amount of resources might not be available from a single operator in the favorable 800 MHz LTE band. A random access driven uplink requires scheduler updates in base stations. Furthermore, standardization efforts are required. Finally, the analysis shows that the combination of broadcast and RACH will likely require more than a single cellular radio in a vehicle.

In terms of reliability, cell broadcasts might suffer from packet loss due to interference, same as with IEEE 802.11p. Compared to 5.9 GHz IEEE 802.11p, cellular based CAM delivery inherits with base station, core network, and backend additional potential points of failures. Imperfect coverage as well as potential cell over-saturation represent additional issues in terms of a vehicular safety system.

The costs investigation shows that cost factors are hardware investments such as the requirement for two radios, required standardization efforts, base station updates, and operational costs for information delivery as well as backend operation. The monetary costs for information delivery are estimated in the 1 Eurocent/km region. While the estimation depends on several factors that are difficult to assess reliably, the fact that this number represents only one of the several cost factors shows that cellular communication driven active vehicular safety is rather expensive.

5.4 Cellular Performance Conclusion

This chapter evaluated the capacity demand to be expected, it investigated the ability of UMTS and LTE to handle the capacity as well as latency demand, and discussed boundary conditions potentially complicating a rollout.

The demand analysis shows that in worst-case conditions $\approx$1700 CAM/Cell/s might need to be transmitted in cross-traffic assistance limited conditions and up to 7200 CAM/Cell/s in case of no load limiting assumptions such as a reduced message delivery rate or CAM delivery in intersection vicinity only.

The UMTS and LTE performance analysis reveals that LTE is theoretically able to handle this demand and provides low round trip times of below 100 ms. UMTS on the contrary has a much higher delay and is not able to handle worst-case capacity demand conditions.

While LTE seems theoretically able to handle the challenging exchange of CAMs, the boundary condition analysis shows that a practical realization would be technically challenging, inherits reliability issues, might require a rollout delaying standardization and would be rather expensive.

6

Evaluation of Ad-Hoc Communication

The feasibility of 5.9 GHz IEEE 802.11p ad-hoc communication driven cross-traffic assistance at inner-city intersections is evaluated in this chapter.

The ability of the ad-hoc communication to inform a crossing vehicle in time depends on the necessity and ability of NLOS reception. NLOS reception is on the one hand dependent on signal propagation, but also on reception behavior under network competition.

The necessity for NLOS reception has not been investigated so far as Section 4.2 showed. More importantly, the knowledge on 5.9 GHz NLOS reception is limited. Especially, no validated NLOS path loss model for 5.9 GHz inter-vehicle communication has been proposed, which would allow for evaluating NLOS reception under network competition via simulations.

The lack of information on NLOS reception necessity is tackled in Section 6.1. The study investigates building positions to answer how often NLOS reception occurs in cross-traffic assistance critical situations. Furthermore, it is intended to provide information on reference scenarios in order to enable representative measurements and simulations.

Following, the general ability of NLOS reception is investigated via extensive systematic measurements in Section 6.2. A methodical selection of tested intersections and parameter values enables to assess the influence of different parameters—for example inter-building distance—on NLOS reception quality. Based on the extensive measurement data, a NLOS path loss equation and fading characterization is derived in Section 6.3.

Finally, the new model is used in a simulation study on NLOS reception under cross-traffic assistance relevant traffic flow patterns in Section 6.4. The study assesses reception quality under deployment conditions.

A conclusion on the identified performance potential of ad-hoc communication with regards to the challenging cross-traffic assistance use case is given in Section 6.5.

6.1   Buildings, Non-Line-Of-Sight and Representative Scenarios

As discussed in Section 3.1.4, propagation at inner-city intersections is not solely, but at least partially characterized by buildings. Building placement determines the field of view into a crossing street and therefore the amount of LOS and NLOS. The incorporation of geometric aspects in the equations of micro-cellular NLOS models for below rooftop base-stations implies that NLOS path loss depends on the field of view. In consequence, it is crucial to know representative scenarios in order to produce meaningful results in NLOS reception investigations.

An application for abstracted scenario knowledge is the definition of representative intersections for radio channel measurements. Measuring in representative intersections allows a generalization of results. Furthermore, selecting different real world intersections of the same type might also allow for assessing if building facades influence reception in a significant way. A second application is the simulation of the ad-hoc communication at intersections. Data is needed that enables the creation of representative simulation setups. If such data does not exist, there is the danger that a simulated scenario is seldom in reality and results cannot be generalized.

This study investigates the characteristics of intersections in a city settlement area to answer the need of NLOS reception and provide the desired data for the measurements in Section 6.2 and the simulations in Section 6.4. Some of the sub-questions that arose were: How many street corners are occupied by buildings? How far away from the intersection are buildings? What are typical building locations?

The study is organized as follows: Firstly, the data basis and its pre-processing are described in Section 6.1.1. Secondly, the data is analyzed and the corresponding results are given in Section 6.1.2. The vicinity of buildings to an intersection is investigated in Section 6.1.2.1. The amount of LOS/NLOS is studied in Section 6.1.2.2. Representative scenarios are investigated in Section 6.1.2.3. Finally, a conclusion is given in Section 6.1.3.

6.1.1 Data Basis and Processing

The city region investigated for this study is the complete administrative area of Munich, Germany, consisting of the complete settlement area without the backcountry.

The data basis is composed of building information and a street data overlay. A map with all building shapes that is publicly available at the City of Munich website was used. After processing the data, the building shape information existed as vector description. Street information was taken from a 2008 street map from a digital map data provider. For each intersection, data about the intersection center and side street direction was extracted. However, there is no information about street widths available in the data.

Building shape and intersection map were stacked on each other. In order to do so, the street information had to be converted from the ellipsoid WGS84 format into the Cartesian Gauß-Krüger format the building information was available in. The precision of the combined map is pretty good. However, it should be noted that there might be slight errors due to the different data sources and the conversion. The resulting data basis is shown in Figure 6.1. A close up look on the building shape resolution and matching grade is available on the left in Figure 6.2.

The following analysis concentrates on intersections with 3 and 4 legs. They represent about 99.5 % of all intersections in the city of Munich. As first analysis step, an algorithm searches the nearest buildings for each intersection. Afterwards, for each corner area—spanned by two side street directions—the nearest

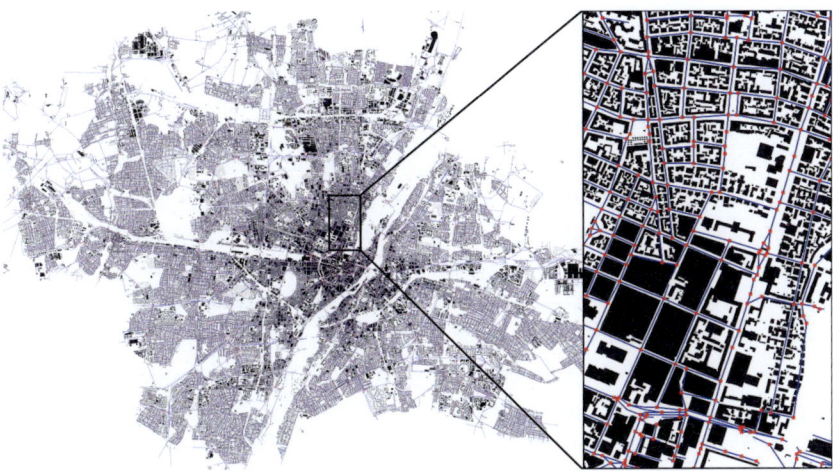

Figure 6.1: Data basis – Overlapped building shape and intersection data of the city of Munich.

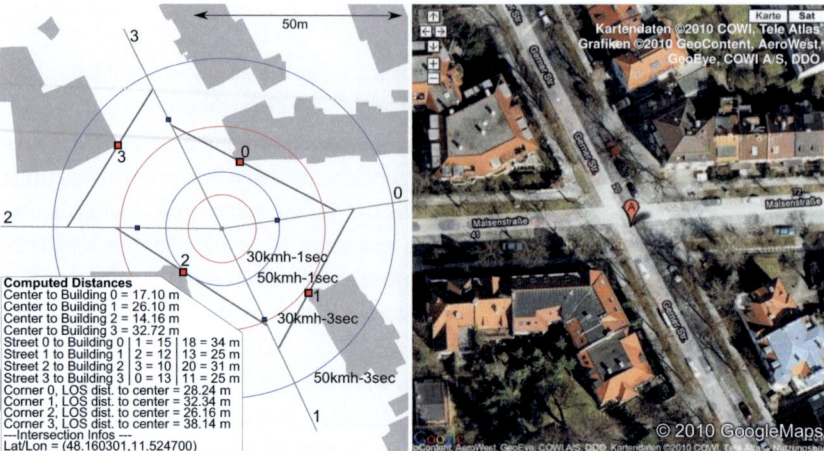

Figure 6.2: Screenshot of HTML-page for verification of map match and data analysis quality of a single intersection. Map quality verification against Google Maps [107].

building vertex point is searched. This information is later on used for classification and further analysis.

The total set of intersections was filtered in order to optimize the data quality of the following evaluation. Intersections with a "corrupt" data basis were excluded. An intersection is classified as "corrupt" if a street leg (direction info) crosses a building. This can happen in case of data source inaccuracies. A possible reason is a special property of the input data: The street direction is determined by the next street segment end-point. If the end point is far away and the street has a turn in between, the resulting line can cross a building.

Intersections with a layout that is "problematic" for an automated analysis were excluded, too: Intersections with one or more corner angles not in the 90 ± 20 degrees range were excluded as a narrow angle increases the probability of a street direction being very near to one side of the corresponding building corridor as a result of map imperfections. In case of 3-leg intersection, the 90 ± 20 degrees criterion was applied to the two smallest angles.

In order to specify the exclusion criteria, the data quality was verified via traversing a subset of automatically generated verification HTML-pages of all intersections. A screenshot of one of them is shown in Figure 6.2. The HTML-pages also include data computed by the evaluation algorithms like the earliest line-of-sight vector at each corner (later on described in Section 6.1.2.2). This allowed to verify the algorithm implementations.

6.1.2   Data Analysis and Results

The resulting data basis after preprocessing is shown in Table 6.1. About 10 % of all intersection data was discarded because a street direction crossed a building. About 70 % of the remaining intersections are "regular" shaped according to the characteristic specified in Section 6.1.1.

Interestingly, 75.4 % of all intersections have three legs. This high number is partly caused by each in-street at roundabouts being handled as a 3-leg intersection. However, this is not considered as a problem, as such a situation is just the same as a street hitting another street. Both reflect a T-shaped "intersection area" with two circa 90 degrees corners and a straight side. Another specialty—not visible in the table—is streets with middle separation. They are represented as two single direction streets in the used map. This leads to multiple crossings and therefore "intersections" at big intersections. It was opted to not correct this, as big intersections with likely high traffic flow are stronger reflected in the analysis this way.

A histogram on the number of corners of an intersection that are occupied by a building provides a first impression on the relevance of buildings in terms of radio coverage from one side street into the next. The histogram for 4-leg intersections is presented in Table 6.2. A corner is classified as not occupied, if the distance from center to nearest building is equal or greater than 50 or 100 m. The statistics show that—dependent on the classification metric—70 to 90 % of all 4-leg intersections have a building at each corner, thus limiting the radio coverage.

Intersections in Munich	Total	Percentage
Total Number	12307	
Without "Corrupt" Intersections	11128	90.4 % of 12307
3 Leg Intersections	8393	75.4 % of 11128
3 Leg with Regular Angle	5619	66.9 % of 8393
4 Leg Intersections	2672	24.0 % of 11128
4 Leg with Regular Angle	2058	77.0 % of 2672

Table 6.1: Data basis – Basic data set characterization numbers.

Occupied Corners	0	1	2	3	4
Criterion: < 50 m	2 %	4 %	8 %	16 %	70 %
Criterion: < 100 m	0 %	1 %	3 %	7 %	89 %

Table 6.2: Occupation statistics for 4-leg intersections.

6.1.2.1   Building Distance Analysis

The distance from the center of an intersection to the nearest vertex point of a building in a corner segment is a generalization of the LOS blocking building location at a corner. For a line of sight analysis, it is irrelevant if the extension of the building shape that is defining the first LOS possibility is located near to the one or the other side street. This generalization helps to reduce the geometric complexity. A special case is the straight street side in case of 3-leg intersections. The point of interest is the building point with smallest orthogonal distance to the straight street, thus defining the nearest position of a building potentially providing a reflection. If there is no building found—or the distance to the nearest building is greater than 100 m—the value is set to 100 m.

The relative histogram of the building vertex distances for 4-leg intersections and the two cases (corner, straight street) in case of 3-leg intersections is shown in Figure 6.3. The value peak is located at the 15 to 20 m bin. There is no major difference between corner occupation at 3-leg and 4-leg intersections. In comparison, the straight street curve is shifted about 5 m to the left, meaning more cases with smaller distances. A cumulative distribution function representation of the data—not given here—reveals that in about 80 % of all cases, the distance is below 30 m.

6.1.2.2   Radio Line-Of-Sight Analysis

One of the questions to be answered was the amount of radio LOS in case of cross traffic assistance. As discussed in Section 2.2.2, driver assistance systems warn the driver about 3 s before a potential collision and the last point of possible system intervention is often considered as 1 s before impact.

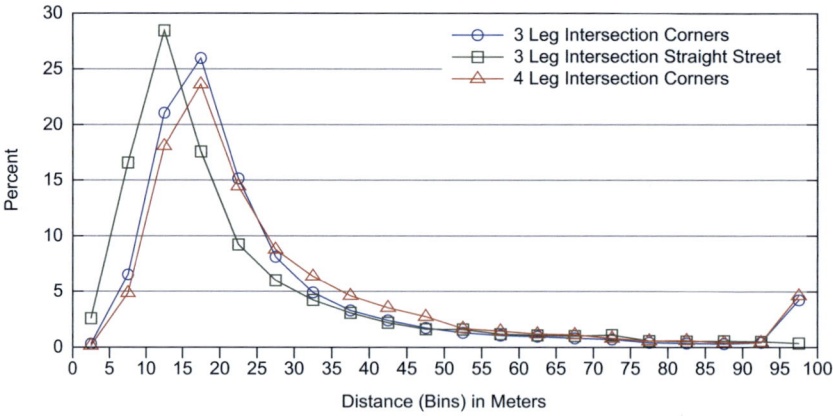

Figure 6.3: Histogram of intersection-center to nearest building vertex distance.

A collision potentially happens if two vehicles approaching an intersection hit the central intersection area at the same moment. Assuming that both vehicles have the same certain speed, it is possible to compute the point on each side street where a radio LOS would be needed for enabling a warning to the driver or for performing an intervention. This is especially important under the artificial assumption that NLOS reception is not possible.

The information about the nearest building vertexes was used to compute the earliest LOS for each intersection corner. It was computed as the line that touches the nearest building vertex and is orthogonal to a vector from intersection center in direction of the middle angle between the corner defining side streets. In consequence, the first LOS line hits both side streets at the same distance from the intersection center. The first possible packet reception point is assumed to be at the crossing between street and earliest LOS line. This point was compared with the needed first point of reception according to the assistance system requirements.

The computation is visualized in Figure 6.4. The vehicle speed and the desired time to collision lead to a certain wanted distance to collision. A CAM message has to be received the moment the nose of the vehicle hits this point to fulfill the assistance system requirement. As the antenna is likely located in the middle of a vehicle, the distance from nose to antenna has to be added to the distance to collision to determine the point on the street where a CAM should arrive. A warning is considered possible, as long as this point is closer to intersection center than the point where the earliest line of sight condition exists (Radio-LOS-Distance).

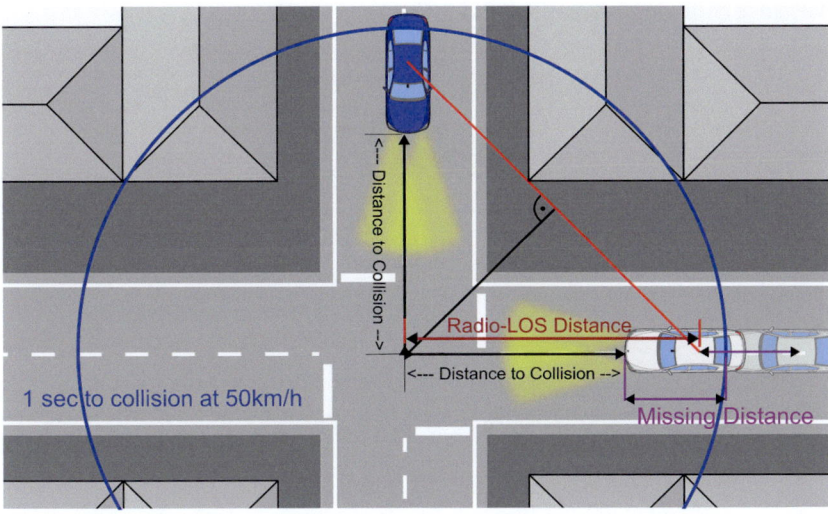

Figure 6.4: Radio LOS against warning point determination.

The verification HTML-pages—presented in the earlier Figure 6.2—also include lines showing the earliest LOS at the corners and four warning distance rings for 1 and 3 s and 30 and 50 km/h each. This way, those HMTL-pages also allowed to judge for these two exemplary speeds if the desired LOS-coverage is given at corners in case an intersection is of specific interest.

The "Radio-LOS Distance" on the side streets was computed for each corner. The resulting numbers are visualized as relative histogram in Figure 6.5. It reveals a concentration between 16 and 30 m distance to intersection center.

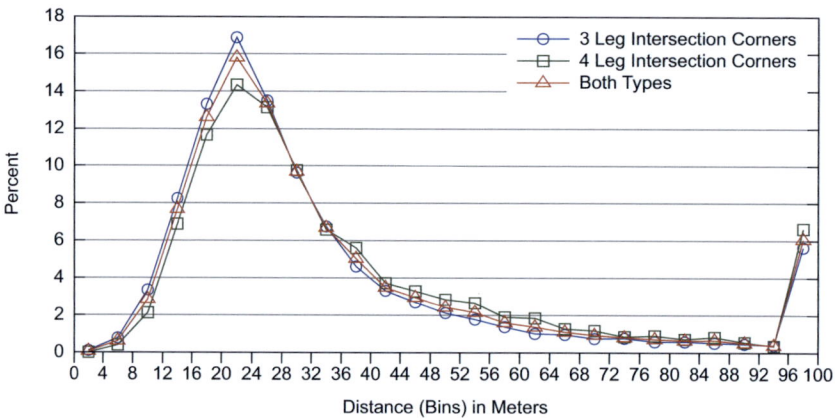

Figure 6.5: Radio-LOS coverage on side streets – Histogram of Radio-LOS-Distance (from intersection-center).

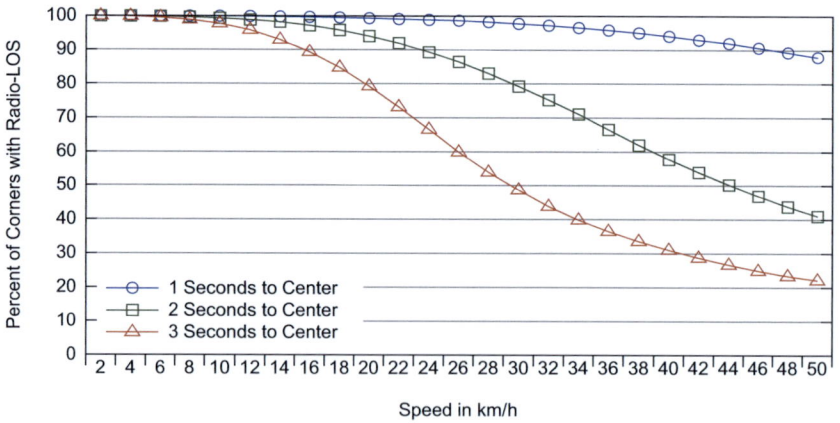

Figure 6.6: Radio-LOS condition at x seconds to intersection center and certain speed and assumed $v_1 = v_2$.

Based on this information, the decision whether there is a LOS condition at a certain time to intersection center and speed combination was made for every corner. The resulting percentage of corners with LOS at a desired point in time before impact is visualized in Figure 6.6. At 50 km/h, only 20 % of all corners provide radio LOS conditions at 3 s to intersection center. At the last intervention time of 1 s to center, there exists a LOS condition at 90 % of all corners, though.

This numbers verify the need to investigate reception conditions in NLOS areas. Especially at the first intended warning point, 3 s before a potential impact, there are a lot of intersections where the LOS between two approaching vehicles is blocked by buildings.

6.1.2.3 Clustering – Finding Representative Scenarios

As described in the motivation to this study, a determination of representative scenarios is beneficial to enable meaningful real world measurements and simulation scenario setups.

A clustering approach was used to find intersections with a similar characteristic. The value used as value domain is the distance from intersection center to nearest building vertex at a corner. This value generalizes the real positioning of the building (whether it is located closer to one or the other street leg), but a single value represents a group of building positions with very similar blocking of the LOS. Thus, the geometric complexity in the clustering process is reduced without sacrificing detail in terms of the most valuable information, being the earliest possible LOS at intersection approaching and the field of view into the side street. The triple (3-leg) or quadruple (4-leg intersection) of the intersection center to building vertex distances for each intersection is interpreted as point in the three or four-dimensional space. The distances at each intersection are sorted in ascending order to simplify the search space and solve the question which corner has to be set as corner 1 and so forth. For 3-leg intersections, the corner distances come first in sorted order, followed by the straight street distance. This way, corners and straight street are kept separate.

Clustering was performed by the popular data-mining tool WEKA [108] in version 3.6.2 from the University of Waikato. The configuration of WEKA was as following: Clustering was done with the "Training Set" method and using the "DensityBasedCluster" wrapper class. The latter has the benefit of providing standard deviation values for the clustering output. "XMeans" was used as clusterer. XMeans [109] is a modified KMeans clustering algorithm. It was modified to enable an automatic discovery of the cluster number. The "cutOffFactor" parameter of XMeans was set to 0.5, the maximum iteration number to 20, the number of clusters was limited to be between three and eight and the seed value was 30.

For 4-leg intersections, the algorithm found four clusters. The complete results are shown in Table 6.3. About 50 % of all intersections turn out to be grouped into one cluster. The distance values in this dominant cluster range from 12.2 to 24.1 m. The standard deviation for this cluster is low with values between 3.5 and 6.2.

As result of the input data construction, the distance values for each cluster turn out to be sorted in ascending order. Because the ordering is a result of the need for a unique corner mapping as input, it should be somehow removed from

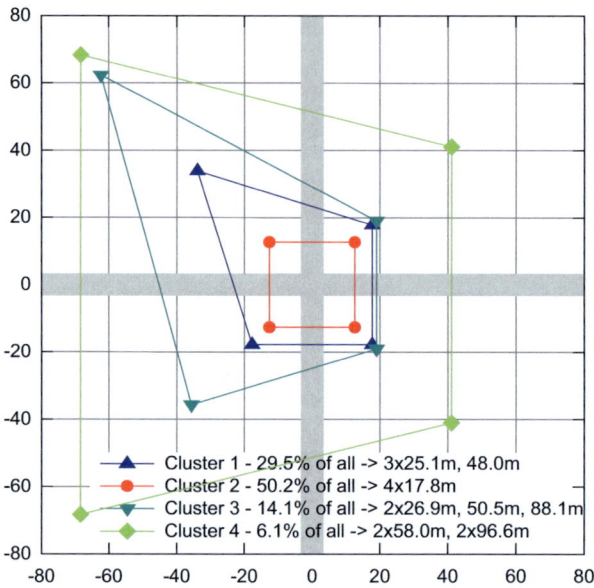

Figure 6.7: Visualization of 4-leg intersection clustering result.

	Cluster		Cluster 2		Cluster 3		Cluster 4	
Number	607		1034		291		126	
Percent	29.5	grouped	50.2	grouped	14.1	grouped	6.1	grouped
Corner 1	18.1	25.1	12.2	17.8	22.1	26.9	45.3	58.0
Std.Dev.	6.8		3.5		9.1		23.4	
Corner 2	24.4	25.1	15.8	17.8	31.7	26.9	70.8	58.0
Std.Dev.	7.8		3.6		12.2		22.9	
Corner 3	32.8	25.1	19.2	17.8	50.5	50.5	94.1	96.6
Std.Dev.	9.0		4.1		19.2		9.6	
Corner 4	48.0	48.0	24.1	17.8	88.1	88.1	99.2	96.6
Std.Dev.	10.2		6.2		12.7		3.5	

Table 6.3: Clustering results for 4-leg intersections. Distances in meters.

the output. In order to do so, a loop algorithm was applied to the clusterer output that averages two neighboring values if the difference between the two is less than 40 % of the bigger value. It terminates if there is no pair left that can be averaged. This way, corner distance values in a cluster that are close to each other are grouped by averaging. As a result, the dominating cluster is characterized by a distance of 17.8 m from intersection center to nearest building vertex at all four corners. This corresponds to an inter-building distance of 25.2 m in all four side streets.

The post-processed (grouped) values from Table 6.3 are visualized in Figure 6.7. The distance to center values were used to compute the nearest point (x,y)

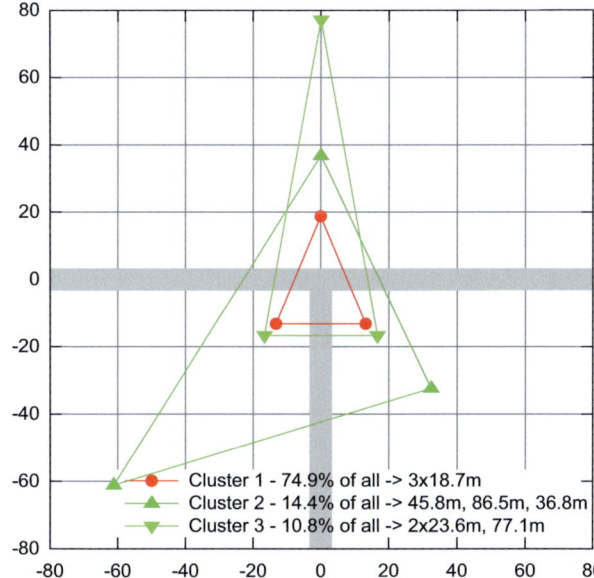

Figure 6.8: Visualization of 3-leg intersection clustering result.

	Cluster 1		**Cluster 2**		**Cluster 3**	
Number	4206		807		606	
Percent	74.9	grouped	14.4	grouped	10.8	grouped
Corner 1	16.0	18.7	45.8	45.8	18.8	23.6
Std.Dev.	6.4		28.8		9.0	
Corner 2	24.3	18.7	86.5	86.5	28.4	23.6
Std.Dev.	10.7		16.0		14.1	
Straight Side	15.9	18.7	36.8	36.8	77.1	77.1
Std.Dev.	8.8		28.8		19.1	

Table 6.4: Clustering results for 3-leg intersections. Distances in meters.

of buildings located in the four corners. The street width in the figure is artificially set to 6.6 m, representing a 2-lane road. It may be wider in some cases in reality. As mentioned before, there was no information about the street widths in the data.

Figure 6.7 shows that there are a lot of intersections with buildings standing relatively close to their streets. Two of the clusters have two to three highly covered corners, while the buildings in the other corners are more far away. Only the most uncommon cluster has two not occupied corners, indicated by distance to center values being almost 100 m, the cut off distance.

The corresponding clustering results for 3-leg intersections are shown as numbers in Table 6.4 and they are visualized in Figure 6.8. The clustering algorithm determined three clusters in this case. The grouped distance value of the most prominent cluster ($\approx$75 % of all intersections) is—at 18.7 m—close to the distance in the most prominent cluster for 4-leg intersections. The other two clusters are characterized by either one corner or the straight street being often unoccupied (indicated by values close to 100 m).

As a summary, clustering reveals that there is a dominating scenario for three and four leg intersections. These scenarios should be a good starting point for simulation setups or field testing. Of course, the value space that was used for clustering, as well as the clustering itself, heavily reduce the real world complexity of buildings positions and their effects on signal propagation. For example, there is no information left if there is a continuous row of buildings starting at the intersection, or if there is only a single building located at the corner. However, the clustering analysis still provides a needed and likely meaningful simplification of a complex environment.

6.1.3   Conclusion

This study provides an analysis of the building occupation of inner city intersection corners at the example of the Munich city area. The analysis shows that only a small percentage ($\approx$20 %) of intersection corner areas provide radio LOS conditions at the moment when a cross-traffic assistant system is intended to warn the driver for the first time. This confirms the intuitively assumed need to investigate the NLOS reception of 5.9 GHz IEEE 802.11p ad-hoc inter-vehicle communication.

Clustering, an often-used data mining technique, was used to find groups of intersections with similar building placement. The results show that there are dominating clusters that incorporate about 50 % of all intersections and therefore allow abstracting a big amount of all intersections in a city. These dominating clusters are characterized by all corners being occupied by buildings that are relatively close to the intersection center.

The provided information about representative scenarios is important for enabling representative NLOS measurements and simulations as performed in Section 6.2 and 6.4. For example, the determined most prominent clusters should provide a good default building placement scenario in the simulations.

The validity of the results is of course to some part bound to the data basis. Cities with more densely packed buildings—probably cities in southern Europe— could very well reveal clusters with smaller distances from intersection center to nearest corner building. The opposite could be the case too. It is up to future research to perform such an analysis with data from other cities and to compare the results with those presented in this study.

6.2   Real-World Measurements of Non-Line-Of-Sight Reception Quality

The building placement analysis in Section 6.1 verified the assumed need for NLOS reception in cross-traffic assistance critical situations. Therefore, in depth knowledge on 5.9 GHz inter-vehicle NLOS reception quality is needed to enable a reliable judgment on the communication technology performance.

The state of the art analysis on NLOS propagation knowledge in Section 4.2.2 showed that no reliable 5.9 GHz inter-vehicle NLOS propagation model exists: Most available models stem from micro-cellular research and differ considerably when applied to 5.9 GHz inter-vehicle communication. Few studies have measured 5.9 GHz NLOS inter-vehicle communication. Those studies were of limited extent and especially lack a profound scenario selection, questioning the generalizability of results.

Such lack of a validated 5.9 GHz NLOS path loss model that is usable for NLOS simulations and the shortcomings of existing measurements motivated to perform an own extensive measurement campaign and deduce a new model based on the gathered data.

In this section, the measurements are described (Section 6.2.1) and the resulting data is analyzed in order to identify different influence factors on NLOS reception quality (Section 6.2.2). The model deduction on top of those results is described in the next Section 6.3.

6.2.1   Measurement Setup

As can be seen from the discussion on previous measurements in Section 4.2.2, there are in general two possibilities to measure a wireless channel. One way is a channel-sounder setup providing impulse response data and the other way to use off-the shelf radio hardware that can provide a signal power indication for received packets.

Using a radio, it is possible to evaluate information about packet reception success and signal power indication. The latter is only available for received packets. Channel-sounders have a higher sensitivity than radios and are therefore able to provide information about signals that are not receivable by a radio. They also provide a much more detailed view of the channel. However, it is difficult to combine the measured channel sounder output with a numerical model of signal processing at the receiver to conclude the real reception performance of a radio.

Another benefit of using a radio is the fact that the provided results are close to channel models as they are used in packet level simulators such as ns-2. As described in detail in background Section 3.1.3, these simulators compute the arriving signal power for one transmitted packet once for each possible receiver. Therefore, the simulation inherits the same per packet simplification as the reception power value available from a radio.

Because the ability to deduce a NLOS channel model for packet level simulations is a main objective and reception rate is one of the major performance metrics for applications, it was decided to measure with radios.

Another major goal is to get results that provide comparability between different intersections and even different intersection legs.[1] If both, transmitter (tx) and receiver (rcv) are mounted on driving vehicles, it is very difficult to control the distance between them during testing and evaluation—certainly the most important influence factor on reception power. Distance between transmitter and receiver also interferes in such a setup with the distance to intersection center, a value that partly defines the NLOS amount of the radio link. Furthermore, for comparability between intersections, exactly the same vehicle coordination would be needed.

These problems were solved by discretization—therefore fixing—of the transmitter position. Two distances to the intersection center were selected as transmitter positions. For each position, a drive through on the crossing street is performed in both directions, producing continuous results in the receiver to intersection center dimension. Each *tx↔center* distance was tested in every side street of an intersection. This way, results were produced that allow comparing the reception performance between different side streets and also different intersections. The measurement design is visualized in Figure 6.9, showing the fixed transmitter positions and the movement of the receiver vehicle.

The two selected *tx↔center* distances are 30 and 60 m. They reflect two different situations in terms of cross traffic assistance: The driver warning assumption of 3 s before a collision and the last point of interception at 1 s ahead correspond to 42 and 14 m at a speed of 50 km/h. Because the halt line is probably a more likely point of collision as the intersection center, and line of sight into a cross street is common

---

[1]Explained in intersection selection in Section 6.2.1.2.

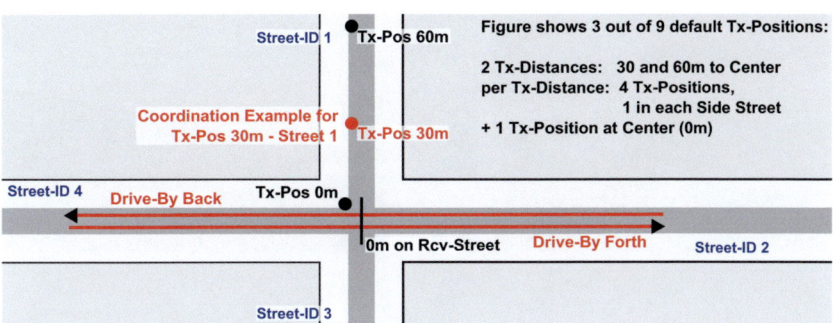

Figure 6.9: Measurement design: Transmitter positioned at discrete distance to center. Receiver driving on crossing street. Example shows transmitter positions in one street-leg. Measurements were done with transmitter placed in all four legs.

at 15 m to center, the numbers were increased to 2 and 4 s. With rounding applied, these numbers lead to the selected 30 and 60 m to intersection center at 50 km/h.

Splitting the distance between transmitter and receiver up into the two dimensions "distance from transmitter to intersection center" ($tx\leftrightarrow center$) and "center to receiver" ($rcv\leftrightarrow center$) was inspired by the NLOS reception models for cellular communication with below-rooftop base stations. All of them compute NLOS path loss based on these two dimensions.[2] The split-up also reflects that a signal has to travel a longer distance in case of NLOS propagation than the direct distance between transmitter and receiver.

6.2.1.1 Used Hardware

Transmitter and receiver unit consisted each of a radio, antenna, antenna-cable, a GPS receiver to determine position and time, and a laptop that initiates transmissions, respectively processes receptions, and logs events.

A tripod was used as transmitter basis. It provides a 35×35 cm metal plate at 1.45 m height as ground for the antenna. A tripod was favorable against a vehicle as it is better placeable at the fixed transmission distances while testing. Also, in some streets, a vehicle would have blocked all traffic. Transmitter positions were pre-determined via satellite images. Because of its drifting, GPS was not accurate enough.

The receiver vehicle was a BMW 5 Series GT with a roof height of 1.56 m. Position was taken from the vehicle GPS via its CAN-Bus. This position is map matched, which means that a digital map and data like wheel spin and steering are also taken into account. The map matched position was much more accurate

---

[2]E.g. in [45], compare background Section 3.1.4, Figure 3.9 respectively.

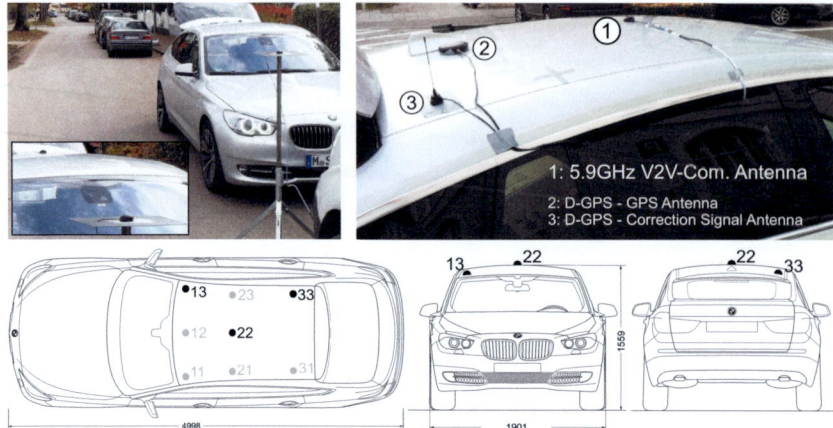

Figure 6.10: Up-left: The BMW 5 series GT and the tripod – Right: Antennas on the roof. Lower part: Antenna positions on roof—13, 22 and 33 have been tested.

in urban street canyons than a differential GPS (D-GPS). Especially, there is no drift if the vehicle stands still. As GPS-time was not available from the vehicle, a D-GPS was installed nevertheless.

A LinkBird-MX V3 [110] communication box by NEC was used. The box contains two DCMA-82-N1 mini PCI cards with Atheros 802.11 radio chips. Each radio is equipped with two antenna jacks, providing switched antenna diversity. In order to be able to match results to antenna position, diversity was disabled and in consequence only one antenna was used.

In order to resemble a close to production system, small low-profile puck antennas from Nippon Antenna were selected. They provide a gain of 0 dB at horizon and +5 dB at 15° according to their data sheet. The antenna cables inherit a loss of 2.4 dB according to their data sheet. For finding a near optimal antenna position, three different positions were tested in free-space conditions (see Section 6.2.2.1). The tripod, vehicle, antennas and tested antenna placements are shown in Figure 6.10.

6.2.1.2 Intersection Selection

A profound intersection selection is crucial to generate reasonable results. All of the NLOS models for below-rooftop base stations in the cellular domain take geometrical aspects into account. One of the major influence factors in the models is the inter-building distance ($\equiv$ side street width—w_t, w_r in Figure 3.9) on the transmitter and receiver side street. The general assumption is: the smaller this distance, the less power in NLOS areas. This also implies that intersections with similar street widths should show similar reception characteristics. It was considered worthwhile to verify this observation by selecting intersections with the same, as well as differing widths.

Probably most important, selected intersections should reflect "typical" inner city intersections to enable a generalization of results. The scenario analysis in Section 6.1 revealed that ≈90 % of all intersections in the city of Munich have buildings at all corners. The measurement focus is on 4-leg intersections, as 3-leg intersection would require a result separation between the straight street and the third leg. Also, 4-leg intersections provide four LOS blocking buildings compared to only two at 3-leg intersections.

The most prominent cluster (50 % of all intersections) present in the scenario analysis results in Section 6.1 has a distance from center to building vertex of 17.8 m. This translates to 25 m inter-building distance in side streets. As less width means more complicated radio propagation conditions, and worst-case conditions are important from an application point of view, the "Main Case" was selected as intersections with all side streets having an inter-building distance between 20 and 25 m. For comparability reasons, a street layout with ≈90 ° angle between side streets was favored.

The data basis from the building position analysis was used to automatically find intersections with the desired shape and inter-building distance in Munich. The resulting intersections were manually inspected via satellite images and then categorized in urban and suburban. As the classification is based on nearest building vertex, and front gardens (with bushes and trees) can further limit the field of view, suburban intersections were suspected to provide worse reception conditions at similar distances into the crossing street.

The intersections to be measured were selected as follows: Firstly, three sub-urban intersections with same "Main Case" dimensioning were selected, having ID 1, 2 and 3 in the intersection list in Table 6.5 and being in the first row of the visualization of intersection layout and properties via satellite images in Figure 6.11. Such testing of multiple intersections with the same layout should show if building placement has most influence or if building facades and similar unique factors are more important.

In order to enable a quantification of the assumed urban / suburban difference, an urban intersection with "Main Case" dimensions was selected as well (ID 10). While the buildings in intersection 10 are placed similar to intersections 1, 2 and 3, those three intersections contain front gardens.

In order to test the influence of inter-building distance of streets, three more urban intersections with larger inter-building distances were selected (ID 11, 20

ID	Streets	Center Lat/Lon	Street Width	Description
1	Pommer / Konstanzer	48.184, 11.560	23 m, 21 m	Suburban (Main Case)
2	Himmelschlüssel/ Josef-Seifried	48.195, 11.532	23 m, 19 m	Suburban (Main Case)
3	Tizian / Kratzer	48.162, 11.525	≈21 m	Suburban (Main Case)
10	Agnes / Teng	48.158, 11.569	24 m, 21 m	Urban (Main Case)
11	Perlach/ Untersberger	48.110, 11.586	27 m, 22 m	Urban Increased Width
20	Klug / Waisenh.	48.164, 11.529	≈30 m	Urban High Street Width
21	Hanauer / Gneisenau	48.179, 11.529	55 m, 30 m	Urban Very Wide, Non-Regular Shape
9	Gotebold / Driesch	48.179, 11.442	18 m	Suburban, Buildings at Only Two Corners
100	Free Space, Country Road	48.247, 11.348		One Street, No Buildings, No Trees etc.

Table 6.5: Selected intersections.

and 21). While intersection 11 only has slightly increased distances compared to intersection 10, intersection 20 already has an inter-building distance of 30 m on each side street. Intersection 21 is characterized by 30 m in one direction and really wide 55 m in the other. Also, this intersection has no exact orthogonality at one leg, thus potentially showing the influence of a more acute angle. Also, this intersection was tested with differing 60 and 100 m $tx \leftrightarrow center$ distance—at 30 m, there was as good as LOS into the side streets.

Lastly, a potential worst-case scenario was selected: A tight suburban intersection with no buildings at two corners (ID 9). In result, there are major reflection areas missing for the 5.9 GHz signal. However, such a scenario is not common.[3]

A free space test site was needed for antenna and plausibility testing. A 1.8 km long country road with plowed soil right and left served this purpose. Despite one small spot to one end, there were no bushes or trees within 200 m at both sides.

In summary, the selected intersections can be classified in three major categories plus the worst-case: Suburban "Main Case", Urban "Main Case" and Urban "Wide". All tests were performed between mid October and mid November 2010

---

[3]Evident in the building placement analysis results in Section 6.1.

ID 1, Suburban, 23,21 m   ID 2, Suburban, 23,19 m   ID 3, Suburban, ≈21 m

ID 10, Urban, 24,21 m   ID 11, Urban, 27,22 m   ID 20, Urban, ≈30 m

ID 9, Suburban, 18 m   ID 100 (other scaling)   ID 21, Urban, 55,30m

Figure 6.11: Google Earth™[92] screenshots of the measured intersections. All but one having same map scale to visualize inter-building distance.

under dry conditions. Trees still had most of their foliage. All intersections were measured under daytime traffic conditions.

6.2.1.3 Parameter Selection

Test parameters and dimensions as shown in Table 6.6 result from the described setup. $Tx{\leftrightarrow}center$ distance was selected as 30 and 60 m as argued above. Also tested were the LOS reception conditions in all intersections ($tx{\leftrightarrow}center$ = 0 m), leading to three different values in total.

It was made possible to test different combinations of transmission power, rate and payload in one run by switching through combinations in each second. Tests in intersection 1 with four combinations based on 20 and 10 dBm and 3 and 6 Mbps showed that data rate has no influence on NLOS reception. Only a slightly higher signal to noise ratio is needed for reception with 6 Mbps. As

Parameter	Value
Tx-Power	20 dBm
Tx-DataRate	3 Mbps (BPSK modulation)
Channel	10 MHz, Number 180 (5.9 GHz center frequency)
Packet size	200 Byte payload + IP/MAC/PHY headers
Tx-TransmissionRate	100 Hz
Tx↔Center distance	0, 30, 60 m (+ partly 100 m)
Tx-Street	1 to 4 (street legs) + 0 (middle of intersection)
Drive direction	Two directions per transmitter position
Communication box	NEC LinkBird v3 (Atheros chipset)
Antenna	Nippon DSRC Puck, horizon: 0 dB gain, 15 °: +5 dB
Rx-Antenna position	Roof center (ID:22 in Figure 6.10)
Cable (box to antenna)	SUCOFLEX 104, 4 m, data sheet: 2.4 dB loss
Transmitter	Tripod, 35×35 cm metal plate at 1.45 m height
Receiver	BMW 5 Series GT, no sunroof
Intersections	4 suburban + 4 urban (increasing width) + free space

Table 6.6: Measurement configuration.

expected, average reception power levels turned out 10 dB lower with 10 dBm transmit power compared to 20 dBm. In order to get high sample numbers per distance, measurements were constrained to a 20 dBm / 3 Mbps configuration in all other intersections. The selected transmission power of 20 dBm is a limitation of the radio. It has a maximum power output of 21 dBm. Channel 180 with 5.9 GHz center frequency was used.

Packet transmission rate was set to 100 Hz and payload to 200 Byte in all tests to keep complexity on a reasonable level. 200 Byte corresponds to the often-assumed 80 Byte information plus security payload for CAMs [93]. The resulting packet has a size of $30(PHY/MAC) + 20(IP) + 8(UDP) + 200(Payload) = 258$ Byte. Hence, the used configuration occupies only $(258 \text{ Byte} * 100 \text{ Hz}) / 3 \text{ Mbps} \equiv 6.6\%$ of the available channel resources.

The test setup leads to $4*2+1=9$ transmitter positions and to 4(SideStreet) $*$ 2(TxDistance) $*$ 2(DriveDir.) + 1(Center) $*$ 2(Streets) $*$ 2(DriveDir.) = 20 runs for a typical tested intersection. In total, 71 transmitter positions were tested and roughly 170 measurement runs performed.

6.2.2 Measurement Results

A "run" consists of one traverse of an intersection on one street. It is identifiable by the association of TxStreet-ID, *tx↔center* distance and a "From" and "To" Street-ID indicating the driving direction.

All results—despite otherwise mentioned—are plotted in a geographic, rather than directional orientation. Therefore, the smaller Street-ID of From and To-Street is always plotted on the left. This becomes especially important when runs are combined in order to provide averaged information: the results are averaged geographically. Therefore, two runs, 3→1 and 1→3 are combined to 1-3, showing the average reception for each side street.

All runs were visualized on a map and as xy-plot. Map visualization is done via a KML file containing aggregated per second results of the run. Reception rate, as well as average received power is visualized as false-color coded dot, respective donut (upper part in Figure 6.12). One main KML file provides information on the

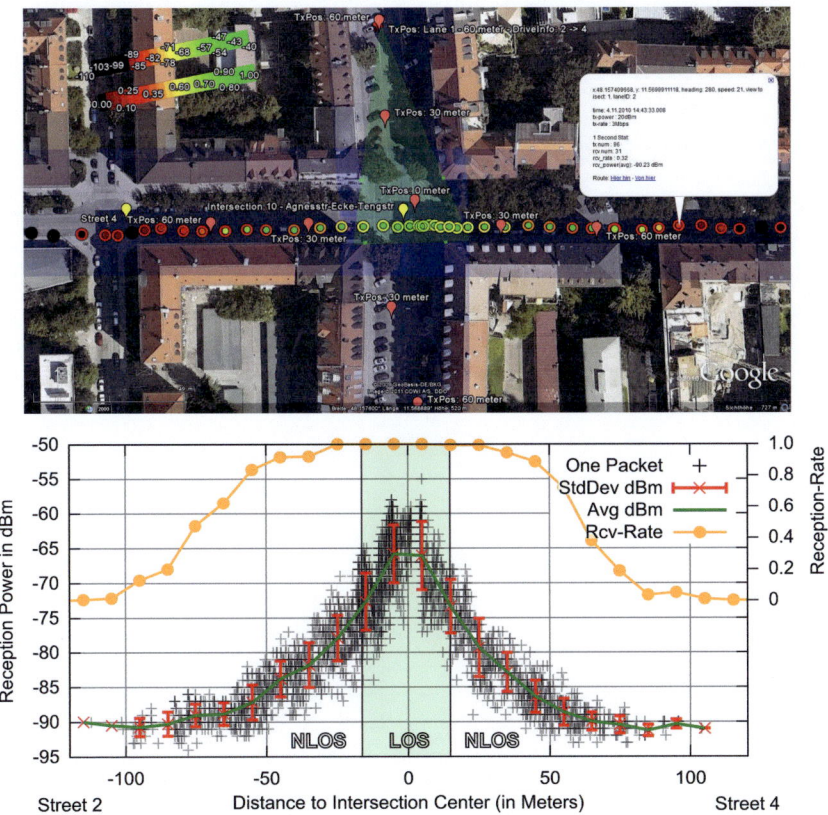

Figure 6.12: Visualization of single run: KML based visualization on top. Each color-coded point provides a link to detailed 1 s statistics. The same run as xy-plot on bottom (note: changed order of streets). Both kinds of visualizations are accessible for all runs via links from a single Start-KML. Available online [10].

transmitter positions, street IDs and area of interest. The xy-plot in the lower part of Figure 6.12 visualizes the power value of each received message, complemented by average and standard deviation and reception rate values. Those are computed for distance-bins of 10 m width. The complete per run evaluation is available at the thesis website [10] (details in Appendix A.1).

The example run in Figure 6.12 stems from intersection 10 with a *tx↔center* distance of 60 m. Clipping at a threshold of ≈-92 dBm becomes visible. Available data sheets (e. g. [111]) for Atheros chipset based 802.11 cards as used in the Linkbird also show a minimum reception threshold of ≈-92 dBm with same signal modulation (802.11p @ 3 Mbps ≡ 802.11a @ 6 Mbps). The small standard deviation at higher ranges is a consequence of low reception rates: if a message could be received, its power is closely above the reception threshold. One should be aware that the average power curve does not correspond to path loss as soon as the reception rate is below 1.0. In general, the curve shows the average power of received messages.

6.2.2.1   Free Space Test and Antenna Position

A free space test was performed to verify a good antenna position and check proper operation of all components. Free space conditions minimize the influence of other effects like reflections. They also allow for determining whether or not the measurement system performance is on par with theoretical predictions.

The three tested antenna positions were: absolute center of the vehicle roof (22), front-right (13) and back-right (33). They are visualized in earlier Figure 6.10.

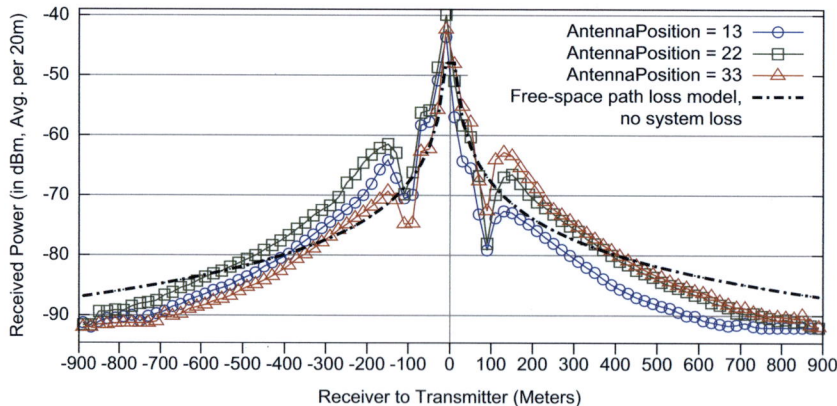

Figure 6.13: Free space test with three antenna positions: 22=CenterCenter, 13=FrontRight, 33=BackRight. Driving direction from -900 to +900 m. Averaged from forth and back run.

Two drive-bys were performed with each positioning, one in each direction. Both runs were averaged in the heading domain, averaging out the influence of left/right and environment differences on the two street stretches. The resulting approach/ depart performance of the antennas is shown in Figure 6.13. While approaching the transmitter, the center position performs best. At 300 m distance, it has 3 dB advantage over the front antenna and 5 dB over the back antenna.[4] While departing, the front position is 5 dB worse than center, while the rear is 1 dB better than the center position. Therefore, the center position provides the best overall performance. This is why it was selected in all NLOS measurement runs.

A comparison to the well-known FSPL model shows that the measurement setup produces results close to theory. Adding approximately 1 dB system loss (-2.4 dB cable + ≈1–2 dB antenna) at receiver and transmitter to the model, values would be very close to the measured ones at high distances. Surprisingly, the real reception power at distances below 400 m turns out even better than theoretically predicted. Of course, despite the prominent drop due to destructive two-ray ground reflection at 90 m. Likely, ground reflection leads to the positive gain at distances around the dip.

6.2.2.2   Reception Quality under NLOS – Measurements Results

The results from single runs are aggregated on two different levels in order to enable a performance comparison on a street level, as well as on an intersection level. Averaging was done over the average-values per distance-bin. This way, fair weighting between runs is ensured, despite differing amounts of input samples per bin.

On street level, for each transmitter position, the back and forth runs were averaged. 30 and 60 m *tx↔center* distance yield four results each—plus two for the central transmitter position. On intersection level, the distance-bin values were averaged from all runs of a certain *tx↔center* distance. Therefore, three data sets per intersection remain, one for 0, 30 and 60 m *tx↔center* distance, respectively.

Street Level   Figure 6.14 shows the street level results for 60 m *tx↔center* distance at intersection 10. This urban intersection has fairly average performance as it can be seen later in Section 6.2.2.2. Considering the high *tx↔center* distance of 60 m, the reception rate over distance turns out fairly well. The reception rate does not drop below 0.5 at distances of 50 m or less into the side street—mostly above 50 m.

The plot also shows that performance is pretty similar despite the transmitter positions being in four different side streets. Six out of eight transmitter to cross

---

[4]The antenna radiation pattern based investigation in [112] reveals very similar results.

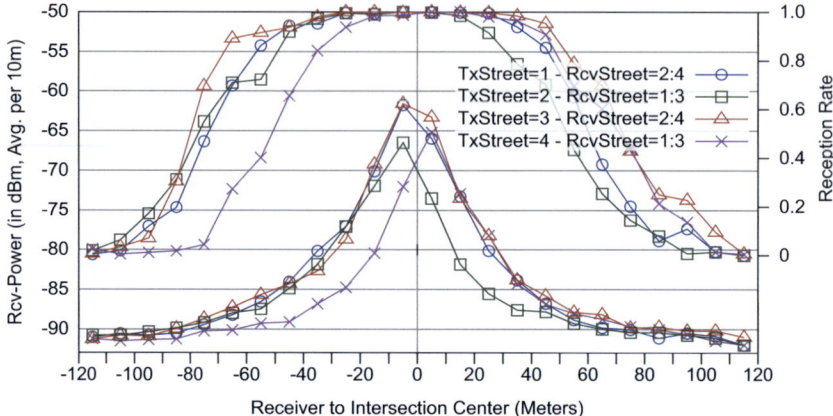

Figure 6.14: Intersection 10 – Streets in an intersection – Reception rate and power over distance for all four transmitter positions with 60 m *tx↔center* distance (back/forth run averaged geometrical).

street leg results are very similar. Only when the transmitter was in street leg 4 and 2, performance in one cross street leg was worse. The other intersections show similar results. As most tested intersections have a regular layout (same inter-building distance on both streets), this confirms the assumption that inter-building distance has most influence on results. If trees, bushes or building facades had major influence, the results would likely turn out more different despite the regular layout.

Intersection Level   The per transmission distance averaged values for the same intersection are plotted in Figure 6.15. The average power plot shows an expectable drop between the 30 and 60 m *tx↔center* distance results due to 30 m more distance to center in the transmitter street and slightly narrower view into the side street. The gap between the 0 and 30 m lines is much wider. As long as no missing data due to non-receptions introduces a slowing of the slope, the reduction is in the 18 to 20 dB range. This reduction amount is of course only partly caused by the penalty due to missing LOS, as the 30 m distance from transmitter to intersection center also leads to a certain loss.

In case of 30 m *tx↔center* distance, the reception rate stays really high (>0.9) for a *rcv↔center* distance of up to 80 m. In case of 60 m *tx↔center* distance, the curve is shifted approximately 40 m to the left. The center tx-position shows that with the used 20 dBm transmit power, over 90 % received messages are feasible at 120 m *tx↔rcv* distance, despite certainly present interference from reflections.

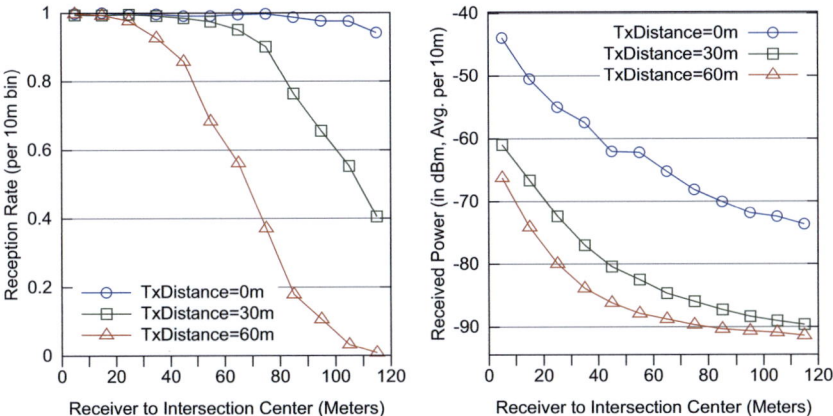

Figure 6.15: Intersection 10 – All data with same *tx↔center* distance averaged – Reception rate on the left, reception power on the right.

Intersection Comparison   After showing the performance in one example inter-section, this paragraph compares the performance in different intersections with each other. Figure 6.16 shows the per intersection averaged results for all eight intersections. The 30 m *tx↔center* distance results are shown on the left, the 60 m ones on the right, reception rate results are located on the top, average reception power of received packets ones on the bottom.

First of all, the comparatively small difference between the three suburban intersections—having the same building positioning—should be noted. Intersection 10, having the same dimensions as the three suburban ones, shows notably better reception rates and power values ($\approx$+4 dB). This is most likely a result of less obstructions and cleaner building facades in the urban setting. Intersection 20, being also urban, but having 30 m inter-building distance instead of 24, 21 m as for intersection 10, has another $\approx$6 dB better values. Intersection 11 has values fitting between the ones of intersection 10 and 20. This matches its inter-building dis-tances being in between 22 and 30 m. For 60 m *tx↔center* distance, there is also a data row for the really wide intersection 21. It performs—as expected—even better.

These observations seem to proof the impact of building position on NLOS reception as presumed from cellular NLOS models for below-rooftop base stations. This is not surprising though: with increasing distance between the buildings of a street, the view angle into a side street is wider, resulting in more LOS and a more open angle for reflected beams, leading to a further traverse into a side street. The plots also show that suburban conditions are worse compared to urban ones.

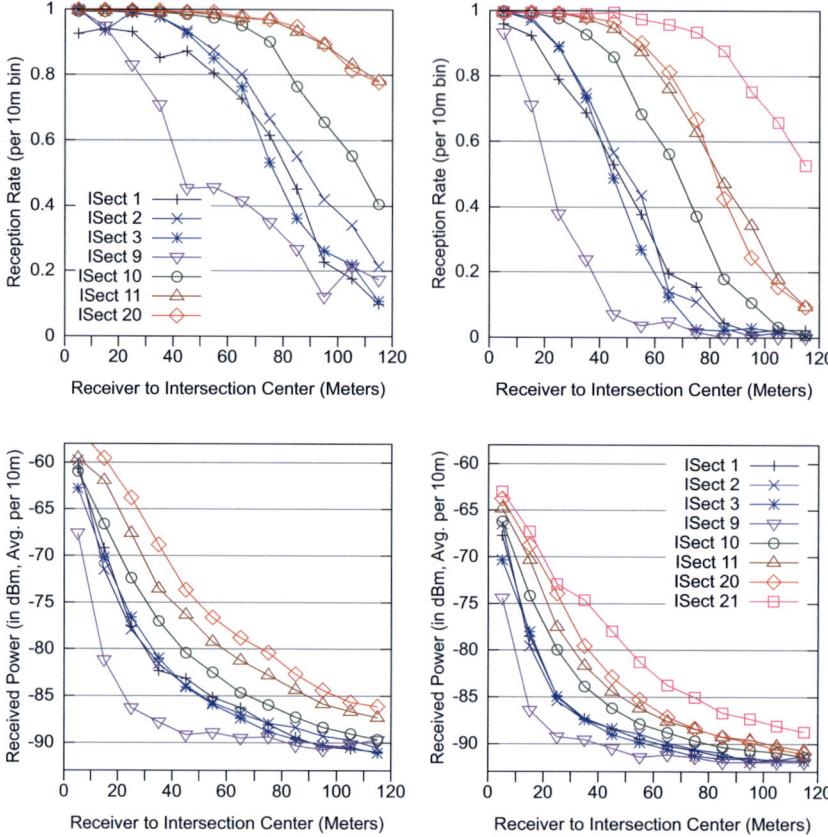

Figure 6.16: Intersection comparison – reception rate (top) and reception power (bottom) – left: 30 m, right: 60 m *tx↔center* distance – per intersection average of all runs with same *tx↔center* distance.

A special case is intersection 9. Missing reflection areas due to non-existence of buildings on two corners of the crossing significantly impact signal power and reception rate (Note that the street legs with LOS were excluded from the averaging for comparability). But, even in this worst-case scenario, there is still connectivity potential left: in case two vehicles approach such intersection in the same moment and are 30 m away from center, the reception rate is already at ≈0.5.

Overall, reception rates turn out pretty well. Considering two vehicles approaching synchronously, reception should start at distances of ≈70 m and more. A reception rate of 0.5 is reached at 50 m to center or more. At this distance, a vehicle needs 3.5 s to reach an intersection center while driving at 50 km/h.

6.2.3   Conclusion

An extensive field test with a profound scenario selection was performed in order to investigate 5.9 GHz IEEE 802.11p NLOS reception quality. The results show that 5.9 GHz IEEE 802.11p NLOS reception is in general well feasible despite the high frequency of 5.9 GHz. If two vehicles synchronously approach an intersection from crossing streets, a reception rate of 0.5 is reached at 50 m to intersection center. This holds for tight suburban intersections with worse than average conditions.

The cross-traffic collision avoidance use case needs information as early as 3 s to a potential collision, corresponding to 42 m at 50 km/h. At this point, reception rates will be already at levels above 0.5. Additionally, the investigation also shows that urban intersections provide even better NLOS reception than suburban intersections with front yards. And, if the inter-building distance rises, reception rates improve even more.

In general, the results verify that intersections with same inter-building distances perform very similar. Combined with the above described observation of better performance with higher inter-building distance, it seems to prove the correlation obtained from cellular below-rooftop base station models: the inter-building distance in a street has a major influence on the path loss under NLOS conditions.

In terms of the tested intersections, a worst-case condition for 5.9 GHz IEEE 802.11p NLOS reception was a side street with no buildings on the opposite side of the intersection. Missing reflection surfaces lead to considerable less signal power in the crossing street compared to intersections with all corners occupied. However, the building placement analysis in Section 6.1 showed that such intersections are very seldom.

6.3   Deduction of a Validated Non-Line-Of-Sight Path Loss and Fading Model

The methodical NLOS measurements and their evaluation in Section 6.2 showed the general ability of NLOS reception in application critical moments and revealed different influence factors on 5.9 GHz NLOS path loss.

In this section, the desired validated 5.9 GHz NLOS path loss model is developed based on the measurement data and the derived knowledge. Furthermore, small-scale fading in NLOS conditions is characterized. In combination a complete NLOS propagation characterization for packet-level simulations is provided.

The propagation modeling is described in Section 6.3.1. Following, the new path loss model is compared to existing models and measurement data in Section 6.3.2, before a conclusion is given in Section 6.3.3

6.3.1   NLOS Propagation Model Development

Subsequently, a new and specific vehicular 5.9 GHz NLOS path loss model—called VirtualSource11p—is deduced from the measurement data in Section 6.3.1.3 and small-scale fading in NLOS areas is characterized in Section 6.3.1.4.

As foundation to the model deduction, data quality is examined in detail in Section 6.3.1.1 and system loss quantified in Section 6.3.1.2 beforehand.

6.3.1.1   Data Quality

The general ability of the measurement setup to deliver reasonable results was already shown via a comparison of free space condition results against the FSPL model in Section 6.2.2.1. However, to deduce path loss and fading from an off-the-shelf radio, it needs to provide reliable and independent reception power values. This motivates a more detailed look at the data quality of the measurements.

Per packet reception power values with 1 dBm resolution were retrieved from the radio via the level value in the *iw_statistics.iw_quality* struct from a *SIOCGIW-STATS* socket call. Measured values equal the values reported in "iwconfig" and the Linkbird "wlan11p" tool. Observed values are in the range of -5 to -92 dBm.

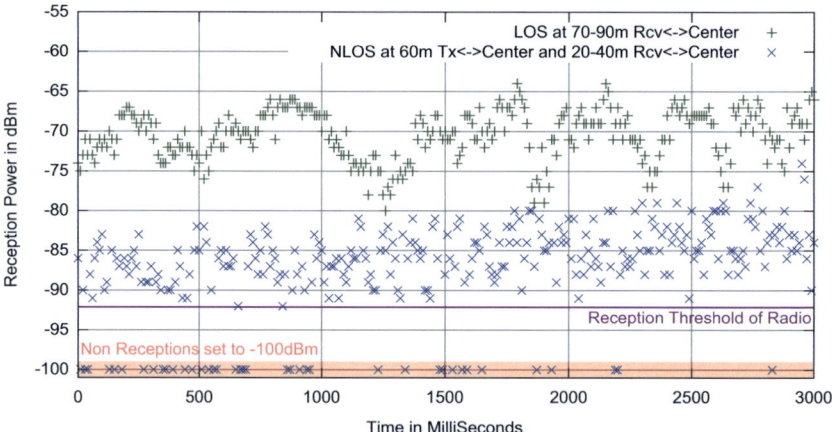

Figure 6.17: Detailed look at the measured power values over time. Data is from intersection 3, for 20 m stretches on street 1 and drive direction from street 1 to 3. The plot reveals how well the radio-chip reports power values: In LOS, the small-scale fading power curve is clearly visible. In contrast, the sample rate of 100 Hz is not high enough to produce a clear curve of the faster fading channel in NLOS, leading to the more chaotic power distribution in the NLOS measurement.

This corresponds well to the reception sensitivity of -92 dBm as reported in data sheets such as [111]. Figure 6.17 shows the good quality of the reported power values over time for two exemplary 20 m street stretches. Differences in small-scale fading between NLOS and LOS are clearly visible. The resulting power histograms (compare Figure 6.22 in later Section 6.3.1.4) show very reasonable results, too. More of these detailed plots are available at the thesis website [10].

There was only one issue: Power histograms revealed that there are no packets reported with -69, -68 and -67 dBm. A figure illustrating this can be seen in Appendix A.2.1. The same gap can be seen in [113]. An explanation would be that the chipset changes its sensitivity in this power range, and reports values above -69 dBm by 3 dB too strong. This was corrected by subtracting 3 dB from all reported values >-69 dBm. The reported reception sensitivity was not changed by the correction.

6.3.1.2 System Loss

The measured value is reception power, where in dBm space:
$$\text{RxPower} = \text{TxPower} - \text{SystemLoss} - \text{PathLoss}$$
Here, system loss refers to antenna gain minus cable loss at receiver and transmitter. In order to determine path loss, system loss needs to be known. Given the values stated in Section 6.2.1.3, the cables lead to a combined loss of ≈ 4.8 dB and the antennas to a gain of two times some value between 0 (0°) and 5 dB (15°).

In order to determine the average loss, the LOS measurements from most intersections were taken (excluding free space, special case 9, and 1) and the deviation between average power curve and the theoretical limit was determined. The fit equation used is:

$$\text{LogDist}(x) = P_{tx} - L_S - PL_{ref} - 10 * E_L * \log_{10}(\frac{x}{1})$$

$$PL_{ref} := \text{FSPL}(1) = 10 \log_{10}((\frac{4\,\pi\,1}{\lambda})^2) = 47.86 \text{ dB}$$
$$\text{FitDimensions}: L_S := \text{SystemLoss}, E_L := \text{LossExponent}$$

The fit equation comprises the common log-distance model and FSPL for determination of reference loss. Unfortunately, curve attenuation interferes with slope variation. Therefore, three fits were performed (both fitted, SL = 0, LE = 2). Figure 6.18 visualizes fit input and results. The fit input was limited to $20 < x <$ 150 m, as packet loss occurred at $x > 150$ m and small distances are inaccurate as the transmitter was not exactly positioned in intersection centers.

The fit reveals a loss of 2.75 dB with LE = 2. With SL = 0, it shows a loss exponent of 2.1, being higher as in FSPL. Subsequently, a system loss of 1.75 dB is assumed, as revealed by fitting both variables. The resulting average gain of

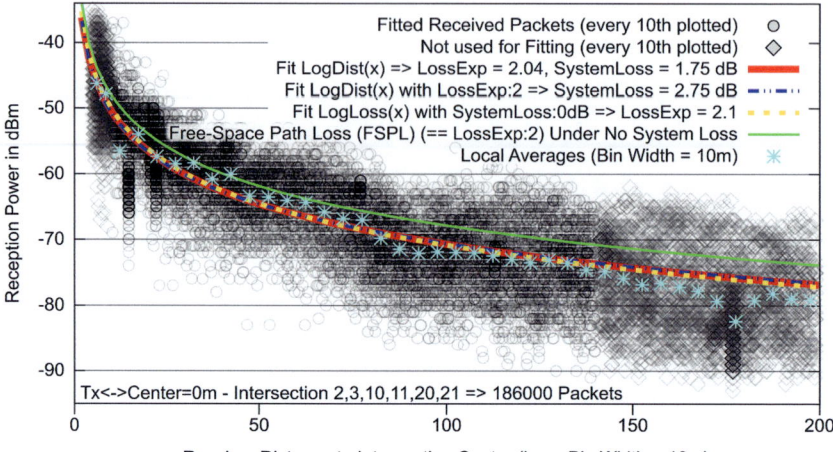

Figure 6.18: Determination of system loss by theory comparison.

1.5 dB per antenna seems realistic, given its characteristic. Note that such a system loss determination absorbs the problem that the real transmitted power might slightly differ from the configured value.

6.3.1.3 NLOS Path Loss Model Development

In order to determine path loss with respect to variable street-width and suburban/urban differences, the intersection wide average power over distance curves of multiple intersections (such as the lower part in Figure 6.16) are fitted to a unified path loss equation. The basis for the used fit equation is the cellular model proposed in [45]. The original VirtualSource equation (as given in [45], but indices modified to Figure 6.19 and as positive path loss in dB) is:

$$
\text{PathLoss} = \begin{cases} 10\log_{10}\left(\frac{1}{\alpha}\left(\sqrt{\frac{2\pi}{x_t w_r}}\frac{4\pi d_t d_r}{\lambda}\right)^2\right), & d_r \leqslant d_b \\ 10\log_{10}\left(\frac{1}{\alpha}\left(\sqrt{\frac{2\pi}{x_t w_r}}\frac{4\pi d_t d_r^2}{\lambda d_b}\right)^2\right), & d_r > d_b \end{cases}
$$

$\lambda :=$ Wavelength	$h_t, h_r :=$ Tx, Rcv Height
$d_b := \frac{4h_t h_r}{\lambda}$ (BreakEven Distance)	$\alpha :=$ StreetParameter

The model takes the distance of transmitter and receiver to intersection center (d_t and d_r), receiver street width (w_r) and distance of transmitter to wall (x_t) as input. The last two values reflect building position influence. Adaption to differing streets is enabled by a street parameter (α). A higher loss is present at

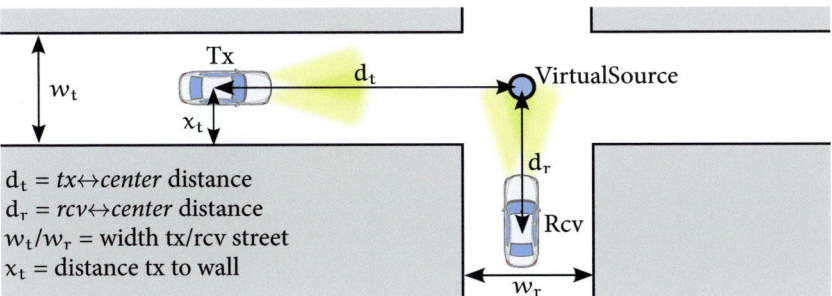

Figure 6.19: Basic VirtualSource1lp path loss model parameters. Figure adopted from [45].

high rcv-distances (due to a diffraction, rather than reflection predominance), determined by a break even distance (d_b).

The geometric input parameters d_t, d_r, w_r, h_r, h_t and x_t are given by the measured data. Therefore, it was first tried to fit the path loss exponent and α. As both are fitted globally, α represents a relative shift of the fitting curve. These first fits showed that especially the influence of street width w_r is not properly reflected by the existing equation. Therefore, the fixed weighting $\sqrt{2\pi}$ of the term $1/\sqrt{x_t w_r}$ was replaced by a fittable exponent. As d_t also influences the "view" and therefore energy into a crossing street, it was also made fittable. A suburban loss factor was added to incorporate the observation of less power in suburban scenarios from Section 6.2.2.2. The following fit equation (in dBm) was found:

$$\text{RxPower} = P_{tx} - \text{SystemLoss} - \text{PathLoss}$$

$$\text{PathLoss} := \text{VirtualSource1lp}(d_r, d_t, w_r, x_t, i_s) =$$

$$C + i_s L_{su} + 10 \, \log_{10}\left(\left(\frac{d_t^{E_T}}{(x_t w_r)^{E_S}} \frac{4\pi d_r}{\lambda}\right)^{E_L}\right)$$

Fit Dimensions: C := CurveShift, L_{su} := SubUrbanLoss, E_L := LossExponent, E_S := StreetExp., E_T := TxDistExp.

Value i_s is specifying suburban ($i_s = 1$) or urban ($i_s = 0$). λ is the wavelength. As d_b is $\approx$180 m for the used setup, which exceeds the highest distance d_r that receptions occurred at, the $d_r > d_b$ equation is of no use for the fitting.

The final fit to determine the five variable parameters is visualized in Figure 6.20. The intersection wide average median reception power per tx-distance curves were fitted. Each of these curves abstracts (averages) eight measurements,

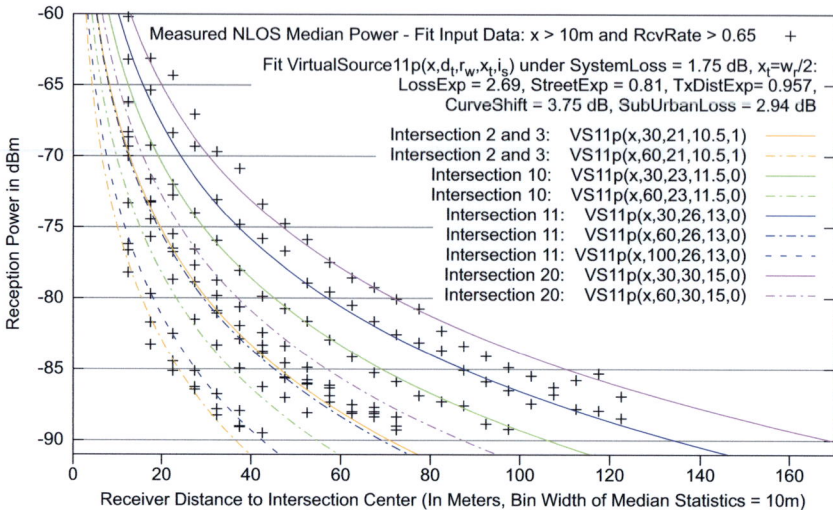

Figure 6.20: Fit of measured values to NLOS path loss equation.

thus providing a stable input to the fit and keeping the complexity on a moderate level. Section 6.2.2.2 revealed that this averaging is viable, as the performance is very similar despite the transmitter being in the different side streets.

The fit input values are from the regular shaped ($\approx 90°$ and $w_t \approx w_r$) intersections with buildings at each corner: intersection 2, 3, 10, 11 and 20, with w_r being 21, 21, 23, 26 and 30 m respectively and intersection 2 and 3 having $i_s = 1$. The fitted measurements have d_t values of 30 and 60 m (plus 100 m for intersection 11).

Each input value (visualized as a cross in Figure 6.20) is complemented by the reception rate in the bin and the intersection wide w_r and i_s values as input to the equation and for pre-selection. w_r is set to $\frac{w_t+w_r}{2}$ as w_t and w_r were selected similar per intersection and intersection wide average values are fitted. System loss is set to 1.75 dB and $x_t = \frac{w_r}{2}$ (as this dimension was not tested).

Intersections 1, 9 and 21 were not fitted due to differing reasons: Intersection 1 was the very first tested intersection. Here, it was measured with alternating transmission power (20 dBm, 10 dBm) and rate (3 Mbps, 6 Mbps) in each second. In consequence, there are spatial gaps in the data for each of the four configurations, leading to empty bins at the 5 m bin width in the fit. Anyhow, the performance of intersection 1 is very close to that of intersection 2 and 3, as can be seen in Figure 6.16. Intersection 9 has missing reflection facades. This dimension was not incorporated in the fit, as it would have complicated the fit by another dimension. Furthermore, only one intersection of such type was tested (as it is rare), leading to insufficient data to provide a reliable fit in this additional dimension.

Intersection 21 was excluded due to two reasons: Firstly, one of the street legs has a non 90° angle. Secondly, the inter-building distance in the two streets differs a lot (55 m against 30 m). It is questionable whether the averaging over the four side street simplification is applicable for this particular intersection. Despite the exclusion of the three intersections, the fit covers 11 data rows from five intersections, stemming from 88 measurement-runs.

The median reception power curve was fitted, as it is more stable at lower reception rates. The average reception power curve suffers (bin values are too high) from incomplete data as soon as the reception rate sinks below 1.0. The median is technically accurate as long as reception rate is greater than 0.5. However, due to small-scale fading leading to variations and potential measurement inaccuracies around the reception threshold of the radio, median values also turn out to be slightly too high at reception rates close to 0.5. This is visible in plots. In order to prevent a negative influence on the fit, an exclusion criterion of reception-rate >0.65 was selected.

Also excluded were small distances to center, as they are in LOS. The Root Mean Square (RMS) error of the fit showed that $x > 10$ m is a good exclusion criterion: The RMS error decreases from 2.4 with $x > 0$ m to 0.8 with $x > 10$ m, but not much further with a higher exclusion distance value. The very low RMS error of 0.8 corresponds to the good fit quality (compare input values to resulting model curves in Figure 6.20). The resulting VirtualSource1lp path loss equation, as determined by the fit, is:

$$
\mathrm{VirtualSource1lp}(d_r, d_t, w_r, x_t, i_s) =
$$
$$
3.75 + i_s\, 2.94 +
\begin{cases}
10 \log_{10}\left(\left(\dfrac{d_t^{0.957}}{(x_t w_r)^{0.81}} \dfrac{4\pi d_r}{\lambda}\right)^{2.69}\right), & d_r \leqslant d_b \\[3ex]
10 \log_{10}\left(\left(\dfrac{d_t^{0.957}}{(x_t w_r)^{0.81}} \dfrac{4\pi d_r^2}{\lambda d_b}\right)^{2.69}\right), & d_r > d_b
\end{cases}
$$

Despite of no available measurement data for high d_r distances, an increased loss at high distances ($d_r > d_b$) due to diffraction rather than reflection being dominant is incorporated (as in [45; 42; 43; 46]).

Note that close to intersection center, loss is really low (similar to FSPL having a heavy slope close to 0). Figure 6.21 depicts a representative example for Intersection 10. In consequence, the VirtualSource1lp path loss equation only applies to NLOS conditions and not to the complete crossing street. At LOS on the crossing street, either the normal LOS path loss should be used with distance as $d_t + d_r$, or a percental value between LOS at intersection center and NLOS value at the first point of NLOS. The latter is potentially more accurate.

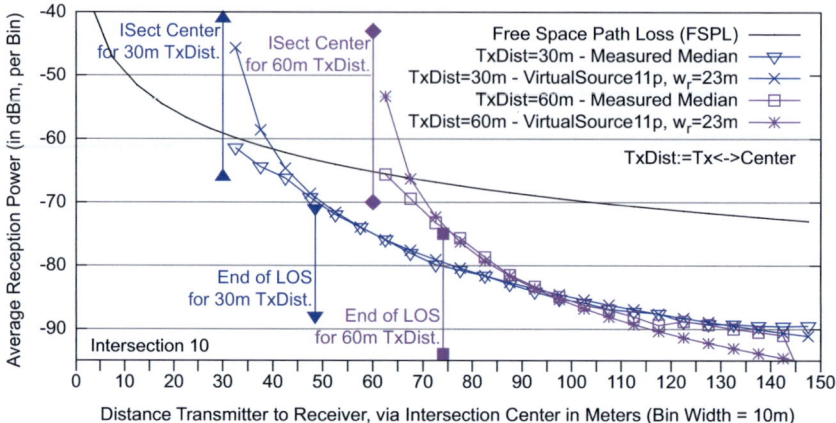

Figure 6.21: Power over distance: Measurements and model. Intersection 10.

6.3.1.4   NLOS Small-Scale Fading Classification

Small-scale fading leads to a distribution of power values around an average value. Figure 6.22 shows the different power probability distributions of received packets for different distances to the center in suburban intersection 3. It reveals e.g. a high variation in the 10–20 m bin as it includes LOS and NLOS conditions, or a variance limitation due to failed receptions (measurement limitation) for larger distances.

In order to determine fading in NLOS conditions, the power probability distribution curves were centered to their average and curves from different inter-

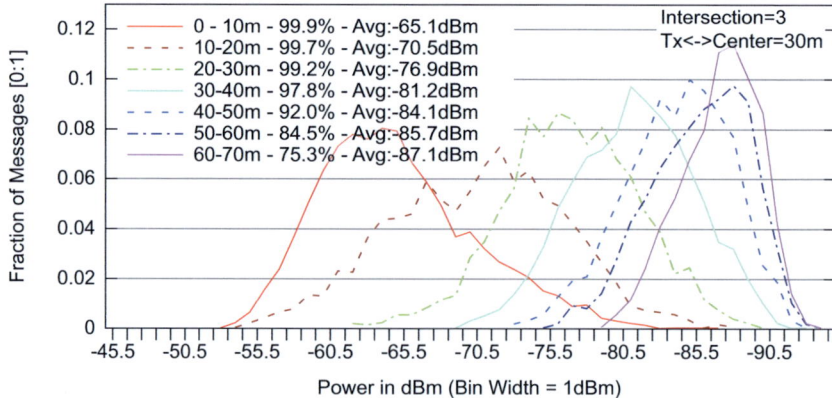

Figure 6.22: Power distribution in different distances to center in NLOS. 30 m *tx↔center* distance in intersection 3. Percent value is amount of received packets.

sections compared (for a certain street stretch in NLOS). Figure 6.23 shows the curves for $d_t = 30$ m and d_r bin 40–50 m. This stretch exhibits NLOS conditions for all intersections and is in most cases (except probably intersection 2) not influenced by the radio reception limit. The curves from different intersections show a very similar shape. While they fit well to both, Nakagami-m and the Normal Distribution, the RMS error is slightly smaller for the Normal Distribution. Using visual judgment, they clearly match the Normal Distribution better. Therefore, fading in NLOS should be modeled as a normal distribution with σ=4.1 dB.

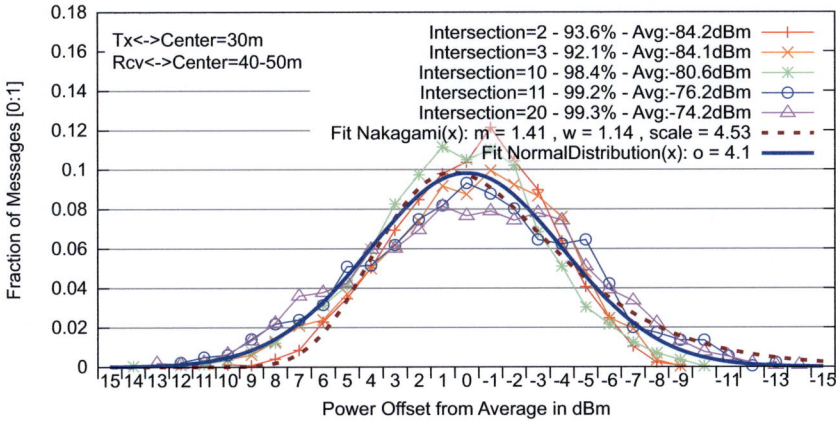

Figure 6.23: NLOS fading determination. Power distribution around average for receptions in 40–50 m to center stretch in cross street. *Tx↔center* distance = 30 m.

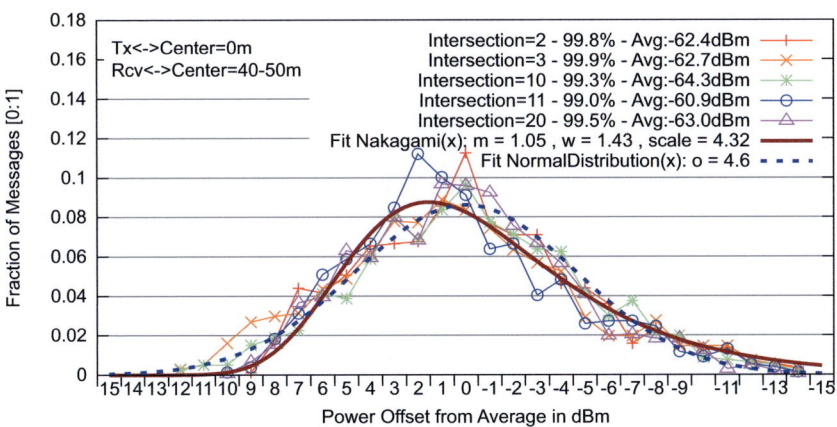

Figure 6.24: LOS fading determination. Power distribution around average for receptions in 40–50 m to intersection center.

For LOS conditions, it was possible to verify that a 5.9 GHz vehicular channel is properly modeled by the often assumed Nakagami-m=1 distribution. The corresponding fit is given in Figure 6.24. It reveals a good visible match to the Nakagami curve with fitted m=1.05.

6.3.2   Path Loss Model Comparison

In this section, the derived VirtualSource11p model is compared to previously proposed NLOS models. One of those was measured under V2V conditions at 790 MHz, the rest are micro-cellular models for urban street canyons where base stations are typically located inside street canyons, for example at signal lights. Note that there is no comparison given to the models in [86; 87], as those models do not take important influence factors such as inter-building distance into account.

The models and their claimed validity (or verification setup) are given in Table 6.7. A model based on vehicle to infrastructure measurements at 790 MHz was proposed in [48] by Toyota staff. Two different micro-cellular models are provided in the ITU-R P1411-5 recommendation for planning of short range communication systems [43]; one in section 4.2.3 for 0.8–2 GHz, the other in 4.2.4 for claimed 2–16 GHz and low height terminals, but receive street width w_r limited to <10 m. The second model seems to be based on [44]. Another urban micro-cell

| | Claimed Validity or Verification(V) | | | | # Verific. | Vehicle |
	Freq. GHz	Tx,Rcv Height	Street Width	Corner Angle	Scenario/ Measure.	G-Plate Anten.
VirtualSource11p	5.9 (V)	1.5,1.5m (V)	15-40 (V)	90° (V)	5/88	Yes
Virtual Source [45]	0.9/1.5 (V)	5-10m, 2-3m (V)	15-40 (V)	90° (V)	3/3	No
Sai et. al. [48] (Toyota)	0.79 (V)	1.8-5m, 1.9m (V)	n.a.	90° (V)	1/>6	Only at Rcv.
ITU-R P1411-5 [43] (4.2.3,0.8-2GHz)	0.8-2	4-50m, 1-3m	n.a.	n.a.	n.a.	n.a. (No)
ITU-R P1411-5 [43] (4.2.4,2-16GHz)	2-16	4-50m, 1-3m	w_r <10m	90°	n.a. (3/3)	n.a. (No)
Winner II - B1 [42] (u. in iTETRIS[84])	2-6	10m,1.5m (V)	n.a.	90°	n.a.	No
Sun et.al. Paper [46] (u. in CORNER[83])	0.9/1.5/ 2.1(V)	n.a.	10-40 (V)	90° (V)	5/5	No

Table 6.7: Street canyon NLOS model comparison.

model stems from the WINNER II propagation measurement project [42]. It has been selected in the iTETRIS EU-project [84] to model urban 5.9 GHz V2V communication by adapting the frequency and transmitter height. At last, [46] is an analytical model based on propagation theory as used in ray-tracing. It was used in a re-parameterized way in the CORNER 5.9 GHz V2V simulation implementation proposed in [83].

All models except the second ITU-R model are only specified for up to 2 GHz and $h_t > 4$ m. Also, those models are not based on measurements with vehicular ground plate antennas as in the measurements in this thesis, except the receiver side in [48]. In iTETRIS, the model was not verified with the new environment parameters; in CORNER only very briefly. In contrast, the proposed VirtualSource11p model was derived from measurements in five intersections and 11 loss-curves, based upon 88 test runs.

The path loss equations of all models were implemented in gnuplot to compare them against the data from the NLOS measurements and the proposed Virtual-Source11p model. Figure 6.25 shows the resulting received power when configured same as the measurements in intersection 10 with $tx{\leftrightarrow}center$ distance $d_t = 30$ m. All models are configured with their proposed default configuration. It can be seen that the models selected in CORNER and iTETRIS differ to the measurements by 10 dB and more in critical NLOS areas. Only the P1411-5 2–16 GHz and the Toyota model come close to the measurements in this scenario. Note that the very low

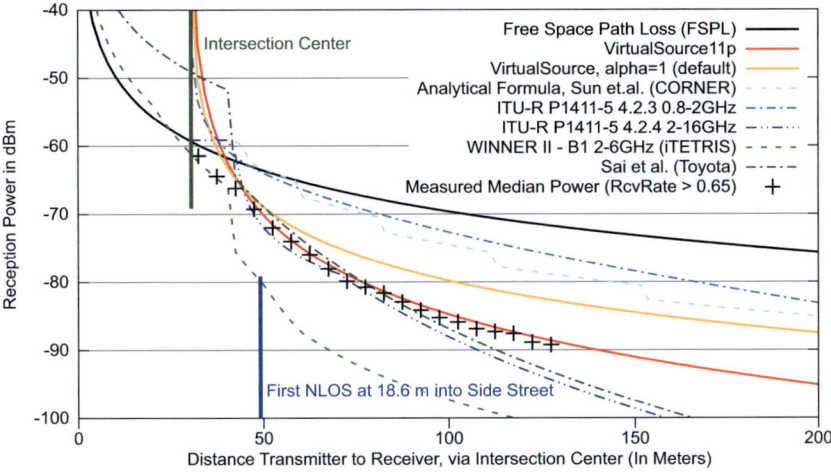

Figure 6.25: Model comparison: 5.9 GHz, 20 dBm tx-power, 1.75 dB SystemLoss, 30 m $tx{\leftrightarrow}center$ distance, 1.5 m tx/rcv-height, 23 m tx/rcv-street-width, urban, intersection 10 measurement.

path loss of the Toyota model in LOS is a strange behavior of their formula when parameterized to 5.9 GHz—at specified 0.79 GHz, the curve is just below FSPL.

Obviously, the VirtualSource1lp model shows a very good accordance to measurements due to its fitting based development. Comparisons to the other measured scenarios reveal similar results and show that the VirtualSource1lp model especially follows changes in the street width better than the P1411-5 2–16 GHz and the Toyota model.

6.3.3 Conclusion

With VirtualSource1lp, a well-validated, low complexity NLOS path loss model for 5.9 GHz V2V communications at intersections is presented in this thesis. The model was deduced from data collected in an extensive measurement campaign, specifically targeted to measure NLOS reception quality (Section 6.2). A founded selection of test intersections enabled to quantify the influence of inter-building distance and suburban/urban differences in a single path loss equation with only a few simple geometric input-values.

Due to its fitting-based generation, the equation corresponds well to measurement data in different scenarios, especially with changing inter-building distances. In contrast, existing street canyon NLOS path loss models for micro-cellular environments at lower frequencies differ mostly substantially from the measurements when parameterized to 5.9 GHz V2V communication. Of course, the proposed model is also limited in its validity to the measurement environment it is based on. While certainly not every special case is covered, the measured intersections were selected as representative as possible, built upon an own building positioning investigation (Section 6.1). To the best of the author's knowledge, this is a novel approach and has not been done before.

In addition to path loss, NLOS fading is investigated, finding a normal distributed power variation around average. In conclusion, this section provides the desired knowledge for including NLOS propagation conditions into packet level simulations of 5.9 GHz inter-vehicle communication.

6.4 Non-Line-Of-Sight Reception under Competition

The ad-hoc background discussion in Section 3.1 showed that NLOS reception in operational conditions is inevitably degraded by competition on the radio channel. Multi-user interference will lead to packet loss due to effects such as hidden-terminal collisions. This will have a negative impact on the reception rates found in the competition free measurements.

The impact of network competition on NLOS reception rates is investigated in this section via a simulation study. Here, the VirtualSource11p propagation model proposed in Section 6.3 is used to enable a realistic simulation of 5.9 GHz V2V NLOS reception. However, the question of reception rate degradation due to competition not only depends on signal propagation, but also depends on the expectable network competition level, which in turn is bound to the question of vehicle density in situations relevant to the application of cross-traffic assistance.

This study—tackling those questions—is structured as follows: Firstly, the network simulation environment needed to properly model NLOS reception under load is described in Section 6.4.1. It contains a description of the needed modifications to the ns-2 (2.34) [30] event simulator to support the VirtualSource11p NLOS propagation model and a discussion about the selection of proper network parameter values. Secondly, the selection of a representative intersection scenario to be simulated is discussed in Section 6.4.2, including a microscopic traffic flow simulation based load level determination. Finally, the results of the network simulations are presented in Section 6.4.3.

6.4.1 Network Simulation Environment for NLOS Reception Quality Assessment

The simulation of NLOS reception under load requires an accurate NLOS path loss and MAC modeling. A proper path loss model is needed, as the loss over distance is stronger in NLOS compared to LOS conditions. Inaccuracies might lead to a big change of NLOS reception range compared to reality. Proper MAC modeling is needed, as the strongest impact factor on reception under competition are MAC level effects like hidden terminal collisions.

The ns-2 [30] packet level network simulator was used in version 2.34. As described in Section 3.1.3.1, this release includes the 802.11 MAC simulation overhaul as proposed in [31], making it to a good choice for MAC dependent simulations. As ns-2 2.34 by default provides no obstacle and NLOS path loss models, the simulator had to be extended. In order to model NLOS path loss and fading, the VirtualSource11p model developed in Section 6.3 was integrated into the simulator.

The ns-2 enhancements are briefly discussed in Section 6.4.1.1. Afterwards, the selection of appropriate network parameters is discussed in Section 6.4.1.2

6.4.1.1 ns-2 Non-Line-Of-Sight Enhancements

The VirtualSource11p path loss equation takes several geometric aspects, such as the distance from transmitter to intersection center ($tx \leftrightarrow center$), from center to receiver, from transmitter to wall and the width of the receive street into account.

Also, the model only applies to NLOS conditions, requiring a LOS/NLOS detection. Thus, it requires a topography module that provides this functionality and is able to compute the distances during runtime.

Therefore, a new, extended topography module was implemented. This new module takes the building shapes and street corridors from the simulation tcl-file. Based on this information, it computes the required distances at runtime. Results are cached in a 2-dimensional matrix based on a 1×1 meter patch simplification in order to reduce complexity to a lookup after the initial insertion.

The VirtualSource11p model itself is implemented as a new propagation module, derived from the present Nakagami propagation module. Based on the topography response, it either takes the existing path loss and fading computation from the Nakagami module, or applies the corresponding VirtualSource11p equations.

6.4.1.2   Network Simulation Parameters

In order to produce realistic results, a proper selection of system parameters in the simulation such as data-rate or SINR for successful packet decoding is important. The parameters were selected as shown in Table 6.8.

A data rate of 6 Mbps was selected, as it was found a good compromise between capacity and signal robustness in [26]. The decoding success SINR value of 8 dB is the ns-2.34 default for a 6 Mbps 802.11p 10 MHz channel. Noise floor was set to the typical -99 dBm value of current Atheros 802.11 chipsets.

In order to get proper NLOS reception performance, the transmission power should be selected pretty high. However, channel load in LOS will rise due to the high power and needs to be monitored during evaluation. The tx-power was

Parameter	Value
Channel	5.9 GHz, 10 MHz bandwidth
Data rate	6 Mbps
SINR	8 dB for decoding success at 6 Mbps
Noise Floor	-99 dBm
Tx-Power	82.64 mW = 19.17 dBm (to achieve 700 m intended range)
Antenna Gain	0 dB (for tx- and rcv-antenna)
Packet Size	228 Byte (200 Byte payload + 28 Byte MAC/PHY header)
LOS Path Loss	LogNormal FSPL with common loss-exponent of 2
LOS Fading	Nakagami-m=1 (common, and Section 6.3.1.4)
NLOS Path Loss	VirtualSource11p (Section 6.3.1.3)
NLOS Fading	NormalDistributed with σ=4.1 dB (Section 6.3.1.4)

Table 6.8: Network parameter values in simulation.

set to provide an intended range[5] of 700 m. At 6 Mbps, 700 m intended range corresponds to 19.17 dBm. This is 2 dB below the maximum output power (21 dBm) of currently available commercial radio hardware (Atheros 802.11 chipsets).

The antenna gain is assumed to be 0 dB, leading together with 19 dBm tx-power to 1 dB "loss" per node against an optimal system. This is realistic given cable loss and most likely no achievable antenna gain in production antennas (compare findings in Section 6.2.2.1).

The payload is set to the commonly used value of 200 Byte, consisting of 80 Byte content (such as in the German sim^{TD} V2V project [93]) plus overhead. Finally, the table states the used LOS and NLOS models and their parameterization. NLOS path-loss and fading are modeled as identified in Section 6.3.

6.4.2   Simulation Scenario Selection

The selection of simulated situations (scenarios) is important to get results that apply to operational conditions. From an evaluation point of view, it is also needed to simulate a controlled environment to get specific and comparable results.

Firstly, the basic intersection setup providing a controlled environment is described in Section 6.4.2.1. Based on this geometric setup, two general transmitter placement configurations are specified for constructing network load. One uses static transmitters to provide a controlled reference scenario that removes vehicle movement from the evaluation (Section 6.4.2.2). The other setup uses moving vehicles as in reality. While load levels in the static scenario are artificially selected, the vehicle density is crucial in the dynamic case. Therefore, Section 6.4.2.3 provides an analysis about expectable vehicle densities in order to achieve a realistic simulation scenario selection.

6.4.2.1   Basic Scenario Setup

The selected prototype intersection is a typical 4-leg intersection with 1-lane streets (per direction) and right-of-way from the right (no traffic light). Such an intersection is expected to predominately produce situations where cross-traffic assistance—demanding NLOS reception—is needed. With traffic light, dangerous right of way violations are less likely. Consequently, the evaluation of 2-lane streets is left to a future analysis, as the likelihood of a traffic light at 2-lane streets is high.

The building placement influences the reception power in NLOS due to the amount of "view" into the crossing street. The VirtualSource1lp equation inherits this by the inter-building distance input value (building canyon width for a street). The main scenario is selected as an intersection with 23 m inter-

---

[5]The construct of "intended range" is described in Section 3.1.3.3.

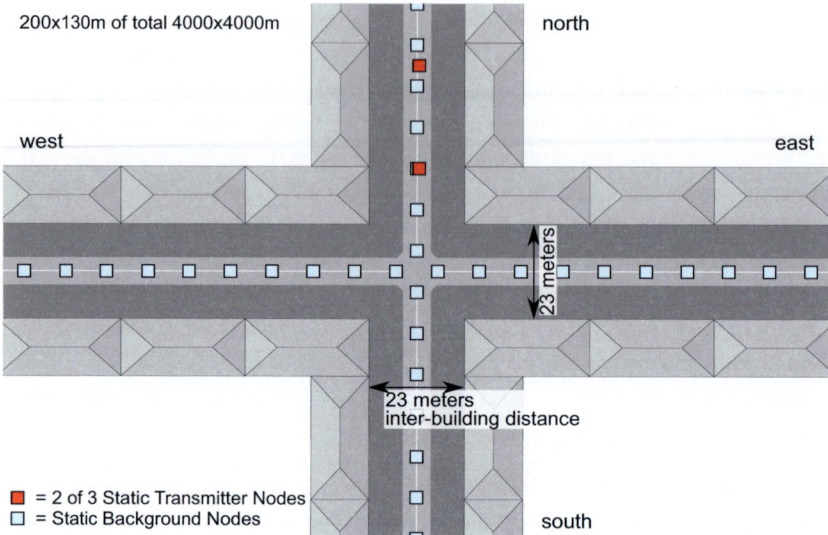

Figure 6.26: The main scenario layout – Static transmitter nodes for evaluation at 25, 50 and 100 m north and background nodes every 10 m. Background nodes are used for monitoring reception and for generating network traffic in the static scenario by transmitting with a certain rate (BgNode-MsgRate).

building distance, corresponding to the main cluster in the building placement analysis in Section 6.1. The cluster corresponds to 50 % of intersections in the city of Munich. A second value of 30 m was also simulated in order to provide comparison results for wider intersections.

Nodes were placed in 10 m steps on each side street to measure reception. Those are background nodes, not representing a "real" vehicle. Evaluation was performed for three static transmitters at a controlled distance to intersection center of 25, 50 and 100 m. 25 and 50 m roughly correspond to 1 and 3 s before impact at 50 km/h, the interception and driver warning points as discussed in Section 2.2.2.

The needed street-leg length is dependent on the transmission power. At the used 19.17 dBm, the signal loss curve crosses the reception sensitivity of the radio at ≈1310 m. Therefore, long street-legs are needed in order to get the full load in the intersection center and NLOS region close to center. It was opted to use 2000 m each, leading to a simulated area of 4000×4000 m. A virtual boarder wrap around of the propagation in the simulator prevented the need for even longer roads. The amount of simulated events is already barely manageable at the selected setup (heap-space limitations). Figure 6.26 visualizes the center 200×130 m of the main setup with 23 m inter-building distance.

6.4.2.2 Static Scenario

In this reference scenario, load is generated via a changing message transmission rate at the background nodes. Important is a proper selection of load levels to prevent an overloaded channel. Results under overload are worthless, as load control should prevent such situations in reality.

A theoretic load metric was used in order to find good message rate values and for enabling the judgment of the load levels present in simulations. A channel load metric allowing to compare scenarios was for example described in [114]. It is extended here by incorporating packet sizes and making it point of interest rather than area specific. Resulting, the theoretic channel usage at a certain point of interest can be expressed as percentage by:

$$\text{ChannelUsage} = \frac{\#\text{TxEvents}}{\text{Second}} * \frac{\text{PacketSize}}{\text{DataRate}} * 100$$

Where:

- #TxEvents := number of transmissions where the point of interest is in their theoretic range.
- Theoretic range := distance where the path loss curve crosses the reception threshold (NoiseFloor+SINR).

Therefore, the formula expresses how long it takes to set all transmissions in one second perfectly timely and spatially aligned onto the channel. In other words, it computes the used percentage of available resources if a perfect MAC is available. In the used setup, theoretic range is 1310 m.

Given the never perfect spatial distribution of tx-events, imperfections due to the distributed MAC and a non-consideration of some effects—such as preamble overhead—in the formula, "Channel-Usage" values should be kept well below 100 %.

A message rate of 0 to 5 Hz with 1 Hz step size was selected. The resulting simulation wide average load indicators are given in Table 6.9. The values were computed from simulation results for five different points: center of intersection and 100 m into every street leg. All three metrics (Channel-Usage, #Tx-Events, #Tx-Nodes) were computed using theoretic range and only events in LOS to the point of interest were considered.

The table shows that the theoretic channel usage value increases to up to 80 % in intersection center. Such a value is already rather high. The #tx-events metric shows that the center node could potentially receive about 2600 messages per second. This number also indicates a high load level. However, the values for the points inside of only one street canyon only rise up to 40 % with 5 Hz.

Bg-Node Msg-Rate	Metric	center	east 100 m	west 100 m	north 100 m	south 100 m
0 Hz	Channel-Usage	0.9 %	0.0 %	0.0 %	0.9 %	0.9 %
	Tx-Events	30	0	0	30	30
1 Hz	Channel-Usage	16.8 %	8.0 %	8.0 %	8.9 %	8.9 %
	Tx-Events	551	263	263	293	292
2 Hz	Channel-Usage	32.6 %	16.0 %	15.9 %	16.9 %	16.9 %
	Tx-Events	1072	526	525	556	555
3 Hz	Channel-Usage	48.4 %	23.9 %	23.9 %	24.9 %	24.9 %
	Tx-Events	1594	786	788	820	820
4 Hz	Channel-Usage	64.3 %	32.0 %	32.0 %	32.8 %	32.8 %
	Tx-Events	2115	1053	1053	1079	1079
5 Hz	Channel-Usage	80.1 %	40.0 %	40.0 %	40.8 %	40.8 %
	Tx-Events	2636	1317	1317	1341	1342
0 Hz	Tx-Nodes	3	0	0	3	3
1–5 Hz	Tx-Nodes	527	264	264	267	267

Table 6.9: Channel load characteristics in static scenario.

A comparison of the values for the four street legs shows that load is equal in both street canyons at any direction from the intersection. Obviously, the 0 Hz scenario is as good as competition free, as only the three evaluation nodes transmit.

6.4.2.3 Dynamic Scenario

The dynamic scenario is intended to show NLOS packet reception rate behavior under realistic traffic. Network load levels here depend on the vehicle movement. The cross-traffic application is most critical in situations with no traffic jam at an intersection. In case of queues, NLOS reception is likely not needed, as at least one of two vehicles involved in cross-traffic assistance is located very close to the intersection center.

In order to find realistic scenarios, the maximum vehicle flow needs to be found that does not produce a steadily increasing queue of standing vehicles at one of the streets hitting the intersection. Such a scenario produces maximum load under the assumption of a need for cross-traffic assistance and therefore NLOS reception. In other words, it is needed to study how high load levels rise in application critical situations in reality.

In order to find such a realistic worst-case, first of all node movement was simulated via the SUMO [89] microscopic traffic flow simulator. On each street end (east, west, north, south), a vehicle inflow is specified as vehicles per minute.

An automatic scenario generation via script files allowed fast testing of differing inflows. A first tool generates a complete SUMO specification based on the script: street description, vehicle type, turn probability, vehicle routes, and the SUMO main configuration file. The turn probability is set weighted by inflow. A street with high inflow will be likely turned at, and vice versa. After scenario specification, SUMO is run scripted and produces a trace. Afterwards, another tool converts the trace to an ns-2 movement tcl file, and produces vehicle flow related statistics. The first 1000 s of a simulation are discarded before an ns-2 movement file is generated. Thus, the scenario is already "filled" and "stable" at ns-2 movement file start.

Experiments showed that in case of a symmetric inflow on all four sides, 6 vehicles/minute is the highest value not producing a traffic jam. This configuration is selected as "high" scenario. A "medium" scenario is selected at 3 vehicles/minute.

An alternative inflow pattern as opposed to symmetric is a high flow on one street, and a low one on the other (set to 1 vehicle/minute). Testing showed that 11 vehicles/minute is the maximum inflow at the high flow street before a traffic jam arises. The goal of this asymmetric configuration is to test if a high load on one street is especially harmful to NLOS reception.

The selected scenarios and their inflow are given in Table 6.10. The complete set of files for each scenario—configuration files, movement traces, building position description, ...—is available at the thesis website [10]. There, one can also find videos showing the traffic flow in the intersection for each inflow setup.

The vehicle density and affinity to small jams directly at the intersection for the different scenarios is investigated in Table 6.11. None of the scenarios has (in average) standing vehicles on the 20–100 m to intersection stretches. In consequence, there are no long jams. The high scenario has a notable amount of standing vehicles in the intersection center. When it was tried to increase the inflow from 6 to 6.5 vehicles/minute, long jams occurred. In the asynchronous inflow cases, there is only a slight amount of standing vehicles in the direct intersection area. The medium case is almost completely free of standing vehicles. Note that the "all vehicles" numbers are unusable as network load indication, as only the area close to center is incorporated here.

Scenario	east	west	north	south
none	0	0	0	0
medium	3	3	3	3
high	6	6	6	6
high_crossing	11	11	1	1
high_tx	1	1	11	11

Table 6.10: Scenario inflow setup in SUMO (vehicles/minute).

Scenario	Counted Vehicles	center ±50 meter	west 20–120 meter	east 20–120 meter	north 20–120 meter	south 20–120 meter
none	all vehicles	0.00	0.00	0.00	0.00	0.00
	standing ones	0.00	0.00	0.00	0.00	0.00
medium	all vehicles	2.71	0.87	0.73	0.70	0.89
	standing ones	0.18	0.00	0.00	0.00	0.00
high	all vehicles	6.98	1.87	1.61	1.41	1.34
	standing ones	1.63	0.00	0.00	0.00	0.00
high_crossing	all vehicles	5.24	3.10	2.88	0.27	0.18
	standing ones	0.18	0.00	0.00	0.00	0.00
high_tx	all vehicles	3.65	0.25	0.22	2.77	2.67
	standing ones	0.10	0.00	0.00	0.00	0.00

Table 6.11: Movement characterization in the selected dynamic scenarios: average vehicle number per area per second.

Table 6.12 shows the resulting values for the same three network load metrics (Tx-Nodes, Tx-Events, Channel-Usage) as given for the static scenario in Section 6.4.2.2. The message rate was selected as the often-assumed 10 Hz in all scenarios.

The table reveals that the load in the center is similar for all three "high" scenarios, despite the different inflows. In the asynchronous cases, load is concentrating in one of the two crossing streets and the level is higher as in the synchronous "high" setup. A comparison to Table 6.9 shows that the load in the "high" case is somewhere in between the 1 and 2 Hz static scenarios. Therefore, the indicators show that the channel is not at its maximum capacity in situations where cross-traffic assistance is most needed and NLOS reception important.

As expected from the traffic jam indicators, these load indicators do not vary much over time. Plots showing this are available on the thesis website [10] (not given here in order to keep this evaluation focused).

6.4.3 Network Simulations and Evaluation

In this section, the simulation runs and statistics generation is shortly explained, before the evaluation results are presented in Sections 6.4.3.1 and 6.4.3.2.

The evaluation discusses the NLOS packet reception rate over distance in the different scenarios and under parameter variations. It is organized as follows: Firstly, the static scenario is evaluated for the main inter-building distance and suburban conditions in Section 6.4.3.1.

Scenario	Metric	center	east 100 m	west 100 m	north 100 m	south 100 m
none	Ch.-Usage	0.9 %	0.0 %	0.0 %	0.9 %	0.9 %
	Tx-Events	31	0	0	31	31
	Tx-Nodes	3	0	0	3	3
medium	Ch.-Usage	12.9 %	6.1 %	6.2 %	7.2 %	7.2 %
	Tx-Events	423	201	205	236	236
	Tx-Nodes	43	20	20	24	24
high	Ch.-Usage	26.6 %	14.3 %	14.3 %	13.5 %	13.4 %
	Tx-Events	876	471	469	445	440
	Tx-Nodes	88	48	47	45	45
high_crossing	Ch.-Usage	25.1 %	22.7 %	22.8 %	3.0 %	3.0 %
	Tx-Events	825	747	750	99	100
	Tx-Nodes	83	75	75	10	10
high_tx	Ch.-Usage	24.7 %	2.1 %	2.1 %	23.0 %	23.0 %
	Tx-Events	814	69	71	757	757
	Tx-Nodes	82	7	7	76	76

Table 6.12: Channel load characteristics in dynamic scenarios.

Following, Section 6.4.3.2 presents the results of the dynamic scenario. Paragraph 6.4.3.2.1 shows the results for the same scenario as the static one, but with dynamic traffic flow. Paragraph 6.4.3.2.2 will discuss changes when stepping to the urban case. Then, in Paragraph 6.4.3.2.3, the same urban scenario with increased inter-building distance is discussed. All those discussions are based on the results for the 50 m $tx \leftrightarrow center$ distance setting. It corresponds to the probably most important point in time while approaching an intersection under cross-traffic assistance, the warning distance at 50 km/h.

Finally, the influence of $tx \leftrightarrow center$ distance on the NLOS reception under competition is discussed in Paragraph 6.4.3.2.4 based on the suburban/23 m inter-building distance setup.

The complete set of all plots is available at the thesis website [10]. Therefore, it contains the here missing 25 and 100 m $tx \leftrightarrow center$ distance results in case of suburban and wide building placement and all reception rate results for LOS.

Simulations and Statistics Generation   Each load scenario was simulated in both, the suburban and urban setting of the corresponding i_s VirtualSourcellp parameter. The suburban setting is characterized by a 3 dB stronger path loss in NLOS. Also, each one is simulated with the main 23 m inter-building distance as well as the extended 30 m setting. Therefore, four simulations were performed for each load scenario. As there are six different message rate settings in the static test suite, 24 simulations result. The dynamic test suite consists of 20 simulations.

The simulated time was 60 s in case of the static scenario and 120 s in case of the dynamic one. As the total node number in simulations raises to a high number of up to 977, this is a good compromise between stable results and simulation complexity constraints such as runtime and trace file size. The first and last 2 s were discarded to exclude eventual ns-2 startup and shutdown side-effects.

For each virtual transmitter (at 25, 50, 100 m), packet reception rate over distance is computed at the background nodes. Starting from intersection center, statistics are separately computed for the transmitter street (LOS), and the crossing street (NLOS).

6.4.3.1 Evaluation: NLOS Reception in Static Scenario

The NLOS reception performance in the static setup as defined in Section 6.4.2.2 is given in Figure 6.27 for the suburban scenario with 23 m inter-building distance. The plot shows the distance to intersection center on the x-axis. Intersection center is at 0 m. Positive distances represent the crossing street, negative ones the street leg the transmitter is placed in. The NLOS area is visualized in blue. The first point of NLOS is computed based on the transmitter position and building placement.

At a message rate of 1 Hz at the background nodes, there is only a slight drop of reception rate in NLOS compared to the competition free channel at 0 Hz rate. The drop becomes much more obvious at 2 Hz. At 50 m into the crossing street, the reception rate drops already 0.3 points from roughly 0.8 to 0.5 due to network competition. At 5 Hz, competition pushes the reception rate down to below 0.2. The huge loss can be explained by power in NLOS decreasing fast. In consequence,

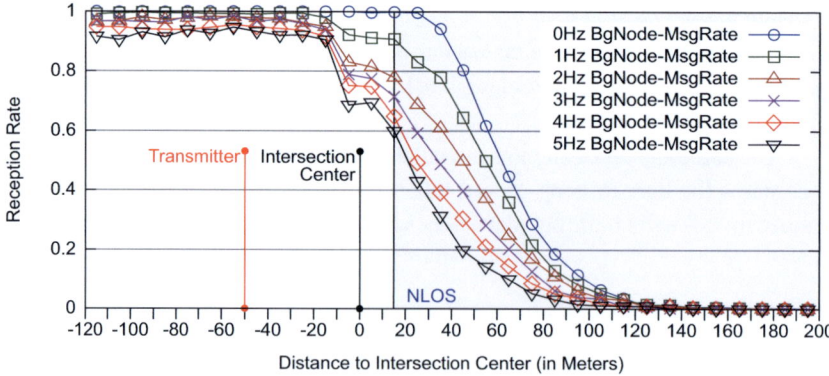

Figure 6.27: Reception rate over distance. **Static scenario**, 23 m inter-building distance, suburban, 50 m *tx↔center* distance.

nodes in some distance (>200 m) do not recognize that the channel is occupied and will transmit. Therefore, the NLOS signal is prone to hidden terminal collisions (a MAC limitation as described in background Section 3.1.2).

The plot also shows that reception rate does not only strongly decrease in NLOS though. In the intersection center, with its increased network competition, the reception rate already drops up to 0.3 points in the 5 Hz scenario. So close to the transmitter, this is a strong sign that the channel is overloaded there. In particular, hidden terminal collisions due to non-detections of transmissions from the crossing street lead to the rather strong degradation. An investigation onto this and the vulnerability of NLOS signals to hidden terminal collisions is available in Appendix A.2.2.

6.4.3.2 Evaluation: NLOS Reception in Dynamic Scenario

This section investigates NLOS reception in the dynamic scenario. One big question is how the introduction of movement, and therefore a varying spatial transmit event distribution, will influence reception. A second question to answer is, how much influence the asynchronous load in the "high_crossing" and "high_tx" scenarios has.

6.4.3.2.1 Basic Scenario – Suburban Results for the same setup (suburban, 23 m) as in Section 6.4.3.1, but with vehicle movement are given in Figure 6.28. In general, there exist the same rate-loss characteristics as in the static setup. The reception rate curve of the "high" scenario is in between the 1 and 2 Hz curve in the static scenario. As the load characteristic comparison revealed the same, this shows that vehicle movement per se has no significant influence on results.

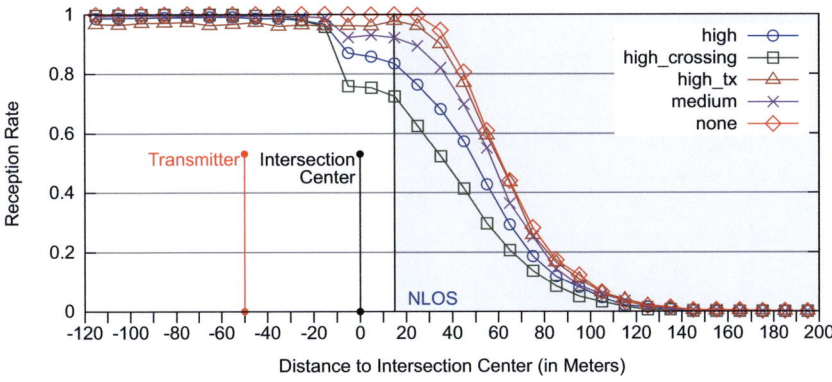

Figure 6.28: Reception rate over distance. **Dynamic scenario**, 23 m inter-building distance, suburban, 50 m *tx↔center* distance.

The "medium" scenario shows almost no reception rate loss in NLOS. In consequence, there seems to be no problem at all in medium to light traffic density conditions.

The two asynchronous scenarios reveal interesting results. The "high_tx" scenario shows almost no loss in NLOS reception rates, despite its very high load on the transmitter street. In case the high load is located in the reception street—the "high_crossing" scenario—, reception rates drop heavily in NLOS; even stronger as in the "high" scenario with comparable load in the intersection center. This shows that the reception performance in NLOS under load is almost completely dependent on the load in the receiver street canyon. On a second look, this is not surprising though, as strong signal components that might destroy an ongoing NLOS reception will primarily originate from nodes in LOS to the NLOS receiver.

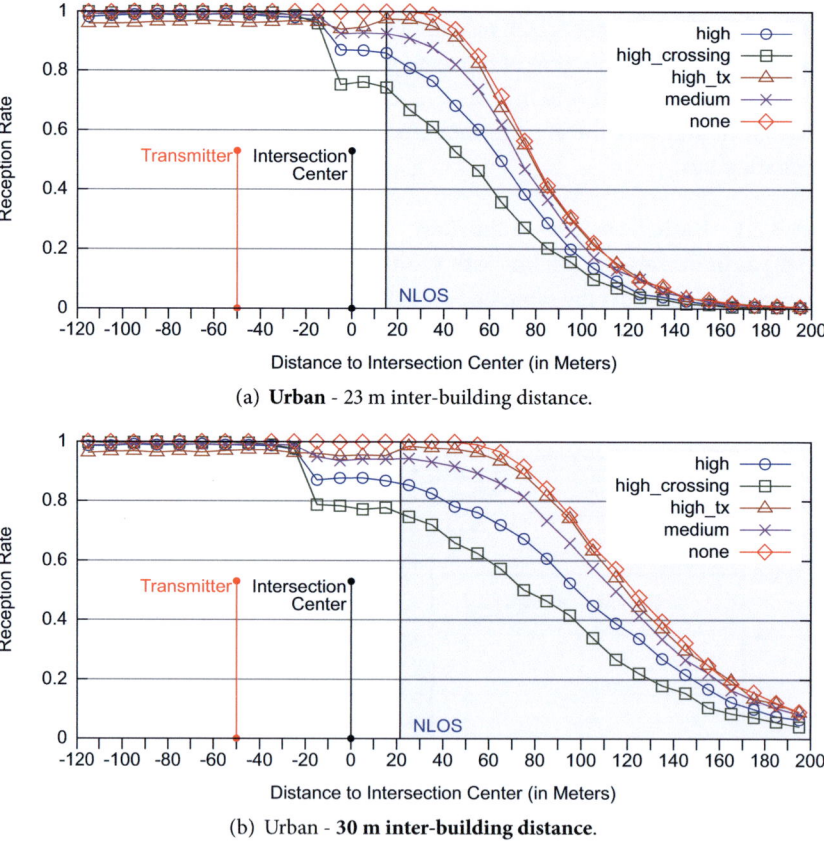

(a) **Urban** - 23 m inter-building distance.

(b) Urban - **30 m inter-building distance**.

Figure 6.29: Reception rate. Dynamic scenario, 50 m *tx↔center* distance.

See Appendix A.2.2 for an investigation on the origin of interfering signals.

In absolute terms, the "high_crossing" scenario leads to the highest performance hit in NLOS, being 0.4 reception rate points at 30 m into the side street. However, the reception rate in this worst-case scenario still stays above 0.5 until roughly 35 m. At 50 m (warning distance) into the side street, the rate has dropped to 0.3. Therefore, an update will arrive every 300 ms in average at 10 Hz message transmission rate. In other traffic scenarios, the rate stays at 0.5 at 50 m. The question to application designers is, whether this is enough for a warning while synchronously approaching at 50 km/h.

6.4.3.2.2   Basic Scenario – Urban   The influence of a transition from a suburban to an urban setting is discussed here. The same configuration as in Figure 6.28 is used in Figure 6.29(a), but with an urban configuration. A comparison of the plots shows that the reception curves are only slightly shifted to the right. This is due to roughly 3 dB less NLOS path loss in suburban compared to urban in the VirtualSource1lp model. The influence of the individual traffic scenarios onto the NLOS reception stays the same.

6.4.3.2.3   Urban With Larger Inter-Building Distance   The influence of an increased inter-building distance is shown in the lower part of Figure 6.29. Despite the change from 23 to 30 m inter-building distance, all parameter are the same. The VirtualSource1lp model predicts more power in NLOS areas in case of better view into the crossing street. The resulting increase in NLOS reception performance is clearly visible. At 50 m into the crossing street, even in the worst-case scenario the reception rate is still above 0.75 now. From a cross-traffic assistance application point of view, such an intersection should provide good reception conditions at warning distance.

The drop in reception rate due to competition stays at the same levels compared to the previously investigated scenarios. The drop is circa 0.4 rate points in the "high_crossing" traffic scenario and 0.2 in the "high" one.

6.4.3.2.4   Influence of Transmitter to Center Distance on NLOS Reception
The transmitter to intersection center ($tx \leftrightarrow center$) distance is a major influence factor on path loss strength in the crossing street (in NLOS), as found in the measurement results in Section 6.2.2.2 and visible in the VirtualSource1lp model equation in Section 6.3.1.3. Figure 6.30 shows the influence of $tx \leftrightarrow center$ distance in the suburban, 23 m inter-building distance setting—therefore in the worst tested NLOS path loss environment. Plots are given for all three static transmitters at 25, 50 and 100 m. They show that the achievable range mainly varies due to the path loss change. Competition is the smaller influence factor in comparison.

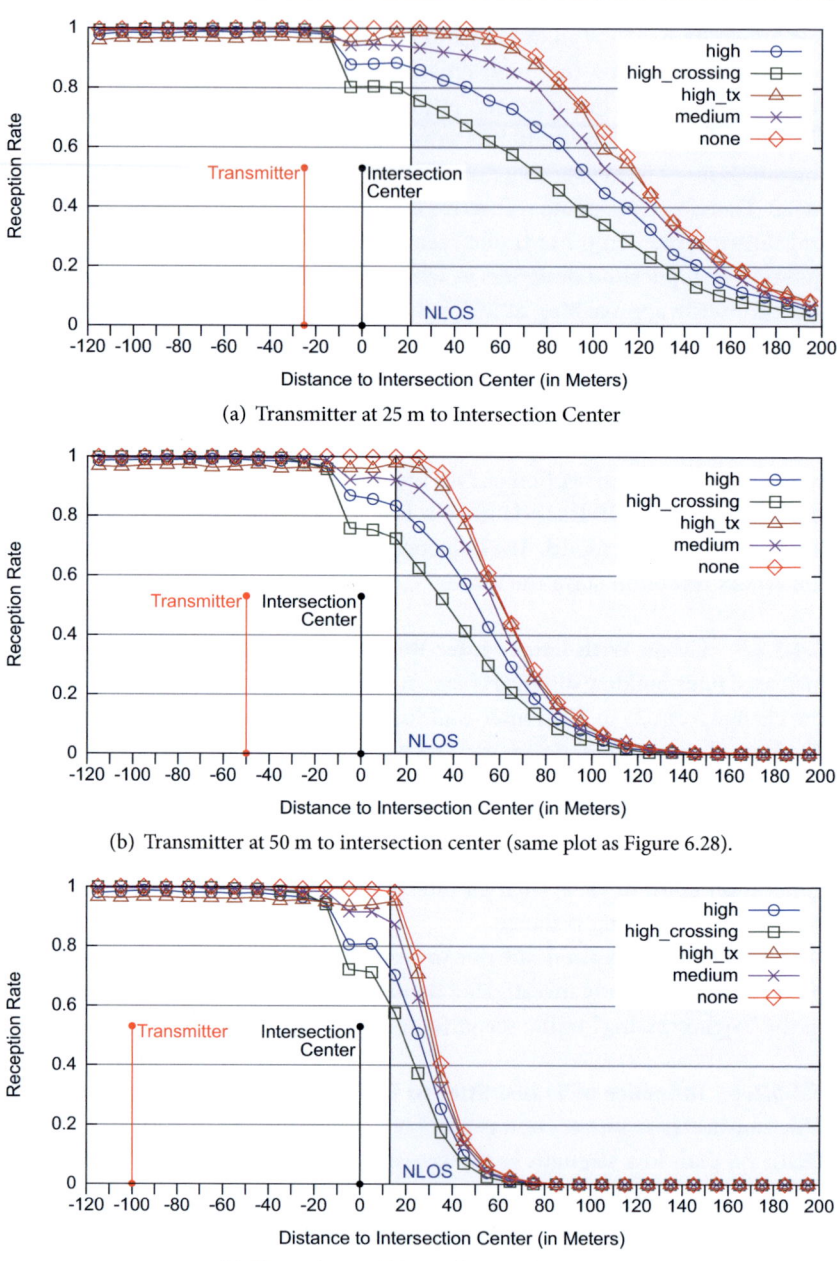

(a) Transmitter at 25 m to Intersection Center

(b) Transmitter at 50 m to intersection center (same plot as Figure 6.28).

(c) Transmitter at 100 m to intersection center

Figure 6.30: Influence of *tx↔center* distance on NLOS reception. Dynamic setup, 23 m inter-building distance, suburban.

At 100 m *tx↔center* distance, NLOS path loss is so strong that network competition cannot degrade reception much further. The 100 m plot reveals that proper NLOS reception should not be assumed when two vehicles are symmetrically approaching an intersection and are located at a distance greater 50 m to center; even given the knowledge that results would be slightly better in an urban setting or with larger inter-building distance.

6.4.4   Conclusion

In this study, the influence of network load on NLOS packet reception rates on a 5.9 GHz IEEE 802.11p channel was investigated. To the best of the author's knowledge, the presented study is the first that is based on a validated and dedicated 5.9 GHz vehicle-to-vehicle NLOS path loss and fading model. As a further novelty, expectable load levels in situations predominantly requiring NLOS reception were investigated. The highest achievable node densities in cross-traffic assistance critical situations (no congestion, junctions without traffic light) were identified with help of microscopic traffic simulation. Furthermore, building placement in simulations was selected based on the environment knowledge gained in Section 6.1. In combination, the selection of realistic network simulation scenarios was ensured.

Network simulations on top of those vehicle movement patterns show that network load levels in the NLOS receiver street canyon are most critical. In the identified worst-case traffic scenario in this perspective, a strong (0.4 rate points) drop in NLOS reception rate at critical warning point distance can be observed. In such traffic scenario, and a critical suburban small inter-building distance environment, the reception rate is still at 0.3 at warning distance, representing a packet reception every 300 ms on average at the simulated 10 Hz message rate. In urban intersections, and especially with increasing inter-building distance, NLOS reception rates stay—despite load—on a likely tolerable level of $\geqslant 0.5$ in critical distance to intersection center regarding a cross-traffic warning.

As maximal application critical traffic flows were simulated under a relative high transmission power and message rate, the results also reveal that load shaping by transmission power reduction—having a negative effect on the NLOS reception range—is not needed in cross-traffic assistance critical situations.

The provided knowledge about NLOS reception performance and a practicable power level under different realistic levels of competition should allow application designers to judge the achievable information level for the investigated cross-traffic assistance application.

In order to allow others the reproduction of the results or doing further investigations, the scenario description files, together with more performance plots and movement videos are provided on the thesis website [10].

6.5   Ad-Hoc Performance Conclusion

The necessity of NLOS reception in terms ad-hoc communication, 5.9 GHz IEEE 802.11p NLOS reception performance, as well as the influence of network competition on NLOS reception were evaluated in this chapter.

The building placement analysis shows that a radio LOS is only available at ≈20 % of all corners areas in the city of Munich. The analysis further reveals that there exist dominant building placement configurations, representing a well-defined reference scenario.

The extensive 5.9 GHz IEEE 802.11p NLOS measurements revealed that NLOS reception is in general well feasible and—despite distance to intersection center—predominantly influenced by the inter-building distance in a street. Reception rates are usually at 0.5 or above at driver warning distance and under synchronous intersection approaching of vehicles from intersecting streets.

Furthermore, it was possible to quantify the influence of inter-building distance and suburban/urban differences on NLOS reception in a single equation describing NLOS path loss, called VirtualSource11p. Together with a characterization of fading in NLOS conditions, a complete model of vehicular 5.9 GHz NLOS propagation is provided.

Reception performance under application relevant network competition levels was investigated by network simulations applying the proposed NLOS propagation model. The study reveals that a harmful transmission power reduction is not needed in application critical conditions. While MAC layer effects considerably degrade reception rates at warning distance in worst-case conditions, an absolute reception rate of 0.3 or more is still existent.

The performed connectivity investigations show that the potential weakness of ad-hoc communication at inner-city intersections, the need for NLOS reception, is likely tolerable. Even in suboptimal conditions, a fair amount of connectivity between two vehicles approaching an intersection is given at cross-traffic assistance critical distances.

7

Suitability Comparison of Cellular and Ad-Hoc Communication

The environment characteristic and performance of cellular and ad-hoc communication in terms of cross-traffic assistance at inner-city intersections was investigated individually in Chapter 5 and 6 respectively. A comparison between the technologies based on the gained knowledge is given in this chapter, before the final conclusion of this thesis is drawn in Chapter 8.

The suitability comparison is given in Table 7.1. Abstract performance factors are compared instead of the individual technical details determining performance. The comparison first lists the basic open questions regarding both technologies at the start of this thesis, before comparing the found performance figures as well as the resulting cost[1] demand. The comparison only covers LTE in terms of cellular communication, as it was found in Section 5.2 that UMTS performs worse than LTE by far and is likely not able to handle the intersection assistance application. Furthermore, LTE is seen as the future of cellular communication and already rolled out in many countries as of now (2011/2012).

Technical Suitability Comparison   The biggest concern in terms of cellular communications as identified in Chapter 5 is the manageability of the capacity demand that is needed for delivering the regular transmitted CAMs. While the environment analysis revealed a high worst-case demand of up to 7200 CAM/Cell/s, the

---

[1]"Cost" should not be interpreted here necessarily as monetary.

technology analysis showed that it is technically possible to deliver such a demand via LTE. However, a non-standard, efficient transmission scheme is needed to keep the resource consumption on a reasonable level while enabling proximity coverage beyond the very few vehicles in close vicinity.

The ad-hoc communication technology analysis in Chapter 5 showed that NLOS reception—the biggest concern in terms of IEEE 802.11p communication—is

	Cellular (LTE)	Ad-Hoc (802.11p)
Open questions in the beginning	CAM induced load? Ability to handle CAM load? Boundary conditions?	Need for NLOS reception? NLOS reception quality?
Environment	High capacity/cell demand (up to 7200 CAM/Cell/s)	NLOS reception is needed at 80 % of all corners
Information delivery	Non-standard, efficient transmission scheme needed (RACH uplink (proposed), broadcast downlink)	NLOS reception works well enough: $\geqslant 0.3$ reception rate in application critical situation
Capacity	Technically manageable with wide (20 MHz) downlink channel	Sufficient: High tx-power possible in critical scenarios
Latency	Reasonable (50–100 ms round trip time)	Very low ($<$10 ms)
Reliability Point of Failure (PoF), Delivery Issue (DI)	PoF: Radio, base station, core network, backend DI: Broadcast loss, no coverage, over-saturation	PoF: Radio DI: Packet loss
Operational costs	Backend infrastructure and consumed bandwidth (worst-case: one 20 MHz system in downlink, $>$8 MHz in uplink (likely over multiple systems))	None
In vehicle hardware demand	At least one dedicated LTE radio and SIM card, likely two of each	One IEEE 802.11p radio, optimally two
Other efforts	Standardization and base station updates (broadcast, uplink scheduler)	Minor, standardization almost done

Table 7.1: Communication technology suitability comparison for cross-traffic assistance at inner-city intersections. Open questions, demand and performance results, as well as cost factors as identified in this thesis.

needed at about 80 % of all corners, but works well enough in order to support the application. In course of this analysis, the investigation of application critical traffic scenarios in Section 6.4.2.3 further showed that a high transmission power can be used in such situations without over-saturating the channel. High transmission power is needed in order to enable the satisfying reception rates in NLOS conditions as measured and found in simulations.

In combination, both technologies are technically able to satisfy the capacity/information demand in the identified application critical situations.

A further performance characteristic used in the comparison in Table 7.1 is latency. A low latency is desired to increase the accuracy of movement predictions. The latency of IEEE 802.11p is low with <10 ms. It is purely dependent on the CSMA/CA access delay. There is almost zero delay on a competition free channel. Channel busy sensing will slightly delay a transmission under competition, but latency will likely still stay below 10 ms as packets are short. In cellular systems, the information is delivered to other vehicles via the backend. In consequence, it passes the air interface two times. The round trip time in cellular systems was found to be too high in UMTS, but being reasonable low in LTE at 50–100 ms. While the ad-hoc communication has a clear latency advantage, application designers might still judge the LTE latency as being tolerable.

A further aspect of technical suitability is the reliability of both systems. While this fact was not investigated in depth in this thesis, it is nevertheless a fact that should be considered. Therefore, factors that impact reliability are listed in Table 7.1. The ad-hoc communication has a clear advantage here as it inherits hardware wise only a single point of failure—the radio, while a cellular solution introduces with base station, core network and backend three additional entities that might fail. Furthermore, eventually missing coverage and the danger of over-saturation of cells (potentially leading to a collapse of the communication) are further problems that do not exist with ad-hoc communication.

Cost Comparison Despite the slight advantage of ad-hoc communication in latency and reliability, both technologies are basically able to support the use case from a technical perspective. In consequence, special attention comes to the costs involved.

The costs to employ an ITS communication technology are manifold. There are hardware costs in the vehicle, operational costs as well as initial costs to bring the technology to market. Hereby, especially operational "costs" manifest themselves not only in money, which is often difficult to assess (compare Section 5.3.3), but can be more generally seen e.g. as amount of consumed resources that one needs to pay for.

In terms of cellular communication, the technical analysis revealed that a single 20 MHz broadcast downlink channel is needed to provide enough capacity in worst-case conditions. In case of reduced requirements, such as communication only in intersection vicinity, a 10 MHz system might be sufficient. In the uplink, it was found that 5000 CAM/s might be transmittable on a 5 MHz channel. Considering the worst-case demand, at least 8–10 MHz are needed. As the number of random accesses is the limiting factor, capacity from multiple systems is needed, or some kind of pre-scheduling to circumvent the random access limit. Considering that a single operator possesses only 10 MHz paired spectrum in the preferable 800 MHz band in Germany [104], those up and downlink bandwidth requirements represent a considerable price tag.

In contrast, the frequencies needed in order to operate 5.9 GHz IEEE 802.11p have been reserved to ITS safety communication free of charge. As the system needs in general no infrastructure, its operation is for free. Therefore, the ad-hoc communication has a tremendous advantage in terms of operational costs.

An often heard argument in favor of cellular systems is the increasing existence of cellular hardware in vehicles: It seems advantageous to use existing hardware, as opposed to add an additional IEEE 802.11p module in order to enable ad-hoc communication. However, the technical investigation of cellular communication revealed that a potentially existing cellular module is likely not sufficient. In order to enable the efficient broadcast based delivery, a radio is needed that constantly monitors a single dedicated cellular channel. As the RACH uplink load likely needs to be split on multiple networks, a second radio is required. Furthermore, the certainly desired parallel usage of voice or user data also implies the need for a second radio.

A single 5.9 GHz IEEE 802.11p radio is required for enabling cross-traffic assistance, as only the common control channel needs to be monitored to retrieve the required CAMs. However, considering the complete set of envisioned ITS applications, a second radio is optimally installed to run further applications on the additionally available service channels. In consequence, both communication technologies require essentially the same number of two radio modules for proper operation.

Finally, there are some additional efforts needed for enabling an efficient cellular CAM delivery. In order to enable the proposed method of a broadcast based downlink and RACH driven uplink, investments in the cellular infrastructure are needed. Current base station software does not support MBMS, and the base station schedulers would need to be modified to enable a special treatment of CAMs in the uplink. Furthermore, that special treatment, as well as the backend handling would require standardization. Of course, there also have been considerable investments made to investigate and standardize IEEE 802.11p communication.

Suitability Conclusion   Both systems turn out to be technically able to support cross-traffic assistance at inner-city intersections with a decent information quality. However, ad-hoc communication inherits a considerable cost advantage. Especially the operational costs of cellular systems due to the found high capacity demand question using them for enabling the investigated use case. The sense of a cellular communication driven approach is further questioned by the slight technical advantage of ad-hoc communication with regards to latency and reliability.

8

Conclusion and Outlook

This chapter closes this thesis. The results are summarized and a conclusion is given in Section 8.1. Finally, a short outlook on open issues and implications that arise from the found results is given in Section 8.2.

8.1 Summary and Conclusion

While the properties of 5.9 GHz IEEE 802.11p ad-hoc based V2V communication in general have been intensively investigated in recent years, little attention was paid to radio propagation at inner-city intersections with potential LOS obstruction. This is particularly important, as the relatively high frequency of 5.9 GHz handicaps NLOS reception. In this scenario, cellular systems promise a better coverage due to high base station positions and a lower frequency. Also, cellular modules become more and more common in vehicles due to a raising demand for Internet connectivity. These facts motivated to compare the ability of cellular and ad-hoc communication for enabling inter-vehicle communication at intersections.

Application   The thesis focuses—by evaluating cross-traffic assistance—on a carefully selected high demand application that challenges the suitability of the different technologies. Cross-traffic assistance manifests itself as a safety application that purely depends on the high load inducing CAMs and needs high update rates. With regards to ad-hoc communication, a need for NLOS reception challenges the information delivery. In terms of cellular communication, the general ability and efficient ways to handle the high load demand as well as latency requirements represented open questions.

Environment The environment turns out to be a strong influence factor on the performance of the communication systems. For example, building placement determines the amount and character of NLOS propagation conditions as well as the combination of cell sizes, street network and vehicle flow determines the amount of vehicles that need to share cell capacity. In consequence, not only the technical abilities of the technologies were investigated in this thesis, but also the environment characteristics that influence performance. Furthermore, cost factors were briefly set into comparison.

Cellular Cellular communication was evaluated by an environment analysis in order to determine capacity demand, by an analysis of the UMTS and LTE standards in order to evaluate if the demand is technically manageable, as well as an analysis of the costs involved in doing so.

The environment analysis combines information about base station positions, street network and vehicle flow on streets for predicting the number of communicating vehicles, and in a second step the V2V communication driven network load per cell. A high load demand was found: There might exist over 700 Vehicles/Cell and up to 7200 CAM/Cell/s might be reached in worst-case rush hour conditions (without applying any application driven limitations such as restricting CAM transmissions to intersection vicinity). The provided knowledge on vehicle amounts per cell seems beneficial beyond the scope of this thesis: For example in order to predict the cell capacity demand of other connected vehicle applications.

In order to interpret the found capacity demand, the capacity and resource efficient delivery of CAMs was evaluated by a technical analysis of the UMTS and LTE standards. The expected latency due to the needed infrastructure detour was investigated in this context, too. The analysis shows that the usage of cell broadcast in the downlink and a random access driven uplink delivery seems beneficial in terms of efficiency. Such a CAM delivery prevents duplication overhead in the downlink and potentially under-utilized static connections. It turned out that UMTS does not provide sufficient capacity, while LTE does due to its higher spectral efficiency and operability on wider frequency bands. However, a lot of resources are needed. Also, capacity is very configuration dependent. For that reason influence factors on performance were discussed. UMTS is characterized by a high latency, while LTE round trip times of 50–100 ms seem reasonably low. In conclusion, LTE can enable cross-traffic assistance from a technical perspective.

However, the proposed kind of information delivery is not supported by current networks: software modifications at base stations would be required. Also, the efficient delivery would likely require an additional radio and SIM in each vehicle. Furthermore, a non-negligible amount of bandwidth would be consumed, directly translating into considerable monetary operational costs.

Ad-Hoc   The ability of the ad-hoc 5.9 GHz IEEE 802.11p communication to enable cross-traffic assistance is strongly bound to the question whether it is necessary to deliver information under NLOS propagation conditions, and if yes, how well this works. By performing a systematic analysis of building placement in the city of Munich this thesis revealed that only 20 % of all corners provide a radio-LOS in the moment it is needed in order to warn the driver. Under the assumption that there will not be a repeater at every intersection, it is therefore needed to investigate the quality of NLOS reception. Before this thesis, there only existed cellular NLOS path loss models for below rooftop base stations, most of them for frequencies of below 2 GHz. A comparison of those models—parameterized to 5.9 GHz—revealed differences of up to 20 dB, questioning their usability in evaluating 5.9 GHz V2V communication.

In consequence, an extensive NLOS measurement campaign was performed at eight intersections in the city of Munich. A systematic selection of measured intersections—based on clustering results from the building placement analysis—enabled a generalization of results as well as the evaluation of influence factors on NLOS reception quality such as inter-building distance or differences between urban and suburban intersections. The measurements revealed that reception rates are at 0.5 or above at application critical distances to intersection center—even in worst-case conditions. In a second step, a NLOS path loss model—called VirtualSource11p—was deduced from the measured reception power values, as well as was NLOS fading characterized. The deduction of the path loss equation via multi-dimensional fitting enabled a reliable quantification of the found influence factors. A comparison to the existing models showed that they differ mostly substantially to the new model and the measurements respectively.

In a last step, the NLOS reception performance under network competition was evaluated. The study is based on packet-level network simulations leveraging the proposed NLOS propagation model. The model was implemented in the ns-2 network simulator. A microscopic traffic simulation (SUMO) was used to find application relevant traffic scenarios, therefore determining relevant network load levels. The simulations revealed that it is possible to use the same high transmission power levels as in the measurements in those situations. While reception rates in NLOS decrease compared to the measurement values due to competition induced packet collisions, the resulting reception rates of 0.3 or higher in the critical phase of intersection approaching seem still tolerable.

Comparison   Based on the individual results, a suitability comparison between IEEE 802.11p ad-hoc and LTE cellular communication showed that while both systems can enable cross-traffic assistance from a technical perspective, ad-hoc communication provides a slight advantage regarding latency and reliability. More importantly however, non-negligible operational costs of a cellular CAM delivery and an eventual need for cellular system updates inherit a considerable cost advantage of ad-hoc communication.

Website   The extensive NLOS reception measurements, cell size analysis as well as simulations comprise a lot of data and intermediate results. A website to this thesis ([10], Appendix A.1) provides an in depth look at the gathered data and results, an interactive graph visualization of the proposed NLOS propagation model, videos of the traffic flow in simulations and similar material. This way, the reader is enabled to gain additional knowledge or review the decision on the presentation of certain plots in this thesis.

Conclusion   In conclusion, this thesis investigates by means of an application with high communication requirements the suitability of ad-hoc and cellular radio technology for V2V communication at intersections. The weakness of 5.9 GHz IEEE 802.11p ad-hoc communication in context of cross-traffic assistance at inner-city intersections is the restricted ability of NLOS reception due to the comparatively high operational frequency. Comprehensive knowledge about inter-vehicle NLOS reception was generated in course of this thesis and transferred into a propagation model for simulations. Network simulations—based on the model—allowed for evaluating NLOS reception quality as to be expected in real situations (under network competition).

Cellular systems are problematic due to the presumable high amount of vehicles per cell and because the information characteristic of CAMs conflicts with the usual point-to-point connection orientation of cellular systems. The thesis analyzes the expectable load and proposes a way of efficient system usage. While capacity is dependent on many variable parameters, the analysis nevertheless shows that LTE is—in contrast to UMTS—technically able to handle the required demand. Also, latency was found to be reasonably low with LTE. However, boundary conditions such as considerable operational costs and standardization needs were identified that complicate using a cellular system for the desired use case.

While the found worst-case reception rates in NLOS are relatively low with 5.9 GHz IEEE 802.11p ad-hoc communication, the technology nevertheless seems to have the edge over cellular systems.

Final Verdict The presented knowledge about the ability of both technologies to handle a high demand application in a difficult communication environment should help to decide on the appropriate technology, or on a meaningful combination of both communication technologies for different use cases.

At the moment, it seems likely that first connected ITS applications (low communication demand ones) will be brought to market via cellular communication. This might strengthen a common question: "What do we need ad-hoc communication for?" This thesis shows that applications based on CAMs will be costly via cellular networks, as well as an ad-hoc network provides on par, if not an advanced connectivity. Therefore, perhaps the question rather should be: "Do we want advanced active safety applications? And if yes, wouldn't it be beneficial to go for ad-hoc communication and think about what other use-cases it will bring us at no operational cost, before we roll out those via cellular networks?"

8.2 Outlook and Implications

Cellular Communication In terms of a cellular V2V communication system this thesis assumed that CAMs issued by a vehicle are reflected back to vehicles located in its surrounding. Vehicles are—just as with ad-hoc communication— enabled to draw a complete environment picture, predict movements of vehicles in the surrounding, and warn the driver in potentially critical situations.

However, this is certainly not the only thinkable approach to enable an active safety application such as the investigated cross-traffic assistance via cellular communication. For example, it is also thinkable to run the applications in a backend and only inform a vehicle in case it enters an unexpected state or a state of potential danger. A benefit might be a reduction of downlink data traffic. Even uplink traffic might be reduced by the backend issuing a CAM transmission frequency reduction in case no potentially dangerous vehicles are in vicinity. However, the data traffic reduction potential for example depends on the size and frequency of occurrence of messages about potential dangers that are issued by applications. Furthermore, a row of other questions arises: Who would operate such a backend, especially considering the involved privacy concerns? Is it possible to reliably process the sheer amount of information and run all the possible applications in parallel for every vehicle? How high are the costs in terms of operating such a backend? The danger information messages need to be standardized. On reception, they need to be translated by the vehicle into appropriate actions. The question arises how complex a functionality verification of the whole distributed process of application processing in the backend, information delivery between vehicle and backend, and

161

in-vehicle translation into an appropriate warning would be considering the active vehicle safety nature of an application such as cross-traffic assistance.

Ad-Hoc Communication   This thesis shows that NLOS reception is in general well feasible in cross-traffic assistance critical distances to intersection center. However, testing was performed with a rather optimal antenna position at vehicle roof center and expensive high quality antenna cables that comprised a loss of only 2.4 dB each. Given the identified rather strong path loss in NLOS, a reception power degradation of only a few dB at both vehicles will considerably degrade the ability of proper NLOS reception in application critical situations. In consequence, a production system needs to be carefully designed to provide a similar antenna gain and/or guarantee a low loss by cables.

The very brief investigation on alternative antenna positions revealed that antenna gain might be degraded by up to 5 dB in the critical driving direction compared to the tested position in case the antenna is mounted at a different position. Such high loss can especially be observed in case the antenna is located at the rear end of the roof, a position currently being common due to aesthetical design reasons. In consequence, given the presented NLOS reception result implications, a proper antenna placement and design will be one of the key challenges for future research. Alternatively, the loss due to long antenna cables could be reduced, or more powerful amplifiers might be used in order to allow for more than the 21–23 dBm maximum output power of most currently available radio hardware. However, using such amplifiers would raise costs and/or inter-channel interference.

In addition to the aforementioned antenna placement and design implications, the requirement of high transmission powers for enabling satisfactory NLOS reception quality leads to implications on channel load control. The current ETSI specification TS 102 687 [115] on load control proposes an open architecture that allows for controlling load on the channel by a number of methods, where message rate and transmission power control are the most important ones. A power control dominated algorithm might strongly reduce the NLOS reception range and in consequence prevent a proper operation of the cross-traffic assistance application. It is highly advisable to consider this fact at the parameterization of the final load control algorithm behavior. For example, it might be wise to transmit at least every second or third CAM with high transmission power despite a stressed channel and reduce the transmission frequency instead.

Conclusion   This brief outlook shows that there exist additional aspects that might be interesting to investigate in terms of cellular communication. And, in terms of ad-hoc communication, the results in this thesis inherit implications onto several parts of an ad-hoc system that should be considered in future research.

A

Appendix

A.1 Thesis Website

As described in Section 1.6, some of the already published parts of this thesis are accompanied by websites. The individual websites are combined into a website accompanying this thesis:

```
http://dsn.tm.kit.edu/download/mangel/thesis/
```

The webpage on this URL puts the existing paper websites into the context of the thesis and links them. The four individual websites and their content are:

- The paper [6] describing the NLOS measurements is accompanied by a website that provides a Google Earth™[92] based visualization of all measurements. A single KML file lets one access individual measurement runs via placemarks at the transmitter locations. For each run, a KML file providing a color-coded visualization of reception rate and power and the xy-plot are linked (compare Figure 6.12 given in the measurement description).
  URL: `http://dsn.tm.kit.edu/download/bmw/nlos_test/`

- The propagation model publications [7; 8] are accompanied by a single website. On the one hand, it provides an interactive visualization (Figure A.1) of the proposed VirtualSource11p path loss formula and the incorporated geometric dimensions as well as some extensions that did not make it into [7] due to space restrictions. On the other hand, it also contains much more detailed information on the measurement results compared to the earlier released measurement paper website. It provides the complete set of plots describing

the measurements. This includes additional plots not present in the papers. For example those ones that allow a high detail look on the measured reception power values over time. Plots from individual measurements or aggregation levels are made accessible via selectors on each varying parameter in the plot set. Most pages let one select two plots side by side in order to enable a comparison of different parameter values. A screenshot of one of those measurement result visualization pages is shown in Figure A.2.
URL: `http://dsn.tm.kit.edu/download/bmw/nlos_model/`

- The website originally accompanying the load simulation paper [9] provides the complete set of plots visualizing reception performance as well as additional plots that show the behavior of the load metrics over time. Furthermore, videos are available that visualize vehicle movement and reception quality at single vehicles in the dynamic scenarios. The video for an individual simulation can be selected by parameter selection lists, just as with plots, as can be seen in Figure A.3. Finally, the files used to set up the simulations are provided in order to allow others to reproduce results for example.
URL: `http://dsn.tm.kit.edu/download/bmw/load_nlos/`

- The paper investigating cellular capacity demand [3] is accompanied by a

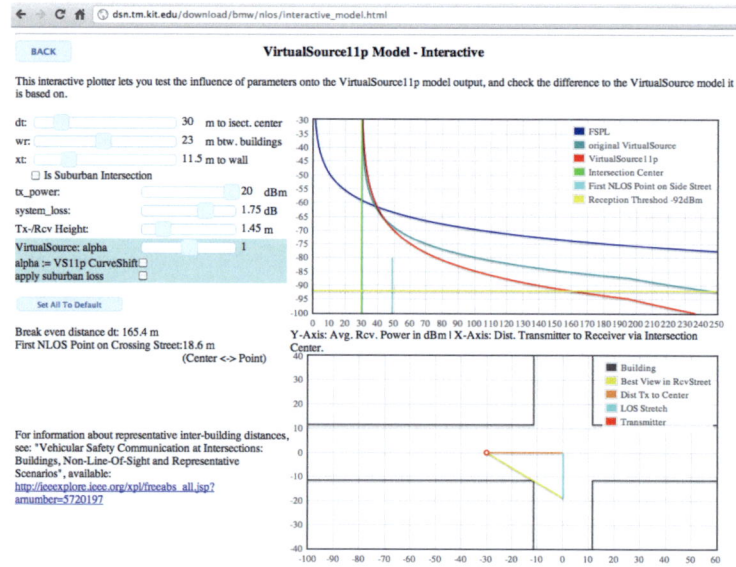

Figure A.1: Screenshot of NLOS propagation model publication [7; 8] website: Interactive visualization of the VirtualSource11p path loss formula and the incorporated geometric dimensions.

website providing a visualization of the Voronoi diagrams [70] that describe the cell approximation of individual network operators. A screenshot showing the KML file based visualization is available in Figure A.4. Furthermore, the complete set of all plots—showing results for each single network operator at a certain technology or antenna configuration—is provided.

`http://dsn.tm.kit.edu/download/bmw/cell_analysis/`

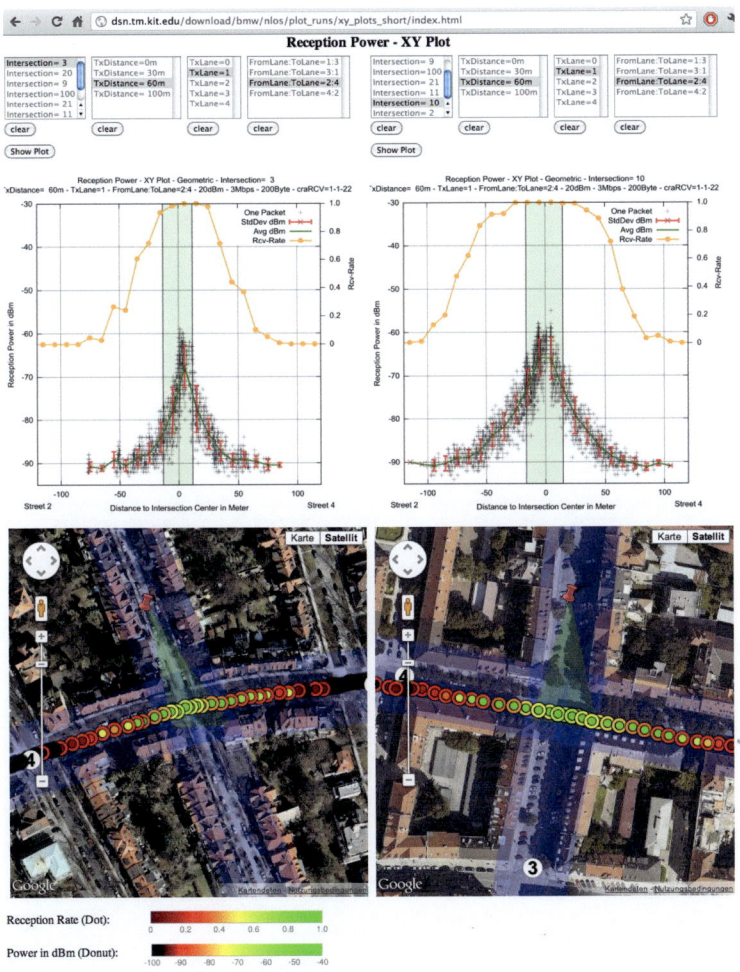

Figure A.2: Screenshot of propagation model publication [7; 8] website: Comparison of two measurement runs. Individual measurements are selectable via a select list for every parameter. For each measurement, the xy-plot as well as a Google Maps™[107] based map-visualization is loaded by hitting the "Show Plot" button.

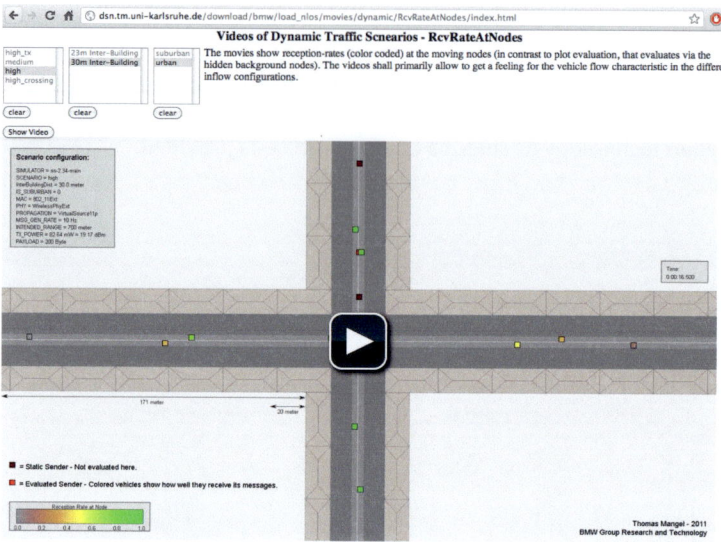

Figure A.3: Screenshot of NLOS reception under competition publication [9] website: Video showing traffic in simulation run with color-coded reception rate. A video showing a particular simulation run can be selected via a select list for each changing parameter in simulation.

Figure A.4: Google Earth™ screenshot of a cellular network approximation via a Voronoi diagram (represented as KML file) as provided on the cellular analysis paper [3] website. Cell sizes in different city regions become obvious.

A.2 Additional Evaluation Aspects

Some aspects were not directly covered in the different evaluation studies, but left to this appendix to assure a focused evaluation in the thesis. Those additional aspects are covered in this section.

A.2.1 Visualization of the Power Value Reporting Gap

The measurement data quality investigation in Section 6.3.1.1 stated that there was a gap in the range of power values reported by the radio. Figure A.5 visualizes this reporting gap and the result of the proposed correction.

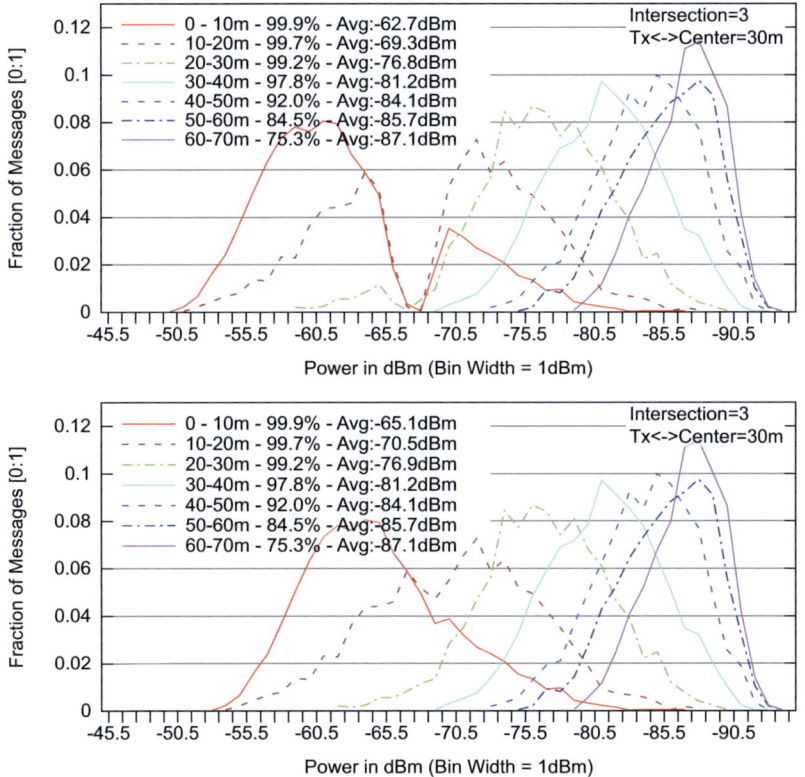

Figure A.5: The plot on top is the not corrected version of the plot in Figure 6.22 (for comparison given on the bottom). The gap becomes obvious. There are almost no values reported by the radio with power values of -69, -68, -67 dBm (this is not due to dropped packets!). The plot in the bottom shows the same data after correcting the issue by subtracting 3 dB from all values reported greater -69 dBm.

A.2.2   Origin of Interference

This section investigates the origin of signals that interfere with an ongoing reception. This investigation was not covered directly in Section 6.4, to keep the focus on the investigated NLOS reception under network competition.

Statistics Generation   In order to investigate the origin of interfering signals, the simulator was modified as follows: In case a signal arrives and another packet is currently decoded, the following is done:

- A destroy event is logged when the new signal destroys the packet (therefore, when it lowers the remaining SINR below the value needed for decoding).
- An interference event is logged in case the new signal would lower the initial SINR value at decoding start (in dB) by more than 10 %.

An example on the computation of the SINR margin reduction is given in Table A.1. For each of the additionally logged events, the position of the transmitter of the interfering signal is logged.

For all messages received in a certain region and originating from the three static transmitters, a statistic is generated (separate for each static transmitter). The regions are ± 20 m around center and 20–60 m into each side street. The statistic separates between the interfering signals originating from the street in LOS or NLOS to the transmitter of the decoded message. The evaluated regions are visualized in Figure A.6.

Two different kinds of statistics were generated: One shows the distribution of the origin of signals that destroy messages, the other of signals that interfere or destroy. The second one turns out a bit more stable, as it includes more events.

Signal Power	Interference Noise Level	SINR	Description
-60 dBm = 10^{-6} mW	-80 dBm = 10^{-8} mW	20 dB	Currently decoded packet – at decoding start
-70 dBm = 10^{-7} mW	-69.6 dBm = $1.1 * 10^{-7}$ mW	10.4 dB	Interfering packet – initial packet still decodable ($10.4 > 8$)
	(new interference noise level: old level + new signal)		Interfering packet cuts $9.6/20 = 48$ % of initial SINR margin

Table A.1: Example of SINR margin reduction by a newly arriving packet. An initial interference noise level of -80 dBm is assumed. The first packet has a signal strength of -60 dBm, the second of -70 dBm. The new packet reduces the SINR margin by 48 %.

Evaluation   It was found in Section 6.4.3.1 that reception rates in the intersection center—a region in LOS to both streets—drop by 0.2–0.3 rate points. While the competition is on a high level in the center (and much higher as in one side street), the drop is nevertheless probably stronger than expected.

Figure A.7 shows the spatial distribution of interference origin for all packets received in ±20 m to intersection center and in case the $tx \leftrightarrow center$ distance is 100 m. Both plots show the static scenario with a 4 Hz message transmission rate at the background nodes. Figure A.7(a) shows the distribution for interfering and destroying signals, while Figure A.7(b) only covers the destroying ones. Color-coding of LOS and NLOS street is same as in Figure A.6.

First of all, it is obvious that the interfering signals originate in almost 100 % of all cases from the NLOS street. This proves the assumption that the strong drop in power in the crossing street (due to NLOS) will provoke collisions: the nodes in the crossing street (west–east) assume that the channel is free, as they do not sense the transmission originating from the north street leg. When they transmit, assuming the channel is free, their signals will destroy ongoing receptions in the intersection center (a region in LOS to the initial transmitter).

While the position of interfering components is distributed over the whole NLOS street, destroying signals originate more likely from regions close to the center. This is not surprising, as the initial signal being decoded in the center is strong (only 100 m from transmitter to receiver) and an interfering signal needs to be relatively strong to destroy such an ongoing reception. Therefore, the distance to center must not be too high.

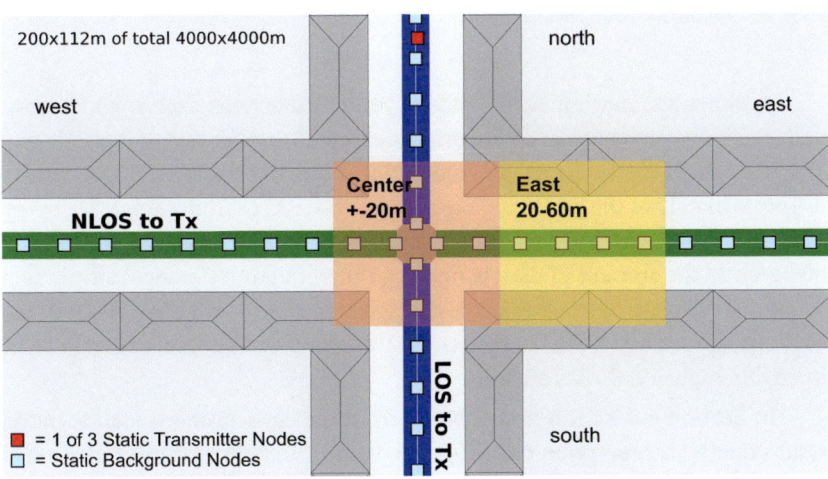

Figure A.6: Evaluation regions visualization.

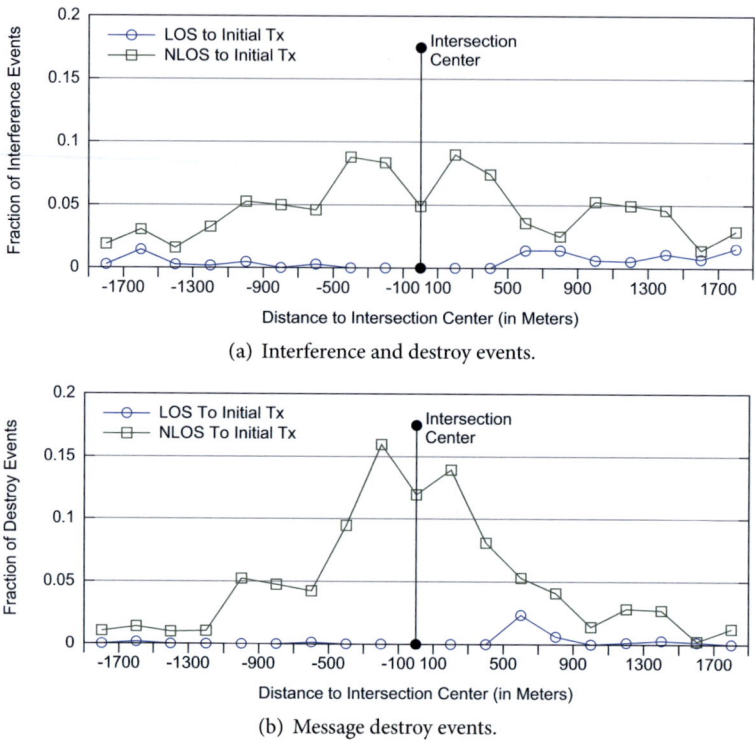

(a) Interference and destroy events.

(b) Message destroy events.

Figure A.7: Origin of interfering messages for receptions in intersection center (± 20 m to center) – 23 m inter building distance, urban, 100 m $tx \leftrightarrow center$ distance, 4 Hz background node message rate.

Another assumption is unfortunately not visible here: One would assume that interfering components do not originate from the center region (both streets). There is a slight dip in the center -100 to 100 m bin, but the value is not close to 0. This is mainly as the NLOS region starts at about 25 m from center. Therefore, the center bin covers 75 % NLOS regions. Using smaller bins was problematic however, as the amount of destructions and therefore interference information is not high enough to provide stable enough statistics in that case. As trace-file sizes already reached 7 GB, the simulation time of 60 s was not increased in order to enable higher statistics stability.

In Section 6.4.3.2.1, it is concluded from the asynchronous load scenario results that NLOS reception rate dropping due to interference is most dependent on the network load in the NLOS receiver street canyon. Figure A.8 reveals that the given explanation, being that interfering signals must be strong and will therefore

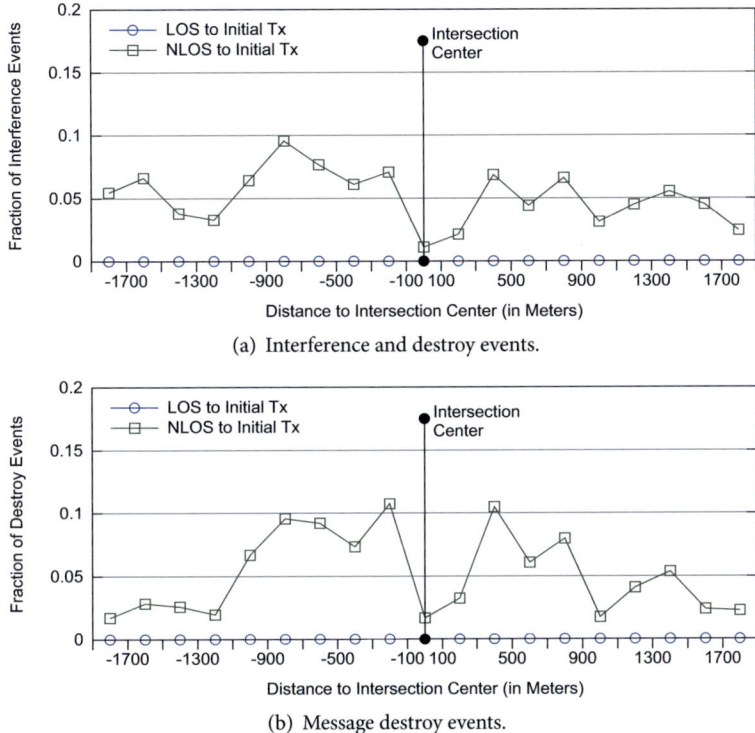

(a) Interference and destroy events.

(b) Message destroy events.

Figure A.8: Origin of interfering messages for receptions on street stretch 20–60 m east – 23 m inter building distance, urban, 50 m *tx↔center* distance, 4 Hz background node message rate.

originate more likely from the same street canyon as the receiver, is likely correct. The two plots show the same information as in Figure A.7, but for receptions in the 20–60 m east street stretch (which is mostly in NLOS) and a *tx↔center* distance of 50 m (having a higher drop due to interference in NLOS compared to the 100 m *tx↔center* configuration).

The plots reveal that for NLOS receptions, interfering signals originate almost completely from the street canyon the NLOS receiver is placed in. In consequence, if load is high there, NLOS reception rates will suffer most, as it could be seen in the "high-crossing" scenario results in Section 6.4.3.2. The plots prove the explanation from Section 6.4.3.2. It is extremely unlikely that a node inside the same street canyon as the evaluated transmitter (in LOS) falsely assumes the channel is free and the power of its transmission is high enough in NLOS to destroy the ongoing NLOS reception.

Bibliography

[1] IEEE Computer Society, "IEEE Std 802.11p-2010: Telecommunications and information exchange between systems - Local and metropolitan area networks - Specific requirements - Part 11: Wireless LAN MAC and PHY Specifications - Amendment 6: Wireless Access in Vehicular Environments," pp. 1–35, 2010. [Online]. Available: http://standards.ieee.org/getieee802/download/802.11p-2010.pdf

[2] CoCar Consortium, "CoCar Feasibility Study: Technology, Business and Dissemination," Public Report, pp. 1–79, 2009. [Online]. Available: http://www.aktiv-online.org/deutsch/Downloads/2009-05-14%20CoCar%20Milestone/CoCar_D04%20public.pdf

[3] T. Mangel and H. Hartenstein, "An Analysis of Data Traffic in Cellular Networks Caused by Inter-Vehicle Communication at Intersections," in *2011 IEEE Intelligent Vehicles Symposium (IV'11)*, Baden-Baden, Germany, Jun. 2011, pp. 473–478. [Online]. Available: http://dx.doi.org/10.1109/IVS.2011.5940495

[4] T. Mangel, T. Kosch, and H. Hartenstein, "A Comparison of UMTS and LTE for Vehicular Safety Communication at Intersections," in *2nd IEEE Vehicular Networking Conference (VNC 2010)*, Jersey City, NJ, USA, Dec. 2010, pp. 293–300. [Online]. Available: http://dx.doi.org/10.1109/VNC.2010.5698244

[5] T. Mangel, F. Schweizer, T. Kosch, and H. Hartenstein, "Vehicular Safety Communication at Intersections: Buildings, Non-Line-Of-Sight and Representative Scenarios," in *8th Int. Conference on Wireless On-Demand Network Systems and Services (WONS 2011)*, Bardonecchia, Italy, Jan. 2011, pp. 35–41. [Online]. Available: http://dx.doi.org/10.1109/WONS.2011.5720197

[6] T. Mangel, M. Michl, O. Klemp, and H. Hartenstein, "Real-World Measurements of Non-Line-Of-Sight Reception Quality for 5.9GHz IEEE 802.11p at Intersections," in *Communication Technologies for Vehicles, (from 3rd Int. Workshop on Comm. Technologies for Vehicles (Nets4Cars 2011))*, ser. Lecture Notes in Computer Science, vol. 6596. Springer

Berlin / Heidelberg, Mar. 2011, pp. 189–202. [Online]. Available: http://dx.doi.org/10.1007/978-3-642-19786-4_17

[7] T. Mangel, O. Klemp, and H. Hartenstein, "A Validated 5.9 GHz Non-Line-Of-Sight Path-Loss and Fading Model for Inter-Vehicle Communication," in *11th Int. Conference on ITS Telecommunications (ITST 2011)*, Saint-Pertersburg, Russia, Aug. 2011, pp. 75–80. [Online]. Available: http://dx.doi.org/10.1109/ITST.2011.6060156

[8] T. Mangel, O. Klemp, and H. Hartenstein, "5.9 GHz inter-vehicle communication at intersections: a validated non-line-of-sight path-loss and fading model," *EURASIP Journal on Wireless Communications and Networking*, vol. 2011, no. 1, pp. 182–193, Nov. 2011. [Online]. Available: http://dx.doi.org/10.1186/1687-1499-2011-182

[9] T. Mangel and H. Hartenstein, "5.9GHz IEEE 802.11p Inter-Vehicle Communication: Non-Line-Of-Sight Reception Under Competition," in *3rd IEEE Vehicular Networking Conference (VNC 2011)*, Amsterdam, Netherlands, Nov. 2011, pp. 155–162. [Online]. Available: http://dx.doi.org/10.1109/VNC.2011.6117137

[10] T. Mangel. (2012) Thesis Website – Inter-Vehicle Communication at Intersections: An Evaluation of Ad-Hoc and Cellular Communication. URL: http://dsn.tm.kit.edu/download/mangel/thesis/

[11] T. Mangel, "A Piggyback-based Feedback Protocol for Vehicular Safety Broadcast Communications," Master Thesis, RWTH Aachen, pp. 1–146, 2008.

[12] H. Kawashima, "Japanese perspective of driver information systems," *TRANSPORTATION*, vol. 17, no. 3, pp. 263–284, Sep. 1990. [Online]. Available: http://dx.doi.org/10.1007/BF02127039

[13] Federal Communications Commission (FCC), "FCC 99-305: Amendment of Parts 2 and 90 of the Commission's Rules to Allocate the 5.850-5.925 GHz Band to the Mobile Service for Dedicated Short Range Communications of Intelligent Transportation Services," pp. 1–14, 1999. [Online]. Available: http://hraunfoss.fcc.gov/edocs_public/attachmatch/FCC-99-305A1.pdf

[14] H. Hartenstein and K. Laberteaux, *VANET: Vehicular Applications and Inter-Networking Technologies.* John Wiley & Sons, Ltd, 2010. [Online]. Available: http://dx.doi.org/10.1002/9780470740637

[15] K. Takagi, K. Morikawa, T. Ogawa, and M. Saburi, "Road Environment Recognition Using On-vehicle LIDAR," in *2006 IEEE Intelligent Vehicles Symposium (IV 2006)*, Tokyo, Japan, Jun. 2006, pp. 120–125. [Online]. Available: http://dx.doi.org/10.1109/IVS.2006.1689615

[16] COMeSafety, "D31 v3.0 – European ITS Communication Architecture: Overall Framework, Proof of Concept Implementation," Project Deliverable, pp. 1–198, 2010.

[17] COMeSafety, "D31 v2.0 – European ITS Communication Architecture: Overall Framework, Proof of Concept Implementation," Project Deliverable, pp. 1–165, 2009. [Online]. Available: http://comesafety.org/uploads/media/COMeSafety_DEL_D31_EuropeanITSCommunicationArchitecture_v2.0.pdf

[18] D. Jiang, V. Taliwal, A. Meier, W. Holfelder, and R. Herrtwich, "Design of 5.9GHz DSRC-based Vehicular Safety Communication," *IEEE Wireless Communications*, vol. 13, no. 5, pp. 36 – 43, Oct. 2006. [Online]. Available: http://dx.doi.org/10.1109/WC-M.2006.250356

[19] ETSI, "TR 102 638 V1.1.1 – Intelligent Transport Systems (ITS); Vehicular Communications; Basic Set of Applications; Definitions," pp. 1–81, 2009. [Online]. Available: http://www.etsi.org/deliver/etsi_tr/102600_102699/102638/01.01.01_60/tr_102638v010101p.pdf

[20] F. Klanner, "Entwicklung eines kommunikationsbasierten Querverkehrsassistenten im Fahrzeug," *Fortschritt-Berichte VDI: Reihe 12 - Verkehrstechnik / Fahrzeugtechnik*, vol. 685, pp. 1–172, 2008.

[21] G. Nitz and F. Klanner, "Evaluation Of Advanced Driver Assistance Systems For Supportive Brake Application," in *Proceedings of FISITA 2008 World Automotive Congress*, Munich, Germany, Sep. 2008, pp. 1–7. [Online]. Available: http://www.atzonline.com/index.php;do=show/site=a4e/alloc=3/id=7924

[22] ELECTRONIC COMMUNICATIONS COMMITTEE, "ECC/DEC/(08)01 - ECC Decision of 14 March 2008 on the harmonised use of the 5875-5925 MHz frequency band for Intelligent Transport Systems (ITS)," pp. 1–5, 2008. [Online]. Available: http://www.erodocdb.dk/Docs/doc98/official/pdf/ECCDEC0801.PDF

[23] T. Strang, "Lecture Intelligent Transportation Systems (ITS) SS 2010 – Wireless Access for Vehicular Environments (WAVE),"

Lecture Slides, STI Insbruck, pp. 1–42, 2009. [Online]. Available: http://www.sti-innsbruck.at/sites/default/files/courses/fileadmin/documents/its-ss10/07-its-WAVE.pdf [Accessed: 2011/10/06]

[24] ETSI, "EN 302 571 V1.1.1 – Intelligent Transport Systems (ITS); Radiocommunications equipment operating in the 5 855 MHz to 5 925 MHz frequency band; Harmonized EN covering the essential requirements of article 3.2 of the R&TTE Directive," pp. 1–41, 2008. [Online]. Available: http://www.etsi.org/deliver/etsi_en/302500_302599/302571/01.01.01_60/en_302571v010101p.pdf

[25] ETSI, "ES 202 663 V1.1.0 – Final Draft – Intelligent Transport Systems (ITS); European profile standard for the physical and medium access control layer of Intelligent Transport Systems operating in the 5 GHz frequency band," pp. 1–27, 2009. [Online]. Available: http://www.etsi.org/deliver/etsi_es/202600_202699/202663/01.01.00_50/es_202663v010100m.pdf

[26] D. Jiang, Q. Chen, and L. Delgrossi, "Optimal Data Rate Selection for Vehicle Safety Communications," in *5th ACM Int. Workshop on VehiculAr Inter-NETworking (VANET 2008)*, San Francisco, USA, Sep. 2008, pp. 30–38. [Online]. Available: http://dx.doi.org/10.1145/1410043.1410050

[27] IEEE Computer Society, "IEEE Std 802.11-2007: Telecommunications and information exchange between systems - Local and metropolitan area networks - Specific requirements - Part 11: Wireless LAN Medium Access Control (MAC) and Physical Layer (PHY) Specifications," pp. 1–1184, 2007. [Online]. Available: http://standards.ieee.org/getieee802/download/802.11-2007.pdf

[28] sim^{TD} Konsortium. sim^{TD} – Sichere Intelligente Mobilität Testfeld Deutschland. URL: http://www.simtd.de/ [Accessed: 2012/03/27]

[29] A. Tsertou and D. I. Laurenson, "Revisiting the Hidden Terminal Problem in a CSMA/CA Wireless Network," *IEEE Transactions on Mobile Computing*, vol. 7, no. 7, pp. 817–831, 2008. [Online]. Available: http://dx.doi.org/10.1109/TMC.2007.70757

[30] NS-2. The Network Simulator - ns-2. URL: http://www.isi.edu/nsnam/ns/ [Accessed: 2011/09/13]

[31] Q. Chen, F. Schmidt-Eisenlohr, D. Jiang, M. Torrent-Moreno, L. Delgrossi, and H. Hartenstein, "Overhaul of IEEE 802.11 Modeling and Simulation in NS-2," in *10th ACM Symposium on Modeling, Analysis, and Simulation of Wireless and Mobile Systems (MSWiM 2007)*, Chania, Greece, Oct. 2007, pp. 159–168. [Online]. Available: http://dx.doi.org/10.1145/1298126.1298155

[32] A. Kochut, A. Vasan, U. Shankar, and A. Agrawala, "Sniffing out the Correct Physical Layer Capture Model in 802.11b," in *12th IEEE Int. Conference on Network Protocols (ICNP 2004)*, Berlin, Germany, Oct. 2004, pp. 252 – 261. [Online]. Available: http://dx.doi.org/10.1109/ICNP.2004.1348115

[33] H. Friis, "A Note on a Simple Transmission Formula," *Proceedings of the IRE*, vol. 34, no. 5, pp. 254 – 256, 1946.

[34] T. S. Rappaport, *Wireless Communications: Principles and Practice*, 2nd ed. Prentice-Hall of India, 2002.

[35] M. Nakagami, "The m-distribution—A general formula of intensity distribution of rapid fading," in *Statistical Methods in Radio Wave Propagation*. Permagon Press, 1960, pp. 3–36.

[36] M. A. Taneda, J.-i. Takada, and K. Araki, "The Problem of the Fading Model Selection," *IEICE Transactions on Communications*, vol. E84-B, no. 3, pp. 660–666, Mar. 2001. [Online]. Available: http://ci.nii.ac.jp/naid/110003218997/en/

[37] V. Taliwal, D. Jiang, H. Mangold, C. Chen, and R. Sengupta, "Empirical determination of channel characteristics for DSRC vehicle-to-vehicle communication," in *First ACM workshop on Vehicular ad hoc networks - VANET '04*, New York, New York, USA, 2004, p. 88. [Online]. Available: http://doi.acm.org/10.1145/1023875.1023890

[38] J. Yin, G. Holland, T. Elbatt, F. Bai, and H. Krishnan, "DSRC Channel Fading Analysis from Empirical Measurement," in *1st Int. Conference on Communications and Networking in China (ChinaCom 2006)*, Beijing, China, Oct. 2006, pp. 1–5. [Online]. Available: http://dx.doi.org/10.1109/CHINACOM.2006.344919

[39] L. Cheng, B. Henty, D. Stancil, F. Bai, and P. Mudalige, "Mobile Vehicle-to-Vehicle Narrow-Band Channel Measurement and Characterization of the 5.9 GHz Dedicated Short Range Communication (DSRC) Frequency Band," *IEEE Journal on Selected Areas in Communications*, vol. 25, no. 8, pp. 1501–1516, 2007. [Online]. Available: http://dx.doi.org/10.1109/JSAC.2007.071002

[40] F. Schmidt-Eisenlohr, *Interference in Vehicle-to-Vehicle Communication Networks: Analysis, Modeling, Simulation and Assessment.* KIT Scientific Publishing, 2010. [Online]. Available: http://dx.doi.org/10.5445/KSP/1000019872

[41] ITU-R, "RECOMMENDATION ITU-R P.1238-2: Propagation data and prediction methods for the planning of indoor radiocommunication systems

and radio local area networks in the frequency range 900 MHz to 100 GHz - ANNEX 1 Propagation impairments and measures of quality," Tech. Rep., pp. 1–15, 2001. [Online]. Available: http://www.itu.int/rec/R-REC-P.1238/en

[42] WINNER – WIRELESS WORLD INITIATIVE NEW RADIO, "D1.1.2 V1.2 – WINNER II Channel Models – Part 1 Channel Models," Project Deliverable, pp. 1–82, 2008. [Online]. Available: http://www.ist-winner.org/WINNER2-Deliverables/D1.1.2.zip

[43] ITU-R, "Recommendation ITU-R P.1411-5: Propagation data and prediction methods for the planning of short-range outdoor radio communication systems and radio local area networks in the frequency range 300MHz to 100 GHz," Tech. Rep., pp. 1–28, 2009. [Online]. Available: http://www.itu.int/rec/R-REC-P.1411/en

[44] V. Erceg, S. Ghassemzadeh, M. Taylor, L. Dong, and D. L. Schilling, "Urban/Suburban Out-of-Sight Propagation Modeling," IEEE Communications Magazine, vol. 30, no. 6, pp. 56–61, Jun. 1992.

[45] H. M. El-Sallabi, "Fast Path Loss Prediction by Using Virtual Source Technique for Urban Microcells," in 51th IEEE Vehicular Technology Conference (VTC2000-Spring), Tokyo, Japan, May 2000, pp. 2183 – 2187. [Online]. Available: http://dx.doi.org/10.1109/VETECS.2000.851659

[46] Q. Sun, S. Tan, and K. Teh, "Analytical Formulae for Path Loss Prediction in Urban Street Grid Microcellular Environments," IEEE Transactions on Vehicular Technology, vol. 54, no. 4, pp. 1251–1258, 2005. [Online]. Available: http://dx.doi.org/10.1109/TVT.2005.851298

[47] L. Denegri, L. Bixio, F. Lavagetto, A. Iscra, and C. Braccini, "An Analytical Model of Microcellular Propagation in Urban Canyons," in 65th IEEE Vehicular Technology Conference (VTC2007-Spring), Dublin, Ireland, Apr. 2007, pp. 402–406. [Online]. Available: http://dx.doi.org/10.1109/VETECS.2007.94

[48] S. Sai, E. Niwa, K. Mase, M. Nishibori, J. Inoue, M. Obuchi, T. Harada, H. Ito, K. Mizutani, and M. Kizu, "Field Evaluation of UHF Radio Propagation for an ITS Safety System in an Urban Environment," IEEE Communications Magazine, vol. 47, no. 11, pp. 120–127, Nov. 2009. [Online]. Available: http://dx.doi.org/10.1109/MCOM.2009.5307475

[49] M. Sepulcre and J. Gozalvez, "Wireless Vehicular Adaptive Radio Resource Management Policies in Congested Channels," in 4th IEEE Int. Symposium on Wireless Communication Systems (ISWCS 2007), Trondheim, Norway, Oct.

2007, pp. 380–384. [Online]. Available: http://dx.doi.org/10.1109/ISWCS.2007. 4392366

[50] J. Gozalvez and M. Sepulcre, "Channel Efficiency of Adaptive Transmission Techniques for Wireless Vehicular Communications," in *15th World Congress on Intelligent Transportation Systems*, New York, USA, Nov. 2008, pp. 1–12. [Online]. Available: http://trid.trb.org/view.aspx?id=898716

[51] B. Bovée, M. Nekoui, H. Pishro-Nik, and R. Tessier, "Evaluation of the Universal Geocast Scheme For VANETs," in *74th IEEE Vehicular Technology Conference (VTC2011-Fall)*, San Francisco, USA, Sep. 2011, pp. 1–5. [Online]. Available: http://dx.doi.org/10.1109/VETECF.2011.6092851

[52] B. Tiwari, "Enabling reuse 1 in 4G Networks," http://www.beyond4g.org, Tech. Rep., pp. 1–5, 2010. [Online]. Available: http://www.beyond4g.org/wp-content/ uploads/2010/07/Enabling-reuse-1-in-4G-Networksv0.1.pdf [Accessed: 2011/12/08]

[53] S. Hussain, "Dynamic Radio Resource Management in 3GPP LTE," Master Thesis, Blekinge Tekniska Högskola, pp. 1–58, 2009.

[54] J. D. Parsons, *The Mobile Radio Propagation Channel*, 2nd ed. John Wiley & Sons, Ltd, 2000. [Online]. Available: http://eu.wiley.com/WileyCDA/ WileyTitle/productCd-047198857X.html

[55] C. Johnson, *Radio Access Networks for UMTS: Principles and Practice*. John Wiley & Sons, Ltd, 2008. [Online]. Available: http://dx.doi.org/10.1002/ 9780470727225

[56] C. Serrano, B. Garriga, J. Velasco, J. Urbano, S. Tenorio, and M. Sierra, "Latency in Broad-Band Mobile Networks," in *69th IEEE Vehicular Technology Conference (VTC2009-Spring)*, Barcelona, Spain, Apr. 2009, pp. 1–7. [Online]. Available: http://dx.doi.org/10.1109/VETECS.2009.5073642

[57] S. Mohan, R. Kapoor, and B. Mohanty, "Latency in HSPA Data Networks," Qualcomm, Tech. Rep., pp. 1–18, 2011. [Online]. Available: http://www. qualcomm.com/documents/files/latency-in-hspa-data-networks.pdf [Accessed: 2011/12/08]

[58] S. Sesia, I. Toufik, and M. Baker, *LTE, The UMTS Long Term Evolution: From Theory to Practice*, 1st ed. John Wiley & Sons, Ltd, 2009. [Online]. Available: http://dx.doi.org/10.1002/9780470978504

[59] XIXIA, "SC-FDMA – Single Carrier FDMA in LTE," Tech. Rep., pp. 1–16, 2009. [Online]. Available: http://www.ixiacom.com/pdfs/library/white_papers/SC-FDMA-INDD.pdf [Accessed: 2011/10/24]

[60] Motorola, "Real-World LTE Performance for Public Safety - Relating Technical Capabilities to User Experience," White Paper, pp. 1–10, 2009. [Online]. Available: http://www.motorola.com/web/Business/Solutions/Industry%20Solutions/Government/Public%20Service/_Documents/Static%20Files/Real%20World%20LTE%20Performance%20for%20Public%20Safety%20FINAL.pdf [Accessed: 2011/12/12]

[61] Real Wireless Ltd, "4G Capacity Gains," Tech. Rep., pp. 1–120, 2011. [Online]. Available: http://stakeholders.ofcom.org.uk/binaries/research/technology-research/2011/4g/4GCapacityGainsFinalReport.pdf [Accessed: 2012/01/19]

[62] C. E. Shannon, "A mathematical theory of communication," *The Bell System Technical Journal*, vol. 27, pp. 379–423 and 623–656, Jul. 1948.

[63] C. E. Shannon, "Communication in the Presence of Noise," *Proceedings of the Institute of Radio Engineers*, vol. 37, no. 1, p. 10, 1949.

[64] SEACORN (a European Commission 5th framework project). EURANE – Enhanced UMTS Radio Access Network Extension for ns-2. URL: http://eurane.ti-wmc.nl/eurane/ [Accessed: 2011/11/23]

[65] M. Mages, "Top-Down-Funktionsentwicklung eines Einbiege- und Kreuzenassistenten," *Fortschritt-Berichte VDI: Reihe 12 - Verkehrstechnik / Fahrzeugtechnik*, vol. 694, pp. 1–155, 2009.

[66] M. Bshara, R. Verschraegen, and L. V. Biesen, "Cell-ID Positioning in WiMAX Networks Analysis of the Clearwire Network in Belgium," in *2009 ICT Mobile and Wireless Communications Summit (ICT-MobileSummit 2009)*, Santander, Spain, Jun. 2009. [Online]. Available: http://wwwtw.vub.ac.be/elec/Papers%20on%20web/Papers/Mussa/ICTMobileSummit09_Paper_ref_56_doc_2219.pdf

[67] J. Markendahl and O. Makitalo, "A comparative study of deployment options, capacity and cost structure for macrocellular and femtocell networks," in *21st Annual IEEE Int. Symposium on Personal, Indoor and Mobile Radio Communications Workshops (PIMRC 2010)*, Istanbul, Turkey, Sep. 2010, pp. 145–150. [Online]. Available: http://dx.doi.org/10.1109/PIMRCW.2010.5670351

[68] A. Baier and K. Bandelow, "Traffic engineering and realistic network capacity in cellular radio networks with inhomogeneous traffic distribution," in *47th IEEE Vehicular Technology Conference (VTC'97)*, Phoenix, AZ, USA, May 1997, pp. 780–784. [Online]. Available: http://dx.doi.org/10.1109/VETEC.1997.600435

[69] Johannes Dölfel, "Development and Evaluation of a UMTS-based Architecture for Vehicular Local Danger Warning," Diploma Thesis, Würzburg University, pp. 1–104, 2007.

[70] F. Aurenhammer, "Voronoi Diagrams – A Survey of a Fundamental Geometric Data Structure," *ACM Computing Surveys*, vol. 23, no. 3, pp. 1–61, 1991. [Online]. Available: http://dx.doi.org/10.1145/116873.116880

[71] M. Chuah, Q. Zhang, and O. Yue, "Access Priority Schemes in UMTS MAC," in *1999 IEEE Wireless Communications and Networking Conference (WCNC 1999)*, New Orleans, USA, Sep. 1999, pp. 781–786. [Online]. Available: http://dx.doi.org/10.1109/WCNC.1999.796757

[72] S. Srivastava and S. Kar, "Analysis of UMTS radio channel access delay," *Computer Communications*, vol. 31, no. 10, pp. 1877–1889, Jun. 2008. [Online]. Available: http://dx.doi.org/10.1016/j.comcom.2007.12.017

[73] R. D. Soares and J. M. C. Brito, "Throughput Analysis of Random Access Channel of the UMTS system," in *2006 Int. Conference on Wireless and Mobile Communications (ICWMC 2006)*, Bucharest, Romania, Jul. 2006, pp. 1–6. [Online]. Available: http://dx.doi.org/10.1109/ICWMC.2006.89

[74] E. Uhlemann and N. Nygren, "Cooperative Systems for Traffic Safety: Will Existing Wireless Access Technologies Meet the Communication Requirements?" in *16th World Congress on Intelligent Transport Systems*, Stockholm, Sweden, Sep. 2009, pp. 1–8. [Online]. Available: http://trid.trb.org/view.aspx?id=906491

[75] S. Sories, J. Huschke, and M.-A. Phan, "Delay Performance of Vehicle Safety Applications in UMTS," in *15th World Congress on Intelligent Transport Systems*, New York, USA, Nov. 2008, pp. 1–12. [Online]. Available: http://trid.trb.org/view.aspx?id=900281

[76] C. Sommer, A. Schmidt, R. German, W. Koch, and F. Dressler, "Simulative Evaluation of a UMTS-based Car-to-Infrastructure Traffic Information System," in *IEEE Global Telecommunications Conference (GLOBECOM 2008), 3rd*

IEEE Workshop on Automotive Networking and Applications (AutoNet 2008), New Orleans, USA, Dec. 2008, pp. 1–8.

[77] CoCarX, "Deliverable D3 – ITS Services and Communication Architecture," Project Deliverable, pp. 1–90, 2011.

[78] D. Valerio, F. Ricciato, P. Belanovic, and T. Zemen, "UMTS on the Road: Broadcasting Intelligent Road Safety Information via MBMS," in *IEEE 67th Vehicular Technology Conference (VTC2008-Spring)*, Singapore, May 2008, pp. 3026–3030. [Online]. Available: http://dx.doi.org/10.1109/VETECS.2008.325

[79] C. Wewetzer, M. Caliskan, K. Meier, and A. Luebke, "Experimental Evaluation of UMTS and Wireless LAN for Inter-Vehicle Communication," in *7th Int. Conference on ITS Telecommunications (ITST 2007)*, Sophia Antipolis, France, Jun. 2007, pp. 1–6. [Online]. Available: http://dx.doi.org/10.1109/ITST.2007.4295880

[80] Teleplan GLOBE, "ASTRIX 5 – Radio Planning Tools," White Paper. [Online]. Available: http://www.teleplanglobe.com/uploads/Whitepapers/Astrix_whitepaper.pdf [Accessed: 2011/11/23]

[81] Contract Telecommunication Engineering, "Pathloss (4.0)." [Online]. Available: http://www.pathloss.com/ [Accessed: 2011/11/23]

[82] R. Miucic and T. Schaffnit, "Communication in Future Vehicle Cooperative Safety Systems: 5.9 GHz DSRC Non-Line-of-Sight Field Testing," *SAE International Journal of Passenger Cars- Electronic and Electrical Systems*, vol. 2, no. 1, pp. 56–61, 2009. [Online]. Available: http://saepcelec.saejournals.org/content/2/1/56.short

[83] E. Giordano, R. Frank, G. Pau, and M. Gerla, "CORNER: a Realistic Urban Propagation Model for VANET," in *7th Int. Conferenece on Wireless On-demand Network Systems and Services (WONS 2010)*, Kranjska Gora, Slovenia, Feb. 2010, pp. 57 – 60. [Online]. Available: http://dx.doi.org/10.1109/WONS.2010.5437133

[84] iTETRIS – An Integrated Wireless and Traffic Platform for Real-Time Road Traffic Management Solutions, "D4.1 – V2V Wireless Communications Modeling," Project Deliverable, 2009.

[85] J. Karedal, F. Tufvesson, T. Abbas, O. Klemp, A. Paier, L. Bernado, and A. F. Molisch, "Radio Channel Measurements at Street Intersections for Vehicle-to-Vehicle Safety Applications," in *71st IEEE Vehicular Technology*

Conference (VTC 2010-Spring), Taipei, Taiwan, May 2010, pp. 1–5. [Online]. Available: http://dx.doi.org/10.1109/VETECS.2010.5493955

[86] C. Sommer, D. Eckhoff, R. German, and F. Dressler, "A Computationally Inexpensive Empirical Model of IEEE 802.11p Radio Shadowing in Urban Environments," in *8th Int. Conference on Wireless On-Demand Network Systems and Services (WONS 2011)*, Bardonecchia, Italy, Feb. 2011, pp. 84–90. [Online]. Available: http://dx.doi.org/10.1109/WONS.2011.5720204

[87] M. Schack, J. Nuckelt, R. Geise, L. Thiele, and T. Kurner, "Comparison of Path Loss Measurements and Predictions at Urban Crossroads for C2C Communications," in *5th European Conference on Antennas and Propagation (EuCAP 2011)*, Rome, Italy, Apr. 2011, pp. 2896–2900. [Online]. Available: http://ieeexplore.ieee.org/xpls/abs_all.jsp?arnumber=5782121

[88] H. Suzuki, H. Murata, and K. Araki, "Performance of Inter-vehicle Communication Technique for Intersection Collision Warning," in *5th Int. Conference on Information, Communications and Signal Processing (ICICS 2005)*, Bangkok, Thailand, Dec. 2005, pp. 603–606. [Online]. Available: http://dx.doi.org/10.1109/ICICS.2005.1689118

[89] D. Krajzewicz, M. Bonert, and P. Wagner, "The Open Source Traffic Simulation Package SUMO," in *RoboCup 2006 Infrastructure Simulation Competition*, Bremen, Germany, Jun. 2006, pp. 1–5. [Online]. Available: http://elib.dlr.de/46740/

[90] Landeshauptstadt München. (2011) Mobilfunkstationen in Betrieb. URL: http://maps.muenchen.de/rgu/mobilfunkstationen [Accessed: 2011/11/24]

[91] DDS Digital Data Services GmbH, "FAW-FREQUENZATLAS 5.0," 2009. [Online]. Available: http://www.ddsgeo.de/produkte/faw-frequenzatlas.html [Accessed: 2011/06/02]

[92] Google Inc., "Google Earth 6.0," 2011. [Online]. Available: http://earth.google.com [Accessed: 2012/03/22]

[93] sim^{TD} Konsortium, "Deliverable D21.4 – Spezifikation der Kommunikationsprotokolle," Project Deliverable, pp. 1–144, 2009. [Online]. Available: http://www.simtd.de/dyn/mediaout.dhtml/-/server/news/publications/news/200912_D214/D214/@teaser_long/@s4/simTD-Deliverable-D21.4_Spezifikation_Kommunikationsprotokolle.pdf

[94] ETSI, "TS 102 637-2 V1.2.1 – Intelligent Transport Systems (ITS); Vehicular Communications; Basic Set of Applications; Part 2: Specification of Cooperative Awareness Basic Service," pp. 1–18, 2011. [Online]. Available: http://www.etsi.org/deliver/etsi_ts/102600_102699/10263702/01.02.01_60/ts_10263702v010201p.pdf

[95] ETSI, "TS 102 637-3 V1.1.1 – Intelligent Transport Systems (ITS); Vehicular Communications; Basic Set of Applications; Part 3: Specifications of Decentralized Environmental Notification Basic Service," pp. 1–46, 2010. [Online]. Available: http://www.etsi.org/deliver/etsi_ts/102600_102699/10263703/01.01.01_60/ts_10263703v010101p.pdf

[96] D. Jiang, H. Wang, E. Malkamaki, and E. Tuomaala, "Principle and Performance of Semi-Persistent Scheduling for VoIP in LTE System," in *2007 Int. Conference on Wireless Communications, Networking and Mobile Computing (WiCom 2007)*, Shanghai, China, Sep. 2007, pp. 2861–2864. [Online]. Available: http://dx.doi.org/10.1109/WICOM.2007.710

[97] R. Schmidt, T. Leinmuller, E. Schoch, F. Kargl, and G. Schafer, "Exploration of Adaptive Beaconing for Efficient Intervehicle Safety Communication," *IEEE Network – Special Issue on "Advances in Vehicular Communications Networks"*, vol. 24, no. 1, pp. 14–19, Jan. 2010. [Online]. Available: http://dx.doi.org/10.1109/MNET.2010.5395778

[98] 3GPP, "TS 25.214: 3rd Generation Partnership Project; Technical Specification Group Radio Access Network; Physical layer procedures (FDD) (Release 9)," pp. 1–98, 2009. [Online]. Available: http://www.3gpp.org/ftp/Specs/html-info/25214.htm

[99] 3GPP, "TS 25.321: 3rd Generation Partnership Project; Technical Specification Group Radio Access Network; Medium Access Control (MAC) protocol specification (Release 9)," pp. 1–191, 2009. [Online]. Available: http://www.3gpp.org/ftp/Specs/html-info/25321.htm

[100] 3GPP, "TS 36.213: 3rd Generation Partnership Project; Technical Specification Group Radio Access Network; Evolved Universal Terrestrial Radio Access (E-UTRA); Physical layer procedures (Release 9)," pp. 1–79, 2009. [Online]. Available: http://www.3gpp.org/ftp/Specs/html-info/36213.htm

[101] 3GPP, "TS 36.321: 3rd Generation Partnership Project; Technical Specification Group Radio Access Network; Evolved Universal Terrestrial Radio Access (E-UTRA); Medium Access Control (MAC) pro-

tocol specification (Release 9)," pp. 1–48, 2009. [Online]. Available: http://www.3gpp.org/ftp/Specs/html-info/36321.htm

[102] Bundesnetzargentur, "Frequenzversteigerung 2010 – Pressebriefing," Presentation, pp. 1–10, 2010. [Online]. Available: http://www.bundesnetzagentur.de/SharedDocs/Downloads/DE/BNetzA/Presse/Reden/2010/FoliensatzPK08042010FreqVersteigerung.pdf [Accessed: 2012/01/16]

[103] Motorola, "Long Term Evolution (LTE): Overview of LTE Air-Interface," Technical White Paper, pp. 1–8. [Online]. Available: http://business.motorola.com/experiencelte/pdf/LTEAirInterfaceWhitePaper.pdf [Accessed: 2011/12/16]

[104] Bundesnetzargentur, "Präsentation zum Ende der Frequenzversteigerung," Presentation, pp. 1–5, 2010. [Online]. Available: http://www.bundesnetzagentur.de/SharedDocs/Downloads/DE/BNetzA/Sachgebiete/Telekommunikation/Regulierung/Frequenzordnung/OeffentlicherMobilfunk/VergabeverfDrahtloserNetzzugang/Frequenzversteigerung2010/PraesentationEndeFrequVerstgrg.pdf [Accessed: 2012/01/16]

[105] X. Meng, P. Zerfos, V. Samanta, S. Wong, and S. Lu, "Analysis of the Reliability of a Nationwide Short Message Service," in *26th IEEE Int. Conference on Computer Communications (INFOCOM 2007)*, Anchorage, USA, May 2007, pp. 1811–1819. [Online]. Available: http://dx.doi.org/10.1109/INFCOM.2007.211

[106] Fraunhofer-Institut für Systemtechnik und Innovationsforschung, "Energieverbrauch der privaten Haushalte und des Sektors Gewerbe, Handel, Dienstleistungen (GHD)," Final Report, pp. 1–27, 2004. [Online]. Available: http://publica.fraunhofer.de/dokumente/N-21164.html [Accessed: 2012/01/24]

[107] Google Inc. (2012) Google Maps. URL: http://maps.google.com [Accessed: 2012/01/24]

[108] M. Hall, F. Eibe, G. Holmes, B. Pfahringer, P. Reutemann, and I. H. Witten, "The WEKA data mining software: An update," *SIGKDD Explorations*, vol. 11, no. 1, pp. 10–18, 2009. [Online]. Available: http://dx.doi.org/10.1145/1656274.1656278

[109] D. Pelleg and A. Moore, "X-means: Extending K-means with Efficient Estimation of the Number of Clusters," in *17th Int. Conference on Machine Learning (ICML 2000)*, Stanford, CA, USA, Jun. 2000, pp. 727–734. [Online].

Available: http://staff.utia.cas.cz/nagy/skola/Projekty/Classification/Xmeans. pdf

[110] NEC, "NEC LinkBird-MX – Test Platform for Evaluation of Vehicular Communications Protocols," Data Sheet, pp. 1–3. [Online]. Available: http://www.nec.co.jp/press/en/0811/images/1301-01.pdf [Accessed: 2012/01/19]

[111] Dd-wrt.com, "Mini-PCI WiFi Module: DCMA-82 – Industrial grade high power 802.11a/b/g 108Mbps wifi mini-PCI module , RoHS compliance," Data Sheet, pp. 1–3. [Online]. Available: http://www.dd-wrt.com/shop/catalog/pdf/ dcma82.pdf [Accessed: 2012/01/19]

[112] O. Klemp, "Performance Considerations for Automotive Antenna Equipment in Vehicle-to-Vehicle Communications," in *20th Int. Symposium on Electromagnetic Theory (EMTS 2010)*, Berlin, Germany, Aug. 2010, pp. 934–937. [Online]. Available: http://dx.doi.org/10.1109/URSI-EMTS.2010.5637361

[113] R. Miucic, Z. Popovic, and S. M. Mahmud, "Experimental Characterization of DSRC Signal Strength Drops," in *12th Int. IEEE Conference on Intelligent Transportation Systems (ITSC 2009)*, St. Louis, MO, USA, Oct. 2009, pp. 1–5. [Online]. Available: http://dx.doi.org/10.1109/ITSC.2009.5309695

[114] D. Jiang, Q. Chen, and L. Delgrossi, "Communication Density: A Channel Load Metric for Vehicular Communications Research," in *4th IEEE Int. Conference on Mobile Adhoc and Sensor Systems (MASS 2007)*, Pisa, Italy, Oct. 2007, pp. 1–8. [Online]. Available: http://dx.doi.org/10.1109/MOBHOC.2007. 4428734

[115] ETSI, "TS 102 687 V1.1.1 – Intelligent Transport Systems (ITS); Decentralized Congestion Control Mechanisms for Intelligent Transport Systems operating in the 5 GHz range; Access Layer Part," pp. 1–45, 2011. [Online]. Available: http://www.etsi.org/deliver/etsi_ts/102600_102699/102687/01.01. 01_60/ts_102687v010101p.pdf

Glossary and Acronyms

Glossary

cell A cell of a cellular system. The term "cell" is used equivalent to "sector" in this thesis. Therefore, a cell is the area where capacity needs to be shared by all users. ii, 3, 5, 22, 24, 42–45, 52, 54, 55, 60–62, 64–70, 72–75, 80, 82–86, 88, 89, 93–96, 132, 152, 153, 158, 160, 165, 166

sector A cell tower does not contain an omnidirectional antenna, but multiple directional antennas in different directions are used to cover the complete surrounding. Each direction is forming a sector. Usual are three sectors per tower. In a system with frequency reuse factor one, each sector provides the full system bandwidth. 70, 84, 88

Acronyms

ACK Acknowledgement. 31

AICH Acquisition Indicator Channel. 77, 78

AU Application Unit. 15

BSS Basic Service Set. 29

C2C-CC Car-to-Car Communication Consortium. 12

CACS Comprehensive Automobile Traffic Control System. 11

CAM Cooperative Awareness Message. i–vi, 1, 3–5, 7, 14, 16, 17, 19–21, 24–32, 39, 42, 44, 45, 53, 54, 58–60, 66, 69–76, 83–96, 103, 116, 151, 152, 154, 157, 158, 160–162

CCU Communication and Control Unit. 15

CP Cyclic Prefix. 48

CQI Channel Quality Indications. 75, 76

CSMA/CA Carrier Sense Multiple Access with Collision Avoidance. 29–31, 33, 153

DCF Distributed Coordination Function. 29, 30, 33

DCH Dedicated Channel. 74

DENM Decentralized Environmental Message. 14, 16, 26, 29, 53, 72

DIFS Distributed IFS. 29, 33

DRX Discontinuous Reception. 83

DSRC Dedicated Short Range Communication. 12

E-DCH Enhanced Dedicated Channel. 74

E.I.R.P. Equivalent Isotropically Radiated Power. 27

ECC European Communications Committee. 26

EDCA Enhanced Distributed Channel Access. 30

eNodeB LTE Base Station. 48, 80, 81

ETSI European Telecommunications Standards Institute. 54, 162

FACH Forward Access Channel. 85

FCC Federal Communications Commission. 12, 26

FDD Frequency Division Duplex. 46

FEC Forward Error Correction. 47, 48

FFT Fast Fourier Transformation. 27

FSPL Free-Space Path Loss. 34, 35, 41, 119, 124, 125, 129, 134, 136

GPRS General Packet Radio Service. 46

GPS Global Positioning System. 12

GSM Global System for Mobile Communications. 43, 44, 46–48, 61, 65, 67, 68, 70

HARQ Hybrid Automatic Repeat reQest. 80, 88

HMI Human Machine Interface. 16

HS-PDSCH High Speed Physical Downlink Shared Channel. 47

HSDPA High Speed Downlink Packet Access. 47, 48, 70

HSPA High Speed Packet Access. 46, 47, 52, 73, 75, 85, 90

IBSS Independent Basic Service Set. 29

IEEE Institute of Electrical and Electronics Engineers. 13

IFS Inter-Frame Space. 29, 30, 188, 190

IP Internet Protocol. 48

ITS Intelligent Transportation System. 11, 12, 15, 16, 18, 19, 26, 51, 53, 54, 153, 154, 161

KML Keyhole Markup Language. 61, 117, 163, 165, 166

LDM Local Dynamic Map. 16

LOS Line-Of-Sight. i, 2, 13, 22–24, 34–36, 39–41, 55, 57, 98, 102–105, 108, 113–115, 120–122, 124, 125, 129, 130, 132, 134–137, 139, 143, 144, 146, 150, 157, 159, 168, 169, 171

LTE Long Term Evolution. ii, 5, 7, 42, 43, 45, 47–50, 52–54, 70–73, 75, 76, 80–92, 95, 96, 151–153, 158, 160

MAC Medium Access Control. 25, 26, 28–30, 32, 33, 135, 136, 139, 145, 150

MBMS Multimedia Broadcast Multicast Service. 54, 73, 85, 91, 154

MIMO Multiple Input Multiple Output. 47, 49

MITI Japanese Ministry of International Trade and Industry. 11

NLOS Non-Line-Of-Sight. i, ii, v, vi, ix, 3–5, 8, 13, 23, 24, 26, 33, 39–41, 55–58, 97, 98, 103, 105, 108–113, 115, 119, 121, 123–125, 128–138, 140–150, 152, 153, 157–160, 162, 163, 168–171

NodeB UMTS Base Station. 45, 46, 77

OFDM Orthogonal Frequency Division Multiplexing. 27, 28, 48, 49, 80

SR Scheduling Request. 76

tx transmitter. 34, 40, 110, 111, 114–116, 118–122, 127, 130, 133, 135, 139, 143–149, 169–171

U.S. United States. 1, 2, 12, 26, 27, 53, 93

UE User Equipment. 42, 44–46, 48, 50, 52, 75–77, 79–81, 83, 92

UL-SCH Uplink Shared Channel. 75, 76, 80, 82

UMTS Universal Mobile Communication System. ii, 5, 7, 42, 43, 45–50, 52–54, 65–68, 70–78, 80, 82–91, 96, 151, 153, 158, 160

USDOT U.S. Department of Transportation. 12

V2V Vehicle-to-Vehicle. iii, iv, vi, 1, 2, 6, 56, 57, 90, 92, 93, 95, 132–135, 137, 157–161

W-CDMA Wideband Code Division Multiple Access. 46, 47

WLAN Wireless Local Area Network. 12